Chaucer
Spenser
Milton

Eve, the Serpent, and Death by Hans Baldung Grien, 1512?
Courtesy of the National Gallery of Canada

Chaucer Spenser Milton

MYTHOPOEIC CONTINUITIES AND TRANSFORMATIONS

A. Kent Hieatt

McGILL–QUEEN'S UNIVERSITY PRESS MONTREAL & LONDON 1975

This book has been published with the help of a
grant from the Humanities Research Council of
Canada, using funds provided by the Canada
Council.

DESIGN BY SUSAN MCPHEE

PRINTED IN THE U.S.A. BY
CAPITAL CITY PRESS, VERMONT

For Alice and Kathy

Milton was the Poetical Son of Spencer. . . .
Spencer more than once insinuates, that the
Soul of *Chaucer* was transfus'd into his Body;
and that he was begotten by him Two hundred
years after his Decease. *Milton* has acknowledg'd
to me, that *Spencer* was his Originall.

John Dryden, Preface to Fables Ancient and Modern

Contents

Illustrations

Eve, the Serpent, and Death   *frontispiece*
Perhaps Adam is a better name than Death for the right-hand figure.
Eve, holding her apple in one hand, subdues Adam through sensuality
to her already sinful will by softly pinching with her other hand the tail
of the phallic serpent. Reacting with red-eyed anger, the serpent pins
Adam to the fatal tree with his coils and closes his fangs viciously and
vengefully on Adam's left wrist, at the pulse. The effect on Adam of this
poisonous hurt is threefold. Erotically aroused and grinning, he convul-
sively grasps Eve's forearm with his left hand, and he plucks an apple
with his right, wholly submitted to Eve's and Satan's will. Instantly,
moreover, he takes on the Body of this Death, expressing the Evil One's
victory over humankind.

Preface

Chaucer, Spenser, Milton does not summarize what is already known about the relationships among the three poets named in the title. The best brief description that I can give of what the book does do is contained in its subtitle. Chaucer's *Parlement*, Knight's Tale, and Marriage Group, and Spenser's *Faerie Queene* III and IV are discussed in part I, in themselves and for the light which they shed on each other. Part II follows the same method with *Faerie Queene* II and Milton's *Comus, Paradise Lost*, and *Paradise Regained*.

The present work thus pivots upon a discussion of three books (and a little more) of *The Faerie Queene*. I am conscious of having paid scant attention in what follows to the most considerable studies of these books in recent years, by scholars for whom I have great respect. Professor Harry Berger's *Allegorical Temper* (New Haven, 1957) is concerned with Book II; Professor Thomas P. Roche, Jr.'s *The Kindly Flame* (Princeton, 1964) is concerned with Books III and IV. I disagree with many of their conclusions, but if my own interpretations are any nearer the mark, this is partly because my book follows theirs. I am conscious of having borrowed an important point from Professor Roche; what I am likely to have borrowed from Professor Berger is difficult to say, because his book was published sufficiently long ago to have become part of the intellectual furniture of the whole present generation of Spenserians. But I should like to pay both of them a more general tribute in this place. I now note that Professor Berger's recent 'Busirane and the War between the Sexes', in the first number of *English Literary Renaissance*, follows in the general drift of its interpretation the same line which I myself have followed here, although his and my approaches differ strikingly.

The situation as regards my friend Professor Alastair Fowler's *Spenser and the Numbers of Time* (London, 1964) is more complicated. In 1960 my book on *Epithalamion* introduced the subject of systematic numerical analysis of Spenser's poetry. Professor Fowler's book followed as an independent, and far more ambitious and elaborate, numerical study of *The Faerie Queene*. Although his recent *Triumphal Forms* (Cambridge, 1970) seems to me the best general book on numerical patterns in poetry (see my review in *Renaissance Quarterly*, 24, 1971, 557–60), and although *Spenser and the Numbers of Time* was a brilliant performance, I disagree with some of the major conclusions of this earlier book. I now find, however, that my present, largely nonnumerical study draws near to several of his incidental conclusions in it. It is best to say this here, because to meet his contentions in detail at a later point would confuse the argument extremely. In particular, in *Faerie Queene* IV my four-groups are his tetrads writ large—a fact which, extraordinarily, escaped me until the last stages of writing the present book. I believe that he has not traced the true consequences of this kind of grouping; on the other hand, I have, perhaps wrongly, not accepted many of the consequences which he draws from the evidence. In any case, he was there before I was. In several other connections his mind (before 1964) and my mind (before 1973) have travelled in parallel channels, and I have tried to acknowledge this in the proper places.

The desire to keep my argument unencumbered and self-contained has kept me from acknowledging the particular contributions of many other fellow workers over many years. I beg their pardons.

Because I have not spent a sizeable part of my scholarly career in the study of Milton, I am the more fortunate in being a member of the faculty of The University of Western Ontario, which owns one of the more remarkable Milton collections of North America and counts on its staff two of the foremost Miltonists of the world: Professors Arthur Barker and B. Rajan. These two friends read part II of my book at an earlier stage and have saved me from many an error. But as I stubbornly resisted their redemptive efforts at various points, and as they never read the final draft, they are to be absolved of all blame. My Spenserian friend Mr. P. C. Bayley, until recently Fellow of University College, Oxford, and now head of Collingwood College, Durham, read the same portion of the book at the same stage, with the same both positive and negative results.

Professor C. B. Hieatt read a draft of the whole book, criticized my prose, and gave specialist aid with part I. As with the rest of my published work, she has given me the most help.

I am grateful to the University of Toronto Press for permission to republish in altered form, as chapter 11, 'Milton's Comus and Spenser's False Genius', which first appeared in the *University of Toronto Quar-*

terly; and to the curators of the Bodleian Library, Oxford, for their kind permission to reproduce the six illustrations in this book.

Various theories presented in the book have been approached from other points of view or have been further elaborated in papers presented at various conferences of the Association of Canadian University Teachers of English, of the Modern Language Association of America, and of the Northeast Modern Languages Association, as well as at the Medieval Seminar of the State University of New York at Albany, as one in a series of lectures sponsored by the English Department of Carleton University in Ottawa, and in colloquia sponsored by my own department. I thank all those involved for the opportunity to clarify my own ideas. Material derived from my other published work is acknowledged in the notes.

I wish to thank my own university for help of various kinds, and the Fellows of University College, Oxford, for making me a temporary member of their Senior Common Room during the time when this book was being written. Various members of the staffs of the Bodleian and of the English Faculty Library, Oxford, have been informedly and constantly helpful during the same period, and I thank them. I should like to express thanks to my colleague Professor A. E. Raymond and to Professor Millar MacLure for particularly kind help at one point, to Professor Bruce Golden for leading me to an illustration, and to my two daughters for obtaining information for me which was available only in America. Many others are thanked at appropriate places in what follows.

Among the hundreds of students who have helped me I should like to single out Mr. Michael Baybak, who now has no professional connection with English studies but who, as an undergraduate in Columbia College, Columbia University, made the initial discovery which started me on the path, through a number of recent studies, to part II of the present book. He and I appear as two of the authors of an article which is cited here several times.

I should like to add my thanks here to my colleague Professor James Reaney for helping me through correspondence when I was away from Canada, and to Professor A. C. Hamilton for his most kind willingness to read the entire book at a late stage when integral changes were no longer possible. His meticulous care has saved me from several misstatements and false deductions in detail, although even he, no doubt, could not take time to find all the errors. Being able to review with him points on which we agree or disagree has been a lively stimulus, more especially since he has been able to bring to bear on my book the knowledge accumulated in preparing his generously annotated forthcoming edition of *The Faerie Queene*. I am grateful to the Columbia University Press for permission to reprint, in appendix B, passages from the translation of the *Saturnalia* by P. V. Evans (New York, 1969).

I am extremely grateful for prompt, generous attention from Miss Beverly Johnston, Executive Editor of McGill-Queen's University Press, and for exacting and sympathetic copy-editing by Miss Audrey Hlady. I must also express my gratitude to other members of the staff of the Press, all of whom have been most helpful.

Textual Note

Except when otherwise stated, quotations from the three indicated authors are drawn from the following editions: *Chaucer's Poetry: An Anthology for the Modern Reader*, ed. E. T. Donaldson (New York, 1958); *The Works of Edmund Spenser: A Variorum Edition*, ed. E. Greenlaw, C. G. Osgood, F. M. Padelford et al., 11 vols. (Baltimore, 1932–57); *The Poems of John Milton*, ed. John Carey and Alastair Fowler (London, 1968). Donaldson and Carey-Fowler have been chosen mainly because they are easier for the nonspecialist to read than are other authoritative editions. A modern-spelling edition of Spenser would have been followed here if a full and authoritative one existed. The contrast suggested between Spenser's language and Milton's by the earlier spelling preserved in the edition of Spenser above and the modern spelling imposed in the edition of Milton is unreal. In quoting Spenser, the letters *i, j, u,* and *v* have been modernized.

For all quotations from Donaldson's edition of Chaucer, Donaldson's line numbering (which corresponds to one of the systems of line numbering in Skeat's edition) is first cited, followed after a semicolon by the line numbering of Robinson's edition (*The Works of Geoffrey Chaucer*, ed. F. N. Robinson, 2nd ed., Boston, 1957). Robinson's line numbering often agrees with one of Skeat's systems of line numbering. For quotations from works of Chaucer which do not appear in Donaldson's edition, Robinson's edition is used.

The information given in the notes of Robinson's edition of Chaucer and the Variorum edition of Spenser has generally been taken for granted. In the absence of a note, the inquiring reader should look there.

Introduction

A striking feature of the English literary tradition is the element of continuity in the development of its greatest works of serious poetic narrative from the later Middle Ages into the seventeenth century. The poet Spenser, although much occupied with Italian, French, and Latin literary culture, was more deeply influenced by Chaucer than is generally realized. Milton was in turn profoundly influenced by Spenser. Perhaps the only way to talk about this is in terms of the myths which these writers devised in order to embody certain vital, but ratiocinatively unoriginal, moral notions. If we discuss Spenser in relation to Chaucer, and Milton in relation to Spenser, we are almost automatically led to consider these mythic embodiments and their successive transformations. This is not necessarily the case, for instance, when we discuss the dependence of Chaucerian poets on Chaucer or of Spenserian ones on Spenser, where relationships of a more explicit or a more formal kind are often of greater interest.

What is meant here needs to be stated very simply if it is not to be misunderstood. Chaucer (who is only vulgarly supposed to have been an amoral relativist) embodied in certain of his most serious works one set of familiar and largely incontestable norms concerned with how we ought to behave towards those who are dear to us. This embodiment takes the form of a series of poetic fables, which amounts to saying that Chaucer found suitable narrative, mythic structures for this set of ideas. Spenser, who honoured Chaucer highly, seized on certain of these structures and variously re-embodied and transformed them so as to create another series, curiously and interestingly related to, and differentiated from, the previous one. Finally, Milton, who venerated Spenser, appears to have absorbed from his works, and to have used in a new form, a mythic structuring of a quite different set of unimpeachable moral notions having to do with the impracticality of invidious aggression or of appetite as a rule of life.

The first of these familiar sets of moral ideas—the one which we are concerned with in the mythic formulations of Chaucer and Spenser—is directed against personal domination. Each of us is tempted to view the person who attracts us merely as an object to possess, and is thus further tempted to coerce or deceive that person so as to bend him to our will. It is generally acknowledged that we ought not to do this, and that doing so destroys the possibility of complete fulfilment in either love or friendship. Another way of describing this first set in relation to sexual life is to say, with Chaucer and Spenser, that sexual relationships are central to our lives in terms of their various pleasures and of the social continuity that they give to a race composed of individual mortal discontinuities, but that these relationships cannot be permanently satisfactory, or even tolerable, unless each of us recognizes his or her actual or potential sexual partner as an individual collocation of partly reasonable desires and habits who is in need of undisturbed liberty of choice. It is wrong to enchant another frivolously and to drive him or her to commitment to oneself unless one makes, or has the will to make, an equal commitment of one's own. It is wrong to master or bully another sexually, without time yielded for persuasion and the thoughtfully given consent of the heart; to do so is likely to lead later to mistrust and jealousy on one or the other side. It is wrong to insulate oneself psychologically from another's tender of love, even if in the end one cannot accept it. It is very wrong to yield facilely to every light-of-love and to tack and shift sexually throughout one's life.

The second set of moral notions, those given mythic formulation by Spenser and Milton, is directed against two opposed tendencies: the passionate propensity to seize credit and get ahead of others violently and fraudulently and, if we do not attain our ends, to resort to vengeance or self-destruction; and the self-indulgent propensity to throw in one's hand and retreat into any available sensual bliss without regard for the consequences for ourselves and for others to whom we have contracted obligations. It is usually agreed under this latter head that to be motivated only by the pleasures which we share with animals is to give up the possibility of self-respect and of a definite line of action. In fact no human can really divest himself of a stirring towards self-direction and focus; its operation in the sensual man, however, is fitful and shameful.

These two sets of ideas probably constitute the only remaining generally received moral norms in Western society, embodying as they do the imperative of the superego not to regard self. Aside from the formulae of institutionalized religion, the mythic formulations given to these ideas by Chaucer, Spenser, and Milton are probably the most impressive, long-standing, and charismatic ones available to speakers of English. Such a heritage is very important to us, because mythic structuring of the norms governing our lives is probably something that we cannot do without.

As such a heritage, the words of these poets deserve to be attended to with some gravity, not necessarily having anything to do with the Arnoldian variety of seriousness. If we have not taken every pain to make sure of these poets' meanings, for instance, there is cause for scandal. Yet, as things stand, there appears to be a wide range of mutually exclusive opinions about the meanings of most of the works by Chaucer, and all those by Spenser, which I am going to consider here. The systematic literary study of Chaucer and Spenser, if not of Milton, seems to be still in its heroic age.

Chaucer and Spenser lie almost as far from contemporary experience as a twentieth-century man can go in his own language. It is perhaps easier to jump to imprecise and overly modernist conclusions about them than about almost any other important writer in English, and the kind of specialist knowledge which will guard against such missteps began to be accumulated rather late, as literary history goes. Our method of studying Chaucer and Spenser, and Milton as well, must be partly historical. It would be better for all concerned if a work by one of these poets gave up its message to every intent reader. It will not; yet to take the trouble to begin to understand his works is to begin to assume a personally important heritage.

No one is really in a position to generalize about the 'worlds' of Chaucer's or Spenser's works, in particular, until we have learned more than we now know about the specifics of what Chaucer and Spenser were trying to say; that is, the need for ordinary exegesis remains vital, in spite of the fatiguing quantity of exegesis that we already have. We need as massive a demonstration as possible of the truth of this exegesis. It is presumed here that the precise interpretation of Spenser, and of those works of Chaucer which are most closely related to Spenser's, is closely related to considerations of parallelism, contrast, and symmetry of ideas, images, and forms, and to familiar medieval and Renaissance categories of thought, and almost not at all to twentieth-century psychological or characterological literary criteria, or to any but the most general of Romantic or Neo-Romantic conceptions. Perhaps this presumption will sound to many specialist readers like coming out firmly for Motherhood, yet it seems to me that some of our latest and most interesting criticism of these two authors has sometimes failed to abide by just this presumption.

What this book presents, then, is something like an iconographical program (as the art historians use the term), with frequent resort to historical and philological procedures. If by inspecting the work of fiction which was foremost in Chaucer's imagination when he was writing the Knight's Tale we can come closer to an understanding of Chaucer's meaning, then a close review of that source is worth the while. If by showing which edition of Chaucer Spenser read we can show what significance Spenser is likely to have found in the incomplete Squire's Tale which he completed in *The Faerie Queene*, then the effort is worth while. If any traditionary item at a decisive point in Chaucer's or Spenser's narratives has not yet been fully studied, then it is worth while to investigate it in greater depth. If something seemingly intended by Chaucer seems to persist in Spenser, or if an episodic structure developed by Spenser seems to be followed by Milton, then meanings which we impute to two of these writers will become proportionately more probable because mutually confirming, always provided that our deductions also follow convincingly from the scrupulous reading of each text by itself. Larger and larger coherent structures may begin to emerge; greater critical precision is perhaps possible. The final intent of this book is not simply to present a set of attractive theories but to find a way of making certain interpretations seem necessary ones.

Certain of the theories presented here may strike some readers as revolutionary, yet in fact many of them are close to what has previously been done in specialized fields. Professor J. A. W. Bennett, for instance, is unlikely to be surprised by the general outline of what is said here about Chaucer and Spenser. A portion of Edwin Greenlaw's article of 1917 (see chapter 13) reads like a general outline of the material here concerned with Spenser and Milton. It will be clear to knowledgeable readers of Milton that what I say of him concerns the functioning of his imagination, not the further interpretation of his works. It is the interpretation of Spenser in the present work that probably contains most novelties. Since he is elucidated both by what precedes him and by what follows, this volume may be said to hinge on him.

In order to talk about the continuities and transformations that lie before us we need specialized terms for only two phenomena, aside from the familiar modern idea of the mythic. The first of these terms, *moralized landscape*, the equivalent of *paysage moralisé*, describes the chosen device of Chaucer, of many medieval poets, and of Spenser for bodying forth a numinous world.[1] *Moralized* refers to the saturation of the components of the landscape with symbolic meaning. *Landscape* is partly unsatisfactory, because outdoor nature is not always meant. What happens in such scenes is that (in waking life, in dream, or in vision) the animate and inanimate entities in a garden, a grove, a watered and delightful plain, a mountain, an island, or a temple, or in a picture of any of these on a wall, in a tapestry, or on a decorated floor, are given symbolic weight, and the area itself is filled with a dense concentration of symbols. One consequence of this concentration is the reader's awareness of the higher than usual significance of what is being imparted. Often in Chaucer, and most frequently in *The Faerie Queene*, these moralized landscapes relate to other kinds or levels of narrative in the same work and also to each other, in terms of contrasting or complementary assertions. Very often the communication in moralized landscape is covert and vatic.

The second specialized term which we need for a compartment of fiction is *chivalric adventure*—the adventure characteristic of a romance. The term indicates the chosen device of Chaucer, of other medieval poets, and of Spenser for putting ideals into action in an imagined world of idealist and élitist narrative. It is typical of the complicated literary situations which we must deal with that moralized landscapes occur most frequently in romances, either occupying the entire narrative space or interspersed with narratives of the world of partly symbolic action, that is, of chivalric adventure.

Neither Chaucer nor Spenser (and certainly not Milton) confined himself to the romance genre, but, in terms of mythic formulations of great ethical significance which are inherited from Chaucer and transformed by Spenser, it is perhaps in the nature of things that what most concern us are these moralized landscapes and chivalric adventures of romance.

Spenser intended that his chivalric fictions should be epic; that is, that they should belong to the same genre—that of heroic poetry—as Virgil's *Aeneid*, which sounds to readers of modern modal criticism like a contradiction in terms. It is not, in fact. Admittedly, it is a convenient taxonomic device for the creators of various useful literary-critical systems to speak of 'romance' in a different sense, as dealing with a sphere of personal adventure pursued with idealized sensibility, in

---

1. A recent work of great interest on the moralized landscape from Boethius to *Pearl* is Paul Piehler, *The Visionary Landscape: A Study in Medieval Allegory* (London, Montreal, 1971).

contrast with 'epic', which refers to a sphere of heroic action entailing leadership of large social units. It is equally convenient, however, for medievalists to use 'romance' to describe a literary form which appeared first in tales of an aristocracy's personal adventures in combat and in love, and which (maintaining one or another of the original features) grew into extraordinarily varied forms, almost as numerous as those of the modern novel. Malory's great collection of romances develops a fertile vein of national conflict, imperial leadership, and great armies in dubious battle, yet remains romance; Wolfram von Eschenbach's romance *Parzival* elaborates a collective Christian ideal; Chaucer's great romance the Knight's Tale is an adaptation of a work which set out to be an epic, the twelve books of Boccaccio's *Teseida,* or *Thesiad.* In the most important vernacular language of the Middle Ages a work like Malory's or the *Parzival* or the Knight's Tale was called a *roman;* we call it a *romance.*

For Spenser, and for Ariosto, there was nothing incongruous about using the conventions of chivalric romance for constructing heroic poetry. The result may remind some readers of the mixture of classical motifs and Gothic structures that one sees in some Tudor, Flemish, French, or German early Renaissance architecture. This may be a useful way of thinking about one kind of heroic poetry, if it is agreed that the grafting of initially alien architectural motifs on an inherited notion of how a building should look can produce something admirable.

In the case of Milton's inheritance from Spenser, the question of literary genre is a far different one. Milton still wished to write heroic poetry, like Spenser and largely unlike Chaucer, but had conceived an aversion to the milieu of chivalric romance. As a result, the combinations of one tradition with the other which today most startle a new reader of Spenser do not arise in *Paradise Lost* and *Paradise Regained.* Also, Milton removed moralized landscape from its formerly numinous and magical milieu, where it had been a largely symbolic structure or metaphor, and installed it in a grandly conceived but nonetheless concrete reality. Thus his Garden of Eden.

Putting the matter in this way may remind some readers of a familiar class of problems. Did Milton write the first English heroic poetry of the Renaissance as this latter term is understood in the visual, and visualizing, terms of the plastic arts? Or is it better to think of Milton as Mannerist or Baroque? For our purposes such speculation is not of much use. After we have decided such a question, we perhaps possess a pleasing general idea, but have not got very deeply into the problems and the appreciation of Milton's actual poetry. Similarly with Spenser: we can find something instructive in thinking of him in one sense as a medieval epigone, continuing and elaborating the devices of Chaucer and Old French poetry into late Tudor times, but this idea, press it as we will, remains a fairly elementary one.

Certainly we ought not to condemn the effort to think about literature in terms of its sister arts or in terms of *Kulturgeschichte*. Experimenting with categories from the systematic conceptual framework of modern art-history is a way for the study of literature to escape from provincialism. Without them the present book, for one, would not have been written. Yet the efforts, going back as far as the 1920s,[2] to define the transition from medieval to Renaissance poetry in a formal sense do not really seem to have helped us to understand the *esse* of our poets. The three poets studied here do indeed differ from each other significantly because they belong to different times, but if those differences are hypostatized ('late medieval decline', 'early Renaissance', 'seventeenth-century Baroque'), they will take one's eye off what is most valuable in these poets and what each has in common with the other. The discussion becomes imprecise; those who know the material tend to lose interest. The most laudable attempts to see medieval or Renaissance literature as parts of a larger cultural tradition most often suffer from the lack of a middle ground relating the objects under the microscope to the towering heights at the rear.

Matters are somewhat different with the attempts to construct great morphologies of literary expression, of which Professor Northrop Frye's is the most notable. Such systems cannot reach their full range without the exotic artifacts of our earlier literature, and the traditional study of the earlier literature by periods may benefit in turn from thinking largely and timelessly. There is also the point that Frye himself is one of the most brilliant critical minds at work in the English-speaking world. If we are ever to make precise statements about poetry as one of the characteristically human activities, we need to read it logically and not just chronologically. Personally, however, I cannot see that my own studies of Chaucer, Spenser, and Milton have been much helped in this way. In studying these poets what has helped in the most subtle and advanced sense seems to have come from reading and thinking about their own works and the works of other writers who were closest to them.

2 E.g., Dagobert Frey, *Gotik und Renaissance als Grundlagen der modernen Weltanschauung* (Augsburg, 1929).

part I

Chaucer
and Spenser

Spenser's Chaucer
and Ours

With the barely conceivable exceptions of Ariosto and Torquato Tasso, Chaucer bulked larger in Edmund Spenser's creative imagination than any other poet. Early and late, Spenser mentioned him approvingly, but other kinds of evidence are more important. Among the best known is the archaizing character of Spenser's language. For a reader of Spenser who knows Chaucer and Middle English well, the continually met Chaucerian words, forms, and turns of speech are a constant indication of an imagination saturated with Chaucer's poetry, although this fluency, without the benefits of historical linguistics, is continually and strangely innovating on the fourteenth-century lexical and morphological original. A prime concern of this book is to say something about Chaucer in his own right, but it seems worth while to start with something of what Spenser found in Chaucer, and how this relates to what we see in him now. In any case, the extreme disarray in which the study of Chaucer's works and of other Middle English poetry finds itself today makes it advisable for anyone writing generally on Chaucer to make his own assumptions clear.

Three propositions are still often put forward about Chaucer and about sixteenth-century literature. [1] In the fourteenth-century, Chaucer escaped from the abstract, moralistic considerations with which fictional worlds and personages were so often carpentered together in the writing of his time, and found his way into a zestfully perceived world of richly individuated, concrete particularities where moral judgement is secondary to an appreciation of what is essentially human. [2] In this preoccupation with the essential humanity of his characters Chaucer was far in advance of his time, recognizing as he did the irrelevance of moral categories to the process of making his characters live. [3] Two hundred years later, in the sixteenth-century literary Renaissance of Elizabethan times, a resurgence of humane values on a broader front ended the domination in the intellectual field of outmoded, ponderous, abstract scholastic philosophical speculation, and brought in a youthful, exuberant appreciation of life and beauty realized in art.

These three still popular ideas are based on a respectable modicum of fact and possess a limited usefulness. In terms of responsible intellectual history, however, three other propositions are closer to the mark. [1] Much of Chaucer's work in generically appropriate cases builds upon (although it is not dominated by) a set of clear philosophical postulates with ethical consequences; [2] the philosophy on which he builds is a 'perennial' one, in which theologians of a much earlier period of the Middle Ages would have found more to interest them than did the daringly advanced late scholastic thinkers of Chaucer's own century; [3] it is precisely this somewhat old-fashioned, Boethian and otherwise Platonizing philosophical setting which gives to Chaucer's fictional world certain features also found in the worlds of graver poets of Elizabethan and even Jacobean times. Each of these propositions is worth some attention.

It is a misapprehension not often repeated today to suppose that Chaucer was only a genial moral relativist. Perhaps the most nearly accurate statement of his position (if not of his personal essence) is that he was a first-rate late medieval courtly poet. As such, in England, as elsewhere in feudal Western Christendom, he would be expected by his primary audience of select laymen to be not only a spinner of delightful tales and an inventor of pleasing devices but also a well of moral doctrine, full of the immemorial testimony of *auctores* and *auctoritee*.

More specifically and personally, Chaucer was a writer who found a satisfying and philosophically adequate complement to his Christian faith, and to his *trouvère* heritage of the cult of secular love, in what amounts to a selective Platonism. His principal source for this was Boethius' *Consolation*, but the rather different Platonism (derived ultimately from the *Timaeus)* of Alanus de Insulis in the *De planctu naturae* and of Jean de Meun in the second part of *Le Roman de la rose* was also important. A poet does not, as Chaucer did, go to the trouble of making a feeling translation of the *Consolation* and a translation of *Le Roman de la rose* without taking their outlook seriously. In *The Parlement of Foules* and the Knight's Tale the mature Chaucer embodied a syncretic vision of the possibility of harmonious human life through the freely exercised human choice of love and friendship within an apparently indifferent but ultimately harmonious macrocosm, ruled over by a well-disposed Nature, or by a 'Prime Mover'.

This vision is strained nearly to disintegration in the sadnesses and ambivalence of his *Troilus*. Certainly the vision takes second place to other considerations (often dictated by genre) in *The Canterbury Tales*. Chaucer is indeed not always and everywhere concerned to press an irreducible core of moral doctrine; perhaps more than any other medieval poet he requires us to make generic distinctions, because his ostensible meanings are always in the service of creating a particular kind of fictional discourse, which may as easily be ironically hyperbolic as gravely idealistic. Nevertheless, even though the vision is subordinated in the most mature of his *Canterbury Tales* to an interest in new ways of treating new materials in fiction, the vision does not evanesce even there—or even, in one obvious instance, when the Boethian view of freedom and the 'Chartrist' view of Nature's imperative laid on us to be fecund become matters of irony at the expense of a rooster in the Nun's Priest's Tale. Essentially the same vision shapes the final synthesis (which in spite of some recent criticism a modern reader may join Spenser in seeing) in the Marriage Group of those tales. What Chaucer had affirmed concerning friendship and love in the Knight's Tale he reaffirms finally in the Franklin's Tale, rhetorically in the narrator's speech on friendship (from which Spenser later paraphrases) and exemplarily in the freely entered upon, mutually supportive relation between man and wife in that tale.

One of the corollaries of Chaucer's view of these matters is that love is not humanly satisfactory unless it is freely sought and given. This proposition is really part of a more generally entertained medieval definition of the *sine qua non* of any secular love characterized by mutual sympathy and sensibility. If, according to this definition, one coerces or guilefully seduces a desired fellow being, the status of that desired being as a free agent is not being recognized and that desire cannot be love. What is essential to a free conjunction of two souls in love is the exquisite sensitivity of each to each which is called *gentilesse* by Guillaume de Lorris (the author of the first part of *Le Roman de la rose),* by Chaucer, and by many other medieval poets, and which Dante and his fellow poets called *gentilezza.* The word *cortaysye* in English usage could on occasion carry nearly the same meaning, and there is nothing surprising in the use, by Chaucer's contemporary the poet of *Pearl,* of this élitist term to characterize man's proper feelings towards the deity: as Christ in His love is supremely *cortayse* to us (457–58), so it behooves us not to demand ocular evidence of the promised future life; even to be able to suppose that Christ would lie to us concerning it is churlish and *uncortayse* (303–4). In secular terms a marriage or any other human relationship of love or friendship which does not in principle avoid disingenuous usurpation of affection and which does not entail continued mutual awareness, considerateness, and freedom comes short of its potential human scope. The doctrine of the Knight's Tale (as interpreted in the next chapter), the attitude of Nature in *The Parlement,* and the dialectic of the Marriage Group all in various ways go to affirm this.

That Chaucer himself should have related this doctrine to an eclectically Platonizing philosophical vision inspired by Boethius and others certainly does not mean that he was caught up vitally in the philosophical currents of his day. His thinking has none of the hard cutting edge of such revolutionary Nominalist scholastics as William of Occam or Robert Holcot. Chaucer never mentions them, or thinkers like them, and his casual mention of Bishop Bradwardine (in the Nun's Priest's Tale, 422; 3242) does not relate to that theologian's chief significance. Except, possibly, for a tendency towards the reforming zeal of Wycliffe,[1] Chaucer's philosophical preoccupations are of the lay kind that students of English literature properly associate with the so-called medieval or Renaissance 'world picture'.

It is not very surprising, then, that a poet like Spenser found the philosophical vision of Chaucer congenial when the forces associated with the historical movement of Humanism in sixteenth-century England had deflected intellectual interest from dialectic, and from both living and dead scholasticism, into rhetoric and the kingdom of letters. The new, fashionable current of Italian, partially literary Platonism which so affected the intellectual life of Elizabethan writers did not contradict the doctrines of such an ancient writer as Boethius but rather

---

1. See R. S. Loomis, 'Was Chaucer a Free Thinker?' in *Studies in Medieval Literature,* ed. MacEdward Leach (Philadelphia, 1961), pp. 21–44.

complemented them.[2] Queen Elizabeth herself translated the *Consolation*; Spenser surely read it, and very likely perused Chaucer's own translation of it, which was always included in sixteenth-century editions of Chaucer's works. It is true that Renaissance Platonic speculations concerning the role of beauty in drawing the lover towards heavenly things would have been news to Chaucer (except in a Dantean sense), but the popular Renaissance notion of human love and friendship as mirrors of the consonance of the universe and of the divine, and the parallel notion of the ordered, rhythmic perpetuation of a temporal and finite world through love, as in a dance, would have struck him as ideas for which he had already found satisfying mythic embodiments in his mature work.

It is Spenser's reflection and transformations of these mythic embodiments which will be traced when I later turn to him.[3] What I am emphasizing here is that Chaucer is sometimes a 'learned' poet not dissimilar to those in the Renaissance who made elaborate symbolic or metaphorical tapestries out of the traditional 'world view'. He was not simply the kind of medieval poet who stayed within the bounds of chivalric love-service, bourgeois satire, and the didactic and exemplary tale. Like his contemporary Boccaccio, Chaucer was drawn to the creation of mythic, metaphorically structured, mysteriously polysemous fictions, and so, of course, were the English poets of the Renaissance. In particular, the spirit of his romances and dream visions is not to be grasped unless one sees that Chaucer is concerned with a grave, mythopoeic reference to ultimate issues, in a manner resembling at a distance that of Spenser, Shakespeare, or almost any other outstanding

2. On Spenser's Platonism, a sound and learned source is Robert Ellrodt, *Neoplatonism in the Poetry of Spenser* (Geneva, 1960). It contains little, however, on *Faerie Queene* II, III, and IV.

3. The generally familiar dependence of Spenser on *The Parlement of Foules* in his *Mutabilitie*, the fragment of a seventh book of *The Faerie Queene*, is probably the most obvious case of Chaucer's influence in the whole of Spenser's work. It is, as well, a characteristic example of a continuation of one medieval Platonizing strain, depending ultimately on Plato's *Timaeus* and concerned with cyclical change analogous to the perfection of eternity, under the control of an ultimately benign power which restrains the tyranny of titanic arbitrary force and is ranked above the pagan gods or astrally powerful planets. *Mutabilitie* is secondary in the present book, because I am concerned first to follow the unfolding of a vision of human love in social circumstances in the central books of *The Faerie Queene*.

On the influence of Boethius upon Spenser himself, or the closeness of Spenser to Boethius, see Brents Stirling, 'The Concluding Stanzas of "Mutabilitie"', *Studies in Philology*, 30 (1933), 193–204; Rosemond Tuve, 'A Mediaeval Commonplace in Spenser's Cosmology', *Studies in Philology*, 30 (1933), 133–47, rpt. in *Essays by Rosemond Tuve*, ed. Thomas P. Roche, Jr. (Princeton, 1970); the Introduction to Edmund Spenser, *The Mutabilitie Cantos*, ed. S. P. Zitner (London, 1968), pp. 38–41.

Renaissance poet. Like them, Chaucer took pleasure in an ample system of symbols which marshal in a unified field individual life, love, friendship, the state, pagan mythology, the spheres of the heavens, astral lore, and a God whose puzzling and apparently arbitrary intermediaries often confuse us but always end by making His final sense. In this inclination towards a learnedly profound and vatic tone Chaucer differs from earlier romance writers like Chrétien or even Gottfried or Guillaume de Lorris, even though he has much in common with them in most other respects.

To realize this helps to make us at home in Chaucer's mental world, but it also brings with it the danger that we should imagine a Chaucer who erects a particular philosophy upon all kinds of terrain, from fabliau to romance. Chaucer's symbolic structures are often, and perhaps always, auxiliary to the creation of a particular kind of fictional discourse, in a particular narrative or poetic mode.

In terms of ideas alone it is easy enough to pull together disparate Chaucerian material. In the Miller's Tale, for instance, Nicholas naturally wishes to seduce Alisoun, the carpenter's wife. When a reputation for starlore enables Nicholas to convince the carpenter that a torrential rain and disastrous deluge are about to ensue, and this conviction becomes rooted in spite of the carpenter's self-proclaimed simple faith and aversion to learned men's prying into God's 'privetee', the situation in terms of ideas alone is very close to that in the Franklin's Tale where, again, an attempt to seduce a wife and overturn the order of marriage is linked with a learned man's astrological calculations so as to induce what seems to be a monstrously high tide—an activity which, the teller of the tale proclaims, belongs to the time of heathen cursedness, not to the beneficial institutions of Christianity. The cursedness of heathen times, again, is in some way related to Chaucer's notions of the tricksiness of the pagan deities in general (for example, Troilus, V. 1849–50) and of the goddess Fortuna in particular. Furthermore, the idea of the overturning of the natural, and consequently of the just, in the service of seduction relates, as idea, to the situation in the Physician's Tale, where Virginia, described as a sovereign creation of Nature, is subjected to the cursed machinations of an unjust judge, who lusts after her; and this particular cluster of ideas, as ideas alone, relates in turn to all the occasions of the betrayal of innocence, in human love (The Legend of Good Women) or otherwise (by mothers-in-law in the Man of Law's Tale of Constance; by Jews in the Prioress's Tale).

Yet the narrative import of each of these incidents is sharply distinguished from the other. In the Miller's Tale the undermining of the carpenter's position, after he has expressed a kind of hybris by recommending his own kind of ignorance, achieves primarily a picture of self-satisfied but credulous dotage. This, in turn, belongs to the world of farce and fabliau, where fools and rogues are the necessary material of the ironic mode. We are able to enjoy, of course, the added fillip that Chaucer brings off this effect as no one else did in the medieval fabliau, through a play of ideas which mean much to him elsewhere, and not simply through farcical plot. In the Franklin's Tale, on the other hand, we are in the world of romance, where the characters are a little larger than in real life. One of Chaucer's striking means of obtaining this effect of magnitude is ambiguously to relate a social reality to grave philosophical generalization, so that the attempt to reverse nature in the Franklin's Tale may well be part of Chaucer's portrayal of a typical shortcoming of noble, but immature, characters: they are self-indulgent in entertaining tragic feelings about the way in which the world is put together. Thus Dorigen in this tale expresses a low order of hybris in saying that she cannot comprehend why God has allowed the black rocks to extend above the water and endanger her husband. In the same way in the Knight's Tale Palamon and Arcite can see no sense in the way the world is put together; only Theseus, with his noble Boethian generalizations, can help to show that the Maker always makes sense, and that it is up to us to make a virtue of necessity. In the process Theseus becomes, as governor and friend, very much larger than life. That Chaucer is here speaking out of reasonable and ideal conviction and not only because he wishes to create a particular narrative effect is what I have already been saying, but the philosophical notions are always related to a narrative effect, even in his romances; and generally this effect is his main aim.

Again, in the Physician's Tale, and in other tales of betrayed innocence, his effort is mainly directed at creating yet another kind of story: what might be described as the formally exemplary tale with mythic overtones of final justification or redemption. Ostensibly concerned to illustrate a particular discursive point of view, he really achieves pathos, in this story and in The Legend of Good Women; or he aims at a pathos relieved by the dramatic reversal of divine intervention—a feeling akin to that of Shakespeare's late romances—as in the Man of Law's Tale.

Of course this rule about Chaucer's primarily fictional concern is not airtight. His exempla are sometimes informed by real conviction and not by partly absentminded acquiescence in their ostensible morals; or the mixture of the exemplary and some other effect is even more complicated. In the Clerk's Tale, what purports to be an allegory of the relation of the Christian's soul to God becomes as well a commentary on the gratuitous suffering imposed by an unconscionably masterful husband on his long-suffering wife; in the Melibee, Chaucer's no doubt serious translation of a doctrinal allegory becomes amusing simply through being placed in the context of The Canterbury Tales: a strong-minded wifely personification called Prudence easily deflates her self-inflated husband, who has displayed a dangerous liking for pleasure and for bellicosity in about equal proportions; and the relation to the context is underlined by Chaucer's use of certain material from this tale in the more explicitly satirical effects of his Marriage Group.

It is untrue, then, that, whenever a certain conceptual configuration can be shown to be common to several works of Chaucer, he is trying to embody some core of doctrine in each of those works. Sometimes this is one of the things that he is doing; sometimes not. Thus, although Chauntecleer's fall from grace through the influence of Pertelote is an instance of Adam's fall under the influence of Eve, Chaucer does not mean it to be so in the way in which the successive falls in the Monk's Tale, for example, are (from the point of view of the Monk) instances of the operation of Fortune. Chaucer, and his Priest-narrator, mean us to understand that by comparing Chauntecleer to Adam they are indulging in ironic hyperbole. They are trying to amuse us. Perhaps more than any other medieval author, Chaucer requires us to make such distinctions of tact and genre as this, because he fables in so many different ways.

In any case, the Chaucer who developed in certain of his works mythic embodiments of a human love and friendship freely entered upon, fully committed, and mutually attentive, and supported by a macrocosm similarly moved by an ultimately charitable impulse, found an eager follower in Spenser. Spenser discovered in Chaucer not only a part of the ready-made, usable national literary past which was demanded in each language of Western Europe at the Renaissance, but also a fictional world adaptable to the particular synthesis of sixteenth-century poetic and narrative fashions towards which Spenser's temperament carried him. This Chaucer is not the uniform Christian allegorist, or the uniformly elusive ironist, or the uniform sceptic drawn by one or another critic today; he is, however, as believable a literary figure for us as he seems to have been for Spenser.[4]

4. The concept of Chaucer as a 'uniform Christian allegorist, is largely the creation of D. W. Robertson and his followers, much of whose work is remarkably useful in other ways. The attack on Robertson's position by E. Talbot Donaldson in 'Patristic Exegesis in the

On chronological grounds it is a fairly safe guess that in reading Chaucer someone like Spenser, who was born in about 1552 and died in 1599, would have used one of the 'Thynne' editions of the 'collected works' of Chaucer, which were the only ones printed between 1532 and 1598. Yet it is worth the effort to demonstrate as fully as possible that Spenser did in fact read one of Thynne's versions and that, further, his acquaintance with Chaucer's works did not extend beyond these editions, because particular characteristics of this family of editions, as against others, appear to function very importantly in the use made by Spenser of Chaucerian material.

The early prints of Chaucer's works which could possibly have been available to Spenser differ drastically from our present idea of what Chaucer really intended. These prints also diverge widely and significantly among themselves in the number of Chaucerian and non-Chaucerian items attributed to Chaucer, in the order of *The Canterbury Tales,* in the attribution of one Canterbury pilgrim's prologue to another, in the interpolation of non-Chaucerian passages in the tales, in typographical errors, and (an item accounting for a number of the other discrepancies) in manuscript tradition. Up to now, no systematic study of this problem in relation to Spenser has appeared.

Of the ten prints (1478?, 1484?, ca. 1492, 1498, 1526, 1532, 1542, undated but ca. 1550, 1561, 1598) of *The Canterbury Tales,* which includes five 'collected works' (or four, if one does not count Pynson's 1526) printed before and during Spenser's lifetime, it seems reasonable to suppose that Spenser read, and built his picture of the Chaucerian canon on, either the 1561, or undated but ca. 1550, or 1542 prints. Yet if he had had access for any length of time to some of those preceding 1532 (for example, 1526), his presumptions in connection with almost all the points listed above would have differed from those deducible from, say, 1561.[5] This different set of presumptions might have led to quite different conclusions about the movement and meanings of many

Criticism of Medieval Literature: The Opposition' (originally published 1951, now reprinted in Donaldson's *Speaking of Chaucer*, London, 1973) perhaps a little outdoes itself in rhetorical polemic but still seems to me sensible. As for 'the uniform sceptic', Sheila Delany, in *Chaucer's House of Fame: The Poetics of Skeptical Fideism* (Chicago, 1972), finds a scepticism in Chaucer concerning the reliability of traditional information, coupled with a religious faith that holds itself apart from rational process (pp. 22–23). She draws an intellectual-historical parallel between this attitude and the attitude of such late medieval thinkers as Occam, Buridan, and Nicole Oresme (pp. 19–21).

5. The contents and order of early editions of *The Canterbury Tales* and of Chaucer's works as a whole are most easily studied in Eleanor P. Hammond, *Chaucer: A Bibliographical Manual* (New York, 1908; rpt. New York, 1933).

of Chaucer's fictions. If he were forced to allow for these possible differences, we should find it difficult, if not impossible, to disentangle the role of Chaucer's work in Spenser's creative imagination in respect to most of the matters with which we shall be concerned.

One piece of evidence helps to limit the possibilities and also shows us something interesting about Spenser's memory and methods. In *A View of the Present State of Ireland*,[6] Spenser makes one speaker in the dialogue say that the quilted leather jacket of the Irish is English in origin. I have added punctuation:

> The quilted leather Iacke is olde Englishe, for it was the proper wede of the horseman, as ye maye reade in *Chaucer* wheare he describeth Sir Thopas apparell and armour when he wente to fighte againste the Geaunte, which Checklaton is that kind of gilden leather with which they use to imbroider theire Irish Iackes; and theare likewise by all that discripcion ye maye see the verye fashion and manner of the Irishe horseman moste livelye set forthe in his longe hose, his Ryding shoes of Costelye Cordwaine, his hacqueton, and his habericion with all the rest theareunto belonginge.[7]

As Josephine Waters Bennett pointed out, Spenser might even have known Chaucer's comic tale of Sir Thopas by heart,[8] yet if he ever did, his memory of it had failed in at least one respect when he was composing *A View*. It is clear that he is quoting from memory, because he has confounded two passages. The 'hacqueton' and the 'habericion' do indeed come from Chaucer's passage (149–50: 860–61) which gives us the many-layered arming of Thopas, but what Spenser calls the 'Checklaton' (which he may have confused in his auditory memory with the 'helm of laton', that is, of brass, hopeless for protection, in the same passage at 166; 877) and the shoes of 'Cordwaine' come from Chaucer's earlier description of Thopas' weeds of peace (21, 23; 732, 734). Moreover, Spenser creates the alliterative phrase 'Costelye Cordwaine', which is not in any version of the original. Apparently he believed that

6. Almost surely written in 1596. See the edition of R. Gottfried, *The Prose Works* (Baltimore, 1949), vol. X of *The Works of Edmund Spenser: A Variorum Edition*, p. 505.
7. Quoted from Gottfried, p. 121.
8. *The Evolution of 'The Faerie Queene'* (Chicago, 1942), p. 12. This is perhaps doubtful. For her point that 'Sir Thopas' was sometimes sung to the harp in Spenser's time she cites Warton citing *The Arte of English Poesie*. All that *The Arte* says is that blind harpers or tavern minstrels 'that give a fit of mirth for a groat' recite stories of 'Sir Topas' and other heroes of romances (II. ix. x).

he was drawing on his predecessor's language when he equipped Belphoebe with the same footwear, 'In gilden buskins of costly Cordwaine' (*Faerie Queene*, II. iii. 27. 3; edition of 1590); [9] and when he had Sir Calidore observe of the appearance of young Tristram: 'Buskins he wore of costliest cordwayne' (*Faerie Queene*, VI. ii. 6. 1; 1596). His ear may have misled him into using 'costly' because, in Chaucer's 'Sir Thopas', an article almost immediately following the buskins is the robe of the material which Spenser calls 'Checklaton', and Chaucer says that this robe 'coste many a jane'—another archaic phrase in which Spenser apparently follows the older poet, in the conversation of the Squire of Dames: 'Because I could not give her many a Jane' (*Faerie Queene*, III. vii. 58. 4; 1590). As for 'Checklaton', Spenser clothes his giant Disdain in it at *Faerie Queene*, VI. *vii*. 43. 3–4(1596): 'in a Jacket quilted richly rare / Upon checklaton'.

The most significant word for our purpose is this 'Checklaton', for which Gottfried gives (on the basis of sixteen texts, none known to be holograph) the variants in the passage from *A View* as 'Shecklaton', 'Checklaton', 'Ehecklaton'. A reading identical with 'Checklaton' in all but accidentals, namely, 'checklatoun', occurs in the 1532, 1542, undated (but between 1542 and 1561), and 1561 prints of Chaucer's collected works and in no other extant printed or MS source during Spenser's lifetime or prior to it.[10] What Chaucer himself intended was a word widely used in the Middle Ages but not in the later sixteenth century—'siclatoun', a kind of fine scarlet or red cloth, or cloth of gold. All extant MSS read 'siclatoun' with variations in accidentals, or at the worst 'sylke latoun'.[11] All prints prior to those of 1532–1561 read only 'syclatoun' or 'syklatoun'. Spenser, then, was obviously following one of the 1532 to 1561 series, and no other source, in this quotation from *A*

9. This and the two following quotations are cited by J. W. Bennett; W. L. Renwick, *Edmund Spenser* (London, 1925); and others.

10. I have checked this in the Bodleian copies of both issues of 1561; in the Huntington Library copies of the same, in the collection 'Early English Books, 1475–1640' (University Microfilms, Ann Arbor, Michigan), Reels 190, 314; in the 1542 and undated Bodleian copies; in all 1542 and undated copies in the cited microfilm collection, Reel 2, Shipment 1 (STC 5069–5074); in all Bodleian copies and all microfilm copies (in Reel 1, Shipment 1, of the cited series) of Pynson's 1526 and ca. 1492; in the same places (Reel 4, Shipment 1) for Wynkyn de Worde's 1498; in microfilm Reels 4 and 1, Shipment 1, for Caxton's 1484? and 1478? editions. Caxton's two editions, being the earliest, are also covered in John M. Manly and Edith Rickert, *The Text of the Canterbury Tales* ... (Chicago, 1940), VII, 185. Walter W. Skeat stated in his note to 'siclatoun' in his *Works of Geoffrey Chaucer*, V (Oxford, 1894), 186, that Spenser's incorrect 'chekelaton' depended on Thynne, but he drew no conclusions from this.

11. See Manly-Rickert, as in n. 10.

View published in 1596. These editions, moreover, belong to one family: the writer of the dedicatory letter in all of them is identified as Thynne, although the 1561 print contains material stated to have been added by John Stow (1525?–1605). As regards matter attributed to Chaucer, the editions are similar or identical in text and arrangement, except for incremental numbers of small non-Chaucerian items and of typographical errors, and except that the non-Chaucerian 'Plowman's Tale' is included only in 1542 (at the end of the *Tales*) and in the undated and 1561 editions (preceding the Parson's Tale). Spenser would have got from any of these editions approximately the same idea of the Chaucerian accomplishment as he would from any other.

It seems extremely unlikely that an author accustomed to buying books in English,[12] who went to Ireland in 1580, who resided there for almost all the rest of his life, who published a continuation of Chaucer's Squire's Tale (*Faerie Queene* IV) in 1596, and who left behind him an imitation (in *Mutabilitie*) of *The Parlement of Foules* did not normally have Chaucer's text at hand in Ireland. Yet whether or not he had it at hand, in Ireland or England, when composing and revising *A View* in 1596, he there quotes Chaucer with the lordly disregard for checking of one who believes that he knows his passage completely. In fact his recall is very good: his confusion of two passages and his addition of an adjective in the spirit of the original are very natural in someone who has lived with a text for a long time and acquires rooted convictions that a passage is in one place when it is actually in another.

But granting that Spenser knew only the Thynne versions of Chaucer in 1596, was it only in those editions that he had read Chaucer in earlier years? If it could be shown that at an early point he was so familiar with 'Sir Thopas' as to have it firmly in his head, then it would be unlikely that he read it at the time in any other edition or in MS, because he would not then have been so sure in 1596 that the reading was (disregarding accidentals) 'Checklaton' instead of 'siclatoun'; he would have been disturbed by the discrepancy, and an earlier edition might indeed have seemed to him, as it sometimes does to us, to possess greater authority than a later one.

12. Gabriel Harvey noted in his copy of *Howleglas* that Spenser gave him this book (a translation of *Till Eulenspiegel*), *Scoggin*, *Skelton* (both 'merrie tales'), and *Lazarillo* (a translation of the Spanish picaresque tale) in December 1578. On the flyleaf of his copy of *The Traueiler of Ierome Turler* Harvey recorded that in the same year Spenser had given him this book on foreign travel, with a description of Naples. See *Gabriel Harvey's Marginalia*, ed. C. G. Moore Smith (Stratford-upon-Avon, 1913), p. 23; Alexander C. Judson, *The Life of Edmund Spenser* (Baltimore, 1945), p. 53.

Spenser was presumably well acquainted with 'Sir Thopas' at least as early as the late eighties. It seems clear, and has been traditionally accepted, that the Ollyphant of *Faerie Queene,* III. vii. 48 (published in 1590), is descended from Thopas' enemy, the giant of the same name, particularly since in the 1590 edition we learn that a 'Chylde Thopas' brought Ollyphant to confusion (line 4 of this stanza, changed in 1596).[13] (Belphoebe's cordovan ['Cordwaine'] buskins in 1590 point in the same direction.) If we might fully assent to J. W. Bennett's appealing contention that the *Ur-Faerie Queene* which Spenser showed to Gabriel Harvey in 1580 was a continuation of 'Sir Thopas', then we should be in the clear for an even earlier period, but this theory is still *sub judice.* Also if, as traditionally accepted, Spenser imitated the 'Thopas' stanza in the 'March' eclogue of *The Shepheardes Calender,* it would seem that he had the tale firmly in mind before 1579. However, this traditional belief appears to be incorrect. W. L. Renwick got the rhyme scheme of 'March' wrong in his table in *Edmund Spenser,*[14] giving instead the scheme of 'Sir Thopas': $a_8\ a_8\ b_6\ a_8\ a_8\ b_6$. In fact the 'March' stanza is a_8 $a_8\ b_6\ c_8\ c_8\ b_6$, which creates a rather different effect. Although the question of availability is a difficult one, it seems preferable to believe that Spenser found the rhyme scheme of the stanza elsewhere, perhaps by halving the stanza of other English tail-rhyme romances, like *Sir Launfal, Syre Gawene and the Carle of Carelyle,* and *Athelston,* all of which have the scheme $a_8\ a_8\ b_6\ c_8\ c_8\ b_6\ d_8\ d_8\ b_6\ e_8\ e_8\ b_6$, creating almost exactly the same effect as the 'March' stanza. It follows that, no matter how familiar he may have been with 'Sir Thopas' by 1579, that familiarity cannot be demonstrated by an appeal to 'March'. We know that *The Shepheardes Calender* was heavily influenced by Chaucer, but that is a separate question from Spenser's choice of an edition of Chaucer in the earlier part of his career.

In sum, it seems probable that Spenser at all times used only the editions between 1532 and 1561 because his verbal memory apparently allowed him no alternative to the unique reading 'Checklaton', which he quotes from memory; it seems extremely likely that he used only these editions from the late 1580s onward, since his familiarity with 'Sir Thopas' (and the corresponding unlikelihood of his having seen any form but 'checklatoun') is warranted by the fact that *Faerie Queene* 1590 contains 'Chylde Thopas', 'Ollyphant', 'many a Jane', and 'costly Cordwaine'; and it seems virtually certain that from 1590 he knew the

13. As J. W. Bennett points out, p. 19.
14. P. 189.

Thynne editions exclusively, during the time when he had in hand Books IV, V, and VI of *The Faerie Queene,* which had not been ready for publication in 1590 and which contain the decisive 'checklaton' (as in *A View*) as well as 'costliest cordwayne'.

Of the four Thynne editions (1532, 1542, undated but ca. 1550, and 1561) the 1542 to 1561 items are the more likely acquisitions for a man born probably just after the middle of the century, particularly since new editions were generally produced only when stocks of the old were exhausted. By the same token, the 1561 edition is more likely than the 1542 and the companion undated ones, although Spenser might have been happier with a secondhand 1542 or undated copy. The inclusion of Lydgate's (correctly attributed) *Siege of Thebes* in the 1561 edition forced upon the publisher a more crowded page and a bulkier volume than the others. Also, the Bodleian copies, and Huntington Library copies inspected on microfilm,[15] of both issues of 1561 (and presumably all other copies on the same quality of absorbent paper) suffer from bad overinking and compensatory underinking in the large-limbed black letter which was traditional for editions of the ancient English poet. Copies of 1542 and the companion undated edition do not suffer from these blemishes.

What follows from a literary viewpoint from the assumption that Spenser used only the Thynne family of editions? For our immediate purpose the most important consequences are that the obvious dialectic of the Marriage Group of *Canterbury Tales* was preserved for him, and that the Squire's Tale, which Spenser was to continue and complete in *Faerie Queene* IV, is located shortly after the tale of the Squire's father, the Knight, and at the beginning of the Marriage Group, as if to introduce it. Unlike 1484?, ca. 1492, and 1526, Thynne places the Franklin's Tale of Arveragus, Dorigen, and Aurelius after Merchant, Wife of Bath (and the appended Friar and Summoner), and Clerk, so that the essential elements of contending male and female mastery in these earlier tales are shown to be deficient when seen against the free, but concessive and collaborative, regimen of the sexually well matched pair in the final tale of the Franklin. This pair's formula is in effect the Boethian one of friendship as found in the Knight's Tale, where friendship is identical with the harmonious love which holds together the universe and which ought to hold together all human aggregations whatever. On the other hand in 1484?, ca. 1492, and 1526, the Franklin

15. In the cited collection, Reels 190, 314.

follows the Merchant but *precedes* Wife of Bath, Friar, Summoner, and Clerk, so that the desirable culmination of the series in the Franklin's Tale is lost.[16] Moreover, in Thynne Spenser did not find what we recognize as the somewhat anxious *gentilesse* of the Franklin and the Host's disparaging reaction to it ('Straw for youre gentilesse!') in the bridging material between the preceding tale and the Franklin's, material which has formed the springboard for some modern critical disparagement of the moral stances developed in the Franklin's Tale itself (see chapter 5, note 7). In Thynne (uniquely among the early prints) the Merchant's Tale follows the Squire's Tale, and this bridging material is foisted on the Merchant, not the Franklin. Finally, and uniquely in Thynne, the position of the Squire's Tale, following on the Knight's Tale, on the two fabliaux of the Miller and the Reeve, and on the Man of Law's Tale, and immediately preceding the Marriage Group (which opens here with the Merchant's Tale), is very likely to have encouraged Spenser to continue the Squire's Tale as a kind of counterpart of the Knight's Tale and as an introduction to the Marriage Group, looking ahead to the final, enlightened version of married love in the Franklin's Tale in terms of freedom and friendly mutual awareness. The net effect of Thynne's arrangement here, even more than of our modern one, is to develop, upon a basis of sexual compatibility in terms of age, an emphasis on free choice uncoerced by power, money, or fraudulent sexual tenders, and on mutual forbearance, as the only rationally acceptable conditions for human love and marriage.

To emphasize such principles only in discursive terms would have amounted to no more than support for a truism, but what caught Spenser's attention (and catches ours in the different arrangement which we know today) was not the logical opposition of mastery and equality but their mythic embodiment through a dialectic of opposed positions embodied in various tales and characters. In a new dialectic in *Faerie Queene* III (of Love) and IV (of Friendship) and in preceding and following sections, Spenser creates a very similar emphasis (with the identical premise of sexual attraction) on the need for mutual awareness and consideration in love and marriage, as opposed to selfishly motivated male or female domination. Naturally the pattern of characters and events through which Spenser develops this vision differs widely from Chaucer's, yet the stories of Britomart and Artegall, of

---

16. The earliest edition of all, Caxton's of 1478?, places the Franklin's Tale at the end of the Marriage Group; and 1498, remarkably, shows the same order for the Marriage Group as is accepted today.

Amoret and Scudamour, of Florimell and Marinell, and of Spenser's false and hateful lovers are tied at fairly close intervals to those Chaucerian concerns, Chaucerian narrative motifs, and even Chaucerian verbal patterns in the Knight's Tale, *The Parlement of Foules*, and the Marriage Group, which I shall be examining in the next chapters.

Many details of the 1561 edition of Chaucer's works are of secondary importance. The title 'The Dreame of Chaucer', for instance, for *The Book of the Duchess*, in this and other early prints, may account for the title *Dreames*[17] for a work of Spenser's which is not extant under this title, although it may have been incorporated in *The Faerie Queene*. On the other hand, the notion, for instance, that the location of fantasy in the front part of the brain in the Knight's Tale ('Biforen, in his celle fantastik', 1376) may have had something to do with the topography of the faculties in the brain of the House of Alma, in *Faerie Queene*, II. x, collapses in the face of the misprint 'Byforne his felle fantastyk' which is common to the 1532–1561 series exclusively.

As for the wealth of non-Chaucerian material that appears in other early Chaucer prints and in 1532–1561 with the implication that it is by Chaucer, Spenser may indeed have made use of it, but he would not have been so inattentive as to consider much of it Chaucerian. As Skeat pointed out,[18] until 1561 the title pages of the Thynne family of editions did not even claim everything within to be Chaucerian, and many of the pieces betray themselves as coming from other hands. If Spenser read *The Testament of Cresseid* and *The Floure of Curtesye* in any of these volumes with sufficient care to be influenced by them, he surely perceived that they were not by Chaucer, because in them Chaucer is praised in the third person as a great predecessor. Spenser would have had to believe in a depth of Chaucerian irony that even we moderns do not credit if he were to think that the following from *The Testament of Love* was written by Chaucer himself (Love answers the speaker's Boethian question concerning the justice of a God who punishes the evil which He Himself has created):

> ...the noble philosophical poet in English, whiche evermore him besieth and travayleth right sore my name to encrease (wherfore al that willen me good owe to do him worship and reverence both;

17. See Spenser's letter to Harvey dated 'Quarto nonas Aprilis 1580'; Harvey's letters to Spenser dated 'Aprilis septimo' and 'Nono Calendas Maias'. The references occur in Gottfried's cited edition of prose works, pp. 18, 459, 471.

18. *Works of Geoffrey Chaucer*, VII (Oxford, 1897), ix–x.

trewly, his better ne his pere in scole of my rules coude I never fynde)—he (quod she), in a tretis that he made of my servant Troilus, hath this mater touched, and at the ful this question assoyled.[19]

The question of the Plowman's Tale (which may, or perhaps more likely may not, be referred to at the end of *The Shepheardes Calender*) certainly needs canvassing in the future. One further detail, however, may be examined as an earnest of what close textual comparison may reveal when the 1561 and earlier Thynne editions come to be really studied. As in no other print,[20] May of the Merchant's Tale in the 1561 edition is allowed a priapically obscene reflection while being swived in the pear tree by young Damian, not knowing that she is in full sight of her aged, jealous husband. The interpolation quoted here seriously alters what Chaucer had evidently intended as noncommittal reportage of her actions so as to leave her true feelings in the realm of her feminine mystique (*tent* is 'probe', by transference the male member).

A great tent / a thrifty and a longe
She said it was the meryest fytte
That ever in her lyfe she was at yet
My lordes tent serveth me nothing thus
It foldeth twifolde by swete Jesus
He may nat swyve worth a leke
And yet he is full gentyll and full meke
This is lever to me than an evynsong
                    [after 1109; 2353]

Spenser probably took this as Chaucer's. The maladroit proposition that May enjoyed her experience more than an evensong (added so as to get back to the rhyme of the second half of Chaucer's own, split couplet) seems to resound in terms of a different office of the day at the point in Spenser's analogous story of old Malbecco and his young wife Hellenore (*Faerie Queene*, III. ix–x) where Hellenore, unknowingly under the eye of her husband, is shown to enjoy the corresponding experience nine times over with one of her friendly band of satyrs: 'At night, when all they went to sleepe', Malbecco 'vewd'

Whereas his lovely wife amongst them lay,
Embraced of a *Satyre* rough and rude,

19. Skeat's transcription, VII, 123.
20. But as in MS Harley 2251 in the British Museum. See Manly-Rickert, VI, 493.

> Who all the night did minde his joyous play:
> Nine times he heard him come aloft ere day,
> That all his hart with gealosie did swell;
> But yet that nights ensample did bewray,
> That not for nought his wife them loved so well,
> When one so oft a night did ring his matins bell.
>   [x. 48]

Spenser may have been led even closer to his bell image (even to the kind of literary reminiscence that an author hopes will reverberate in the knowledgeable reader's mind) by another obscene interpolation a few lines later in the Merchant's Tale. Like the first one, this is found in no other prints than those of 1532–1561. Having reproached May for her behaviour, old January has received her ready answer that in order to restore his sight magically it was necessary for her to 'strugle' with a man in a tree. January's indignant reaction to her attempt to redefine her action is genuinely Chaucerian in the first line (1132; 2376), but thereafter is apparently spurious in its present position. The point seems to depend upon the elongated shape of a certain type of small bell or may amount to no more than scribal botching;[21] 'bell' is punned upon (I have introduced punctuation):

> 'Strogle!' quod he; 'Ye, algate in it went,
> Styffe and round as any bell:
> It is no wonder though thy belly swell,
> The smocke on his brest lay, so theche
> And ever me thought he poynted on the breche.'

Careful examination of the 1532–1561 editions will no doubt yield many results more striking than this one.

---

21. Professor J. A. W. Bennett has pointed out to me the resemblance to the description of the Friar's 'Semycope', General Prologue, 263.

3

The Knight's Tale, the *Teseida*, and Platonizing Influences

It is impossible to understand the dependence of Spenser's imagination on Chaucer's without properly understanding Chaucer's Knight's Tale. There are, however, many conflicting interpretations of this work today. I trace here the direction in which Chaucer, as a medieval writer of romances, moved from the previous version of the story known to him to his own version. This seems the simplest way of defending a partly traditional interpretation of what Chaucer meant, which interpretation, in turn, Spenser seems to have followed in developing certain parts of *The Faerie Queene*.

Typically a great medieval romance was not a transformation of a commonplace tale but started in a symbiotic relationship of its author with some distinguished earlier narrative, in the reading of which we ourselves can get some inkling of how the later author admired it, but was also perhaps exasperated by it to the point of creativity. The subtlest and most sensitive contemporary criticism of medieval romances was in fact that of the greatest romance writers themselves. In composing new narratives they implicitly judged their predecessors' work by exquisitely modulating its incidents or by turning its plots inside out in accordance with one or another new vision of life and art. Wolfram working with Chrétien's narrative to produce the *Parzival*, or Gottfried working with Chrétien's and others' materials to produce the

Tristan, no doubt seemed to the most knowledgeable part of his audience to have distilled the quintessential poetic and narrative truth latent in an initially remarkable, inherited story.

For the French and German vernaculars these great accomplishments belong to the twelfth and thirteenth centuries. The parallel phenomenon did not appear in English until the fourteenth century. Concerning English romances, the problem of the transformation wrought by a fourteenth-century poet on whatever his imagination started with in shaping *Sir Gawain and the Green Knight* is so fascinating that it has become necessary, in the face of the fact that this material no longer exists, to invent it. In the case of Chaucer, the other great fourteenth-century English romance writer, this kind of implicit literary criticism is much easier to disentangle, because we know that the gestation of his two great romances entailed a close and productive relationship with two works by Boccaccio. Chaucer's use of a version of the *Filostrato*, which is at the base of his *Troilus and Criseyde*, has been carefully studied; his use of the *Teseida*,[1] which is at the base of the Knight's Tale, has received less attention.

If we are to make any sense of Chaucer, we have to begin by recognizing that he was cast in much the same mould as Wolfram or Gottfried and that the interplay between his imagination and Boccaccio's work is not only interesting and in fact startling, but also helps to keep us from misunderstanding what Chaucer was trying to do. To take one obvious example, it has been contended that Theseus in the Knight's Tale took a ridiculous step when he substituted a tourney with a hundred fighters on each side for Arcite's and Palamon's forest combat *à outrance*:[2] Theseus seems to have been simply multiplying the chances for slaughter. But if this is what Chaucer was trying to show about Theseus, then we are entitled to ask why Chaucer reduces the number of deaths in the fighting of this tourney from nine in the *Teseida* to zero in the Knight's Tale.[3]

---

1. Quotations from the *Teseida* follow Giovanni Boccaccio, *Teseida delle nozze d'Emilia*, ed. A. Roncaglia (Bari, 1941). However, all conclusions here have been tested against the variants listed, on the basis of a collation of twenty-eight MSS, in Giovanni Boccaccio, *Teseida, edizione critica*, ed. S. Battaglia (Florence, 1938), and also against Battaglia's attempt to construct a stemma, in his Introduction, pp. xlvi–lxxviii. The very important studies by R. A. Pratt of Chaucer's use of the *Teseida* are cited in the next chapter, n. 3, where they are most relevant.

2. Dale Underwood, 'The First of *The Canterbury Tales*', *ELH*, 26 (1959), 461.

3. The number of dead in the *Teseida* is said to be the same as the number of Niobe's dead children for whom she provided urns (X. viii). If Chaucer did not know how many that was, or see Boccaccio's gloss, he at least knew that there was a funeral for more than one or two bodies (X. i–ix).

Boccaccio made much of the nocturnal funeral for those nine young men; in the Knight's Tale, on the other hand, the initial secret fight, in which one or both combatants would have died, finds with Theseus' help an institutionalized sublimation in a tournament in which, just as he planned, the two chief competitors and all their followers are left alive at the end of the fighting; yet a decisive verdict in favour of one of them is reached so as to end the quarrel. It has nothing to do with Theseus that a tricksy planetary god then arranges for Arcite to be thrown disastrously from his horse. Given the literary assumption of two men's indissoluble love for one woman, and given the fact that, literarily, no honourable solution was available except through personal combat, Theseus did the best he could for them; and Chaucer emphasizes the point by discarding the idea of nine deaths and a melancholy funeral. The differences in the limitations on weapons to be used in the battle in Chaucer's and Boccaccio's accounts also seem to be revealing.[4]

A more important transformation of Boccaccio's equation of forces belongs to a more complicated set of facts about the Knight's Tale. We know that one of its episodes, apparently original with Chaucer and certainly not contained in the *Teseida,* has strong affinities with an episode in another of Chaucer's works, the Prologue to *The Legend of Good Women,* belonging, probably, to the *Canterbury* period. At a certain point in the Knight's Tale, Theseus' wife Hippolyta, his sister-in-law Emelye, and the ladies following them kneel as a group before him, weeping and lamenting, in order to beg his mercy for Arcite and Palamon. He has just caught these two fighting in the forest (in flat violation of his authority as the local feudal ruler), and they have just revealed themselves as his enemies, violating his will in other particulars. Correspondingly, in the similar incident in the Prologue to *The*

---

4. One weapon that Boccaccio eliminated is indeed reinstated: the lance. Boccaccio presumably had in mind the thrown spear that wreaks so much havoc in Classical epic; Chaucer, on the other hand, could not imagine how to describe a tourney without the preliminary medieval charge of horsed knights with lances levelled at their opponents, and perhaps he could not resist the resulting picturesque touch (1747–50; 2605–8). Boccaccio's Teseo permits the use of sword, mace, and double-edged axe, but nothing else (VII. xii). Chaucer's Theseus prohibits the axe and is much more circumstantial: no one (on pain of death) may bring into the lists arrows, a dagger, or a short sword which would customarily be used for stabbing (1686–91; 2544–49). No one may charge more than once with the lance. Teseo proclaims that anyone captured or driven outside the area defined for fighting may not re-enter the battle (VII. cxxxii). Theseus provides that anyone who is captured by the opposing side must be taken to one of the two stakes at the ends of the field, and must not re-enter the battle (1693–96; 2551–54). In addition if one of the leaders is taken (as happens) or killed, the battle is to stop (1697–99; 2555–57).

Legend, Chaucer, kneeling in his shirt among the daisies while the Love God wrathfully accuses him of disobeying his behests, is interceded for by the flower-lady Alceste. The reasoning which finally moves both rulers to mercy is similar even at the verbal level, but its operation in the two cases is strikingly different. It is Theseus who tells himself that circumstances alter cases, that any all-powerful ruler is a tyrant (an operative word, this) unless he tempers justice with mercy, and that men such as young Arcite and Palamon are driven by a force stronger than their reason. The narrator observes of Theseus: 'pitee renneth soone in gentil herte' (903; 1761). No such internal conversation occurs, however, in the case of the Love God: it is the lady Alceste who must put to him the case about tyrants of Lombardy and about the impropriety of punishing so harmless a figure as the plump penitent before him. It is about her that the same remark is made, or repeated: 'pitee renneth soone in gentil herte' (491; G 491). Both Theseus and the Love God elicit the kind of startled respect called forth by the personal appearances of anyone with self-assured power, but the Love God is capable of enormities; Theseus, on the other hand, has the ability to reason his own aroused lordly will into submission, as Chaucer says (1762–69).

In the Knight's Tale it is in fact the sadistic treatment doled out by the despotic Love God himself to his subjects Arcite and Palamon that has brought them into mortal combat; and it is what the Love God has done to them that Theseus will attempt to right, to the extent that a mature and understanding fellow human can help a man in love. Shortly before Theseus interrupts the combat, the narrator generalizes on the jealousy of Arcite and Palamon as well as on Love himself and on rule:

> O Cupide, out of alle charitee!
> O regne, that wolde no felawe have to thee!
> Ful sooth is said that love ne lordshipe
> Wol nought, his thankes, have no felaweshipe.
>   [765–78; 1623–26]

That is, the God of Love has no supply of *caritas*—of love of the charitable kind; Love desires to have no companion in his reign (both the God of Love, and any jealous lover under his rule, are intended; the one infects the other); neither Love (continues the narrator) nor those in a state of ruling or lordship willingly accept companionship (friendship, fellowship of equals). Yet this generalization seems to be promptly contradicted by the behaviour of Theseus, already noted. By reasoning himself out of his rage and by warning himself of the injustice of tyranny, he shows himself to be an out-of-the-ordinary ruler because of his *gentilesse* (903; 1761). He immediately produces agreeable banter on the subject of the Love Despot's arbitrariness in inciting two of his servants to bloodying each other for hours on end over a woman who is not even conscious of their existence. Such a lord may well be called 'a god for his miracles'! Theseus then acknowledges his own former subjection to this nonsense, offers his friendship to the two former friends to the point of granting them their freedom at some danger to himself (since they are the survivors of the Theban royal line; and he has fought the Thebans), and finally sketches out for them the plan for the institutionalized sublimation of their struggle—the tournament —which has just been mentioned.

This scene in the Knight's Tale has very little to do with the *Teseida*. Boccaccio's Teseo was not really angry with Arcita and Palemone, for he was not really a feudal ruler who saw secret fighting as an infringment on his rights. He in fact complimented them on their courage in combat (V. lxxxv). Teseo had not been, like Theseus, appealed to by a group of kneeling, weeping, lamenting, imploring women, and his effortless pardon was concerned only with Palemone and Arcita's role as his former enemies (V. lxxxviii–xcii).

The parallelism between Chaucer's two scenes, one in the Knight's Tale and the other in the Prologue to *The Legend*, is important to my case and has had to be described. Nevertheless, this parallelism is familiar, and it has long been recognized that the repetition of the circumstances implies their importance in Chaucer's imagination. It has not been previously noticed, however, that an additional scene in the Knight's Tale, the third in my series here, is parallel to the other two of Chaucer's in a way that does not follow Boccaccio in several crucial respects. The earlier part of the *Teseida*, like the *Thebaid* of Statius, and unlike the Knight's Tale, gives us the story of Theseus' previous conquest of a realm of women who had murdered their men and taken over the rule. These women were the Amazons, whose queen Teseo subdued and married. Boccaccio devoted more than eleven hundred lines to this part of the story and highlighted it by placing it at the very beginning of the tale, but Chaucer concerns himself with it almost not at all. The conquest of the Amazons and Theseus' return to Athens with his new wife and with her sister Emelye are summarized by the Knight-narrator in twenty-one hurried lines, without really taking us out of the pilgrimage frame: at the end of those lines he in fact puts us back in the midst of the pilgrims' storytelling contest:

I wol nat letten eek noon of this route—
Lat every felawe telle his tale aboute,
And lat see now who shal the soper winne.
And ther I lefte I wol ayain biginne.
[31–34; 889–92]

With that over, the Knight plunges into his story proper, and does not once leave it until he concludes, over twenty-two hundred lines later. What he does first in it, without the lengthy preparation of the same incident in the *Teseida* and the *Thebaid*, is to introduce us abruptly to Theseus' encounter with the weeping, lamenting Theban women waiting for him at the Temple of Clemency, where the parallel scene occurs. Unlike the women of the other two authors' accounts (*Teseida*, II. xxv; *Thebaid*, XII. 540–45), these are *kneeling*, in the road, two-by-two, awaiting Theseus.[5] Just as Palamon describes himself and his companion in the later scene as 'caitive' wretches (859; 1717) so these women also are described by their spokeswoman as 'caitives' (66; 924); they have been victimized, they make a poor showing (in black), their spokeswoman has been the wife of a king, and the others have similarly been highly placed (as Palamon and Arcite are 'kings' sisters' sons', now reduced to wretchedness). In Theseus there is the preliminary whiff of anger (Teseo was said simply to be 'stupefatto', II. xxvi):

'What folk been ye that at myn home-cominge
Perturben so my feeste with cryinge?'
Quod Theseus. 'Have ye so greet envye
Of myn honour, that thus complaine and crye?'
[47–50; 905–8]

And this anger is then extinguished by 'pitee'—compassion. In the case of his treatment of Palamon and Arcite what we have heard is the

5. Chaucer may have got the germ of this idea from the *Roman de Thèbes*, although we are not sure that he read this romance. I use the edition of L. Constans (2 vols.; Société des Anciens Textes Français, 29, 1890). In this romance it is King Adrastus who makes an appeal on behalf of the Theban women to Theseus, who is returning with his host from having subdued a rebellious vassal (9905–34). Adrastus, meeting Theseus in open country, recognizes him, rides towards him, descends from his own horse when he has come closer, runs up to Theseus on foot, and then falls humbly at his feet ('Vint corant vers liu a pie; / Vers le duc cort isnèlement. / A ses piez chiet mout humilement', 9942–44). Theseus immediately descends from his own horse; after an explanation the gentle duke is moved to pity ('li gentiz dus tot escota, / En son cuer grant pitié en a: / Par la main prist rei Adrastus, / De la terre le leva sus', 9995–98). It has been previously suggested that Chaucer got from the *Roman* the idea of having Theseus ride a horse rather than a chariot. See F. N. Robinson's note to 949 ff., in his edition of *The Works of Geoffrey Chaucer*, 2nd ed. (Boston, 1957).

famous, repeated Chaucerian sentence: 'Pitee renneth soone in gentil herte'; with these ladies, what is asked for, and received, is 'Som drope of pitee, thurgh thy gentilesse' (62; 920).

The most striking parallels between the two scenes, however, are that these Theban women are the victims of a political tyrant as Arcite and Palamon are victims of the Love Despot, and that what is being demanded of Theseus in both scenes is that he should right wrongs committed by tyrants. Creon, newly ruler of Thebes, has perpetrated a selfishly arbitrary act against women: he will not allow the dead bodies of their menfolk, killed in war, to be consumed by fire in the traditional manner, but has left them for dogs to eat.

In terms of the new emphasis with which Chaucer here transforms the story from Boccaccio's version, Theseus is a ruler susceptible to compassion through a *gentilesse* which, narratively, is first actuated by the pleas of kneeling women; and he is, in terms of the same emphasis, moved to act against the tyranny of a ruler opposite in kind to himself, who is arbitrarily afflicting others. Near the beginning of the tale Theseus in his generosity moves against Creon and his forces, defeating them and killing Creon in personal combat, so that the Theban women may suitably carry out the funerals of their shamed menfolk. He rights a wrong and sees to it that justice prevails. Similarly with the Love God later in the tale.

Another tract of narrative in which Chaucer rearranges the emphases of the *Teseida* concerns a harmonious relationship near the beginning of the tale, and its sudden collapse. The earlier friendship between Arcite and Palamon is much more strongly drawn by Chaucer than it was by Boccaccio for their counterparts, who performed their prodigies of friendship only at the end. When, in the Knight's Tale, the two are first found by the pillagers in the heap of Theban bodies, they are wearing identical armorial bearings and are immediately identified as the sons of two sisters (161; 1019). A little later, we are told that they are not only cousins but friends and brothers by a ritual oath, sworn never to hinder, and always to aid, each other (271 – 83; 1129 – 41). Both the relationship and the oath are Chaucer's invention, as far as we know.

This loving friendship, however, is abruptly overturned as soon as they see Emelye in the garden below their prison. In the *Teseida*, on the other hand, the two men uttered their love-plaints to each other in an extended amity which seems very curious to anyone coming to this work only after reading the later one. Just as not much had earlier been made of their friendship, so nothing was made here of their hostility. It was only when Palemone went to encounter Arcita in the forest, at a very advanced point when the two young men had already both left prison, that it occurred to one of them to be jealous of his companion and to attack him; the companion responded to the challenge with great reluctance. In the case of Chaucer's two plighted brother-cousin-friends, on the other hand, it is as though the first kind of affection could not exist in the presence of the second, erotic one, and is driven out by aggressive competitiveness. Palamon and Arcite have become the votaries of a Cupid, one of whose tyrannical conditions is that each of his subjects should be out of charity with his neighbour—with his former friend or 'felawe'. What, in fact, has been quoted previously here concerning this 'Cupide, out of alle charitee' was ostensibly intended by the narrator to describe Arcite and Palamon themselves.

So far, then, we have seen a certain parallelism. Two kinds of love are in opposition in Chaucer's tale, and are inimical to each other. The harmonious love called friendship, which exists as a given at the beginning in the earlier career of Palamon and Arcite, is driven out by the exclusive and competitive kind of love associated with the imperious Love God. Correspondingly, Theseus as a ruler exhibits charitable friendship towards those whom he might have hated or repulsed, but both Creon and the Love God, with whom he contends, are self-seeking tyrants.

The last of Chaucer's realignments of the patterns of force in the *Teseida* which needs to be considered here concerns the roles of the pagan gods in general. Boccaccio often showed them as gracious to man. Chaucer makes them uniformly indifferent or malign. In doing so, he brings them closer to the usual medieval estimate of them. Particularly those members of the ancient pantheon who were planetary gods (here Mercury, Venus, Mars, and Saturn) were considered to exert astral influence upon the earth so as to help in creating the superficially senseless pattern of events called Fortune. Beyond the concentric heavenly spheres of these pagan deities, however, the true God, who wishes to be our friend, creates for man the ultimately charitable pattern of Providence, which, ultimately only, is subserved by the events associated with Fortune herself. The classic definition of this dichotomy is given by Boethius, but it is the first half of the dichotomy with which I am now concerned.

From one point of view—that of the speaker at the beginning of the *Consolation*, or that of Palamon and Arcite in their despair—the world makes no sense, and its divine rulers seem cruel or arbitrary. Two of these rulers in the Knight's Tale are not in themselves planets but only the son and the wife of planetary deities. Arcite and Palamon are victims not only of an arbitrary Cupid but also of a vengeful Juno, who is also driven by jealousy and exclusivity in love. We hear at one point concerning Palamon himself

> the fir of jalousye up sterte
> Within his brest, and hente him by the herte
> So woodly that he lik was to biholde
> The boxtree or the asshen dede and colde.
>
> [441–44; 1299–1302]

He is led immediately after this fit to reflect on Juno, who hates him and all Thebans (as he hates Arcite) because she is in the same plight as he is: she, too, is (with double verbal repetition) 'jalous and eek wood' (471; 1329). She is obsessed by her own desire for lordship in love, and does Thebes as much damage as possible, because of Semele and Alcmena, who had drawn the attentions of her gallant husband.

The planetary gods who do malice to Palamon and Arcite are more important than Juno. One of the quietest yet most effective of the transpositions which Chaucer performs upon his source is to eliminate the Mercury who in answer to Arcita's prayer becomes the benign guide of his soul at the end of the *Teseida*, and to introduce a Mercury who, in the midst of the Knight's Tale, is the instigator of Arcite's journey back to Athens and to his death. There was no divine messenger in Boccaccio's romantic account of Arcita's visiting the seashore yearningly, speaking to the breeze from Athens that may have touched Emilia, finding a ship newly arrived from there, gaining news of the death of Emilia's official suitor, and making up his mind privately to return, etc. (IV. xxxi–xxxix). In place of all this Chaucer gives us a divine intervention of deliberately cruel ambiguity, with an appropriate evocation of the occasion when Mercury put Argus to sleep in order to kill him:

> Him thoughte how that the winged god Mercurye
> Biforn him stood, and bad him to be murye:
> His sleepy yerde in hande he bar uprighte;
> An hat he wered upon his heres brighte;
> Arrayed was this god, as he took keep,
> As he was whan that Argus took his sleep;
> And saide him thus, 'To Atthenes shaltou wende:
> Ther is thee shapen of thy wo an ende.'
>
> [527–34; 1385–92]

Palamon and Arcite make clear in very Boethian speeches, which are much more extensive than those found in the *Teseida,* that the gods known to them are all cruel or indifferent:

> Thanne saide he, 'O cruel goddes that governe
> This world with binding of youre word eterne,
> And writen in the table of adamaunt
> Youre parlement and youre eterne graunt,
> What is mankinde more unto you holde
> Than is the sheep that rouketh in the folde?
> For slain is man right as another beest,
> And dwelleth eek in prison and arrest,
> And hath siknesse and greet adversitee,
> And ofte times giltelees, pardee.
> What governance is in this prescience
> That giltelees tormenteth innocence!'
>   [445–56; 1303–14]

These planetary forces are harrowingly enumerated in the Temples of Mars and Diana; the victims of Venus through unfortunate love are similarly enumerated in her Temple. The outrageous solution of the strife between Mars and Venus—to let Arcite win but then to kill him—is the strongest example of their arbitrariness, which emerges in fictional reality as mere childishness. The entire conference of the gods is, significantly, Chaucer's invention.[6] The strife becomes so grave 'That Juppiter was bisy it to stente' (1584; 2442), that is, was occupied in controlling it. Chaucer, however, keeps Jupiter in the background as one pagan deity who could later be represented, among the non-Christian Greeks, as a surrogate for the true Lord of the universe. Saturn, instead (1592; 2450), steps forward and recommends himself as a problem solver simply on the strength of his gifts, which are indeed miraculous in the ironical sense in which Theseus had said Cupid might be called a god 'for his miracles':

> 'My cours, that hath so wide for to turne,
> Hath more power than woot any man:
> Myn is the drenching in the see so wan;
> Myn is the prison in the derke cote;

---

6. The germ of this in the *Teseida* consists of only four lines (VII. lxvii. 5–8) with no hint of irony: 'e si ne nacque in ciel novella lite / intra Venere e Marte, ma trovata / da lor fu via con maestrevol arte / di far contenti i prieghi d'ogni parte'.

Myn is the strangling and hanging by the throte;
The murmur and the cherles rebellinge;
The groining and the privee empoisoninge;
I do vengeance and plein correccioun
Whil I dwelle in the signe of the leoun;
Myn is the ruine of the hye halles,
The falling of the towres and of the walles
Upon the minour or the carpenter;
I slow Sampson, shaking the piler;
And mine be the maladies colde,
The derke tresons, and the castes olde;
My looking is the fader of pestilence.'
[1596–1611; 2454–69]

What he proposes is a successful operation in which the patient dies for
the sake of the *amour propre* of his absentminded physicians. So that
Mars may show his power in giving the promised victory to Arcite,
Palamon must be defeated; but so that Venus may lose no jot of
reputation after having promised Emelye to Palamon, Arcite must be
mortally wounded upon the field of his victory (and suffer a lingering
death thereafter). Saturn, as he himself says, stands ready to fulfil his
divine granddaughter's desires (1619–20; 2477–78). The interests of
those outside his exalted family do not enter into his calculations.

Upon the picture of malignant or indifferent heavenly and earthly
rulers and of the collapse of the young protagonists' friendship in
combative *amor* supervene, of course, the friendly mediation of Theseus
but also the final providential pattern of the God who is love and to
whom Theseus is merely vicar in Athens. All is knitted together in the
best consolatory tradition of romance in the duke's great speech on the
occasion of his 'parlement' and 'eterne graunt', of quite different tenor
from what Palamon had originally intended by those words. The despair is shown to be shallow and parochial, which had led Arcite to say

That ther nis erthe, water, fir, ne air,
Ne creature that of hem maked is,
That may me helpe or do confort in this,
[388–90; 1246–48]

and which will lead Dorigen in the Franklin's Tale to guess that whatever controls the tides of that water must wish to destroy humanity and
her lover. The apparent senselessness of the world is no more than

apparent, and the incomprehension which had led Palamon and Dorigen to throw up their hands and resign explanation to the argumentative experts ('The answere of this lete I to divines,' Knight's Tale, 465; 1323; 'To clerkes lete I al disputisoun,' Franklin's Tale, 182; 890) is shown to be the answer of those who have not been able to maintain their liberty of spirit, as a mature Theseus can do.

The First Mover or Jupiter or 'Prince' (Theseus begins) has bound with the fair chain of love the 'fir, the air, the water, and the lond' (2134; 2992) in sure limits, so that they make a harmony together. Or, as Chaucer translates Boethius in the same context, 'the see, gredy to flowen, constreyneth with a certein eende his floodes, so that it is nat leveful to strecche his brode termes or bowndes uppon the erthes' (II. Metrum 8). That Mover is to be praised and thanked for what he has done and what he is about to do. In the finite, temporal, and corruptible world, in a way first described in Plato's *Timaeus* and honoured repeatedly in the Middle Ages in the figures of Nature and Genius, that Prince has necessarily subjected us to temporal limitation, but has given us, as the best possible substitute for perpetual duration, endurance through successive regenerations:

> Wel may men knowe, but it be a fool,
> That every part deriveth from his hool;
> For Nature hath nat taken his biginning
> Of no partye, or cantel of a thing,
> But of a thing that parfit is and stable,
> Descending so til it be corrumpable;
> And therfore for his wise purveyaunce
> He hath so wel biset his ordinaunce
> That speces of thinges and progressiouns
> Shullen enduren by successiouns,
> And nought eterne, withouten any lie.
>   [2147–57; 3005–15]

Almost all of this passage depends on Boethius (*Consolation*, II. Metrum 8; IV. Prosa 6, Metrum 6; III. Prosa 10). The obvious application of this to the immediate situation is that Arcite's death is the common fate. His 'freend' (2192, 2193; 3050, 3051; the word is repeated) ought not to be rebellious against the Prince of all, indeed ought to rejoice insofar as Arcite has died at the height of his reputation and has left 'this foule prison of this lif' (2203; 3061). Providentially, perhaps death was the only way out for one of the two fixed lovers. A less obvious but equally important application is that two of his friends, that is, his 'cosin and his wif',[7] ought to enter upon the social state which institutionalizes these 'successiouns', so as to make 'of sorwes two / Oo parfit joye, lasting everemo': 'the bond / That highte matrimoigne or mariage', love without discord or exclusivity.

The sign manual of this love is selfless charity, opposite in spirit to the Love God and all the 'payens cursed olde rites' and 'hir goddes' (*Troilus*, V. 1849–50) who drew the prayers of Palamon, Arcite, and Emelye to Mars, Venus,[8] and Diana, and who will cause Aurelius in the Franklin's Tale to pray to unregarding Apollo (Franklin's Tale, 323–71; 1023–71). This charity is thus expressed:

And thus with alle blisse and melodye
Hath Palamon ywedded Emelye;
And God, that al this wide world hath wrought,
Sende him his love that hath it dere abought.
[2339–42; 3097–3100]

With some straining this may be taken as a request to the true Creator, the Godhead, to convey to Palamon in perpetuity the love for which he, Palamon, has had to pay so dearly. Much more centrally, however, and with a revision of pronominal reference, these lines constitute an appeal to that same Creator of the world to send to Palamon the love of Christ, who out of His love for us all redeemed the world at the cost of great suffering and of His own life. He is described similarly in the injunction to love Him at the end of the *Troilus*:

And loveth him, the which that right for love
Upon a crois, oure soules for to beye,
First starf, and roos, and sit in hevene above.
[V.1842–44]

The situation among Theseus, Emelye, and Palamon bears one significant resemblance to that of Nature and the falcons in Chaucer's *Parlement of Foules* (see next chapter), except that we are now at a later stage in the progress of a love affair. There, Nature had allotted to the formel, not yet ready for Cupid's works, a year to decide among her

7. 'Wif' is presumably Chaucer's slip. In the *Teseida* Emilia is betrothed to Arcita, although there is no marriage celebration.

8. It should be incidentally noted that Palamon unavailingly prays to Venus (for whom he mistakes Emelye at first sight) to be released from the 'tirannye' of Theseus' prison (1104–11). Quite contrary to the tenor of this prayer, it is only his future friend Theseus who will help him.

three lovers, although Nature obviously inclined towards the first of them; here, in the Knight's Tale, the year appointed before the tournament was to be held has long since passed (in fact, several years have passed since the tournament, though only days had passed in the *Teseida*), and the suitors are reduced to one. Theseus is thus justified (with the unruffled agreement of his 'parlement') in urging the overdue decision on the devotee of Diana as though it had already been made; but that urging includes, of course, a genial invitation to show independently the 'gentilesse' through 'pitee' that he himself has already twice manifested:

'Lat se now of youre wommanly pitee.
. . . .
For gentil mercy oughte to passen right.'
[2225, 2231; 3083, 3089]

The relation between love and friendship is very plain here. The state of harmony which had been represented by Arcite and Palamon's preliminary brotherhood in friendship, without jealousy or striving between them, is reinstituted at the end of the story in terms of Palamon and Emelye's perfect and permanent love, without 'jalousye or any other teene' (2349; 3106).

Yet friendship is at least as important a motif, emphasized positively and negatively throughout the tale. Arcite and Palamon are, and then are not, close friends; Arcite's liberation from prison is accomplished because of his friendship with Perotheus; and Perotheus' intervention is successful because he and Theseus have been friends, 'Sin thilke day that they were children lite':

For in this world he loved no man so.
And he loved him as tendrely again;
So wel they loved, as olde bookes sayn,
That whan that oon was deed, soothly to telle,
His felawe wente and soughte him down in helle.
[338–42; 1196–1200]

Palamon escapes from prison 'By helping of a freend'; Cupid and other lords have no desire for friends; Palamon and Emelye both mourn Arcite as their friend; chiefly, Theseus offers his unreserved friendship (966; 1824) to his two former enemies as he pardons them in the forest. From this point on he will do all that he can for them. In this connection Chaucer created a symmetry by an already mentioned addition to the tale, which Spenser later uses: the original two friends, Arcite and Palamon, were sons of two sisters; the surviving two friends, Palamon and Theseus, are married to two sisters. Theseus' bliss had been made complete at the beginning of the tale by his marriage to the Amazon Hippolyta, whose sister is Emelye. The four are thus joined in marriage and friendship, and the relationship of these two bonds brings us to the verge of the Franklin's speech (see page 69), in his own tale at the end of the Marriage Group, on the need for selfless friendship if love and marriage are to endure (it also brings us close to a variety of topics in *The Faerie Queene*).

One other kind of loving relationship in the Knight's Tale brings us back to the political level on which Creon acts the part of tyrant and Theseus that of merciful ruler. It is original with Chaucer that Theseus' occasion for bringing together Palamon and Emelye at the end of the tale is a '*parlement*'

> At Atthenes, upon a certain points and cas;
> Among the whiche points yspoken was
> To have with certain contrees alliaunce,
> And have fully of Thebans obeisaunce:
> For which this noble Theseus anoon
> Leet senden after gentil Palamon,
> Unwist of him what was the cause and why;
> But in his blake clothes sorwefully
> He cam at his comandement in hie.
> Tho sente Theseus for Emelye.
>
> [2113–22; 2971–80]

It may be asked why Theseus has injected a 'parlement' to achieve unity with Thebes into the business of bringing about a marriage.[9] Certainly

9. For a possible contemporary historical allusion to the 'parlement', see Robinson's note to 2973. But as Albert C. Baugh (*Chaucer's Major Poetry*, New York, 1963) points out in the corresponding note in his edition, it is hardly necessary to seek an historical reference. In any case, an explanation in terms of the story is needed. Note that the *Teseida* has no 'parlement'. Teseo and the nobles who had been in the battle simply go to where Emilia is sitting with other women (XII. iv)—not the place for a formal council. In the Knight's Tale, Palamon and Emelye are summoned to the 'parlement'.

It has apparently not been noticed that a hint for Theseus' final speech came to Chaucer from Teseo's speech to Palemone and his company after the battle (IX. lii–liii). Teseo says that Providence in creating the world may have known the end of every seed ('semenza'); in any case, it is certainly true that we are guided at the pleasure of the Fates, and any man who tries to act contrary to the Fates' decree is deceived (cf. Knight's Tale, 2187–88; 3045–46). Teseo's intention here is to comfort the losers. He continues in stanza lvii to say that their defeat was a thing 'avanti assai pensata / nel chiaro e santo divino intelletto'. Another likely borrowing that has not been noticed depends on a partial correspondence between *Teseida*, I. xxxviii, and Knight's Tale, 780–88; 1638–46.

the answer is that if the former discord between Thebes and Athens, brought about by Creon's despotic act, is to be replaced by harmony, then a marriage between the only surviving member of the Theban royal family (as we know Palamon to be) and the sister-in-law of the duke of Athens is a solid basis for this political realignment. Or to put the matter slightly differently: while the two friends at the beginning of the tale were of the one city of Thebes, the two friends at the end of the tale are of two different cities; and it is through the love and friendship among these two friends and their two wives that the two cities of Thebes and Athens will be bound together forever. To love and friendship, then, we may add national peace among Greeks, as a king's subject would see it in a nascent national state like England, endangered above all by internal contention. It is thus that Chaucer embodies at the end of his tale (as he had done in the midpoint of his *Troilus*) the three forms of harmonizing love which, according to the *Consolation,* will mirror in the human heart the harmony of the rest of the universe, bound in its course, and restrained from chaos, only by love:

Hic sancto populos quoque
Iunctos foedere continet,
Hic et coniugii sacrum
Castis nectit amoribus,
Hic fidis etiam sua
Dictat iura sodalibus.
O felix hominum genus,
Si vestros animos amor
Quo caelum regitur regat.
                    [II. Metrum 8. 22–30]

This is translated by Chaucer as

This love halt togidres peples joyned with an holy boond, and knytteth sacrement of mariages of chaste loves; and love enditeth lawes to trewe felawes. O weleful were mankynde, yif thilke love that governeth hevene governede yowr corages.[10]

The same thoughts appear in the *Troilus* at III. 1746–64. The love and lordship that do not willingly endure 'felaweshipe' yield in the conclusion of the Knight's Tale to a heavenly ruler and an earthly one who extend the hand of friendship to their subjects and enable us to become loving 'felawes' one of another.

10. Quoted from Robinson's 2nd edition. See the Textual Note at the front of this book.

As to the *Troilus*, in a sense it is because the evocation of Boethius' three forms of human love—marriage, friendship, and the political unit—occurs at the midpoint of the story, rather than at the end, that we have little to say here about that great romance, even though Chaucer worked so much Boethian material into the version of it which we now possess. Because the world of Troilus and Criseyde contained no politically pacifying force like Theseus, but rather the ultimate political disaster of war, Criseyde's troth broke under too great a strain and her union with Troilus was destroyed. The friendship that Pandare offered Troilus was irrelevant and pointless under these final circumstances. All three forms—fully committed sexual love, friendship, nation —collapsed. The ascetic condemnation of earthly bliss, which is a minor element in Theseus' final speech, and is confined to the beginning of *The Parlement of Foules*, is front stage centre at the conclusion of the *Troilus*.

In Book IV and elsewhere in *The Faerie Queene*, components of the pattern of the Knight's Tale are fundamental—a stage of anarchic love, another stage of friendship and love among four persons in accord with Nature and courtesy, a Theseus figure, and a fixed combat to put an end to sexual competition. Yet Spenser made little or no use of the *Troilus*. The reason, perhaps, is that the pathos from which there is no awakening does not belong to the theory of epic upon which *The Faerie Queene* depends. For the philosophical pathos of the reflection that, in the light of eternity and the 'Sabaoth sight', all earthly to-and-fro is vanity, there is of course a place at the end of *Mutabilitie* (as there is in the Knight's Tale). But in a revelation of what man's erected, divinely inspired wit can show that the world should be if it were not for the Fall (to paraphrase Sir Philip Sidney), the final insufficiency of Troilus, and the unavailability of a Theseus figure (or, in Spenserian terms, of an Arthur figure) to help such a young hero, would be a grave violation of the spirit of *The Faerie Queene* and probably of what Spenser himself can best give us.

4

The Parlement of Foules

All of both Chaucer's and Spenser's gravest, explicitly philosophical fictions fall easily into the class of either chivalric romance or moralized landscape. The moralized landscape of Chaucer's that is of greatest importance to us here is the dream vision *The Parlement of Foules*,[1] belonging to the same chapter of his intellectual development as the Knight's Tale, the *Troilus*, and the Prologue to *The Legend of Good Women*. It is likely that all of these were written within the space of ten years in Chaucer's life, and quite possibly within five. Chaucerians are perhaps closer to a consensus on the significance of *The Parlement* than on that of the Knight's Tale, but we must still go carefully. The general traditions of moralized landscape and of dream vision, so helpful in accounting for run-of-the-mill examples of such writing, are not always of much use in determining what Chaucer was doing here. One must attend vigilantly to the foreground of *The Parlement* itself and to its place in Chaucer's *œuvre*. The work influenced Spenser's imagination

---

1. Fundamental for its study are Charles O. McDonald, 'An Interpretation of Chaucer's *Parlement of Foules*', *Speculum*, 30 (1955), 444–57, rpt. in Richard J. Schoeck and Jerome Taylor, eds., *Chaucer Criticism*, vol. II (Notre Dame, 1961), and in Edward Wagenknecht, ed., *Chaucer: Modern Essays in Criticism* (New York, 1959); J. A. W. Bennett, *The Parlement of Foules* (Oxford, 1957). A very useful edition is that of D. S. Brewer (2nd. ed., Manchester and New York, 1972). R. A. Pratt's relevant work is cited in n. 3.

profoundly, and not only where he most closely imitated it in *Mutabilitie*.

It seems more likely than not that the occasion for *The Parlement of Foules* was some historical celebration, presumably of a marriage, as is obviously the case with one of its imitators, Dunbar's *The Thrissil and the Rois*. For that matter, the earlier version of the Knight's Tale, mentioned in the Prologue to *The Legend of Good Women* under the title of *Palamon and Arcite*, may also have been written to celebrate a wedding. The historical facts are still worth looking for and may yet be uncovered. Meanwhile, I continue here the modern habit of discussing *The Parlement* as a literary embodiment of a set of ideas, which it must be, no matter what their historical application.

Certainly these ideas are close to the ones just discussed in the Knight's Tale, even though we are not now dealing with a mere transposition of that chivalric adventure into dream vision. Also, either before or at some stage in the composition of *The Parlement* Chaucer had surely completed a careful reading of the *Teseida*,[2] for his Temple of Venus in *The Parlement* is a fairly close imitation of Boccaccio's (IX. ccxi–ccxciv), much closer than that in the Knight's Tale itself. *The Parlement*'s knightly eagle suitors for the love of one formel eagle, all of them exclaiming 'al redy Sire' at the possibility of fighting for possession of her, come from the same mould as Palamon and Arcite. Similarly, the role of Nature here is close to that of Theseus. In personality Nature is straightforward and colloquial, like him, and is concerned to help all living beings, but here in particular to help a small group of aristocratic males who are in competition with one another, and a virginal, sexually reluctant female who is the object of their love. In connection with his other birds in *The Parlement*, Chaucer was, it is true, mobilizing a very widespread tradition, but even here he may sometimes have had the *Teseida* particularly in mind. When Boccaccio's Emilia urges upon Palemone a version of Chaucer's goose's solution (*Parlement*, 567) to the quandry of the three aristocrats, Palemone's answer is close to that of Chaucer's turtledove (582–85): Emilia suggests that the other Greek cities, full of beauties more praiseworthy than her own, will be able to make just restitution for the harm that has been done him in his love (IX. lxviii–lxix); Palemone answers

'Da me amata sarete soletta,

---

2. He had already used the *Teseida* briefly in *The House of Fame* and *Anelida and Arcite*. See Robinson's notes.

né mai fortuna cangerá disio.
Se' fati v'hanno per altrui eletta,
in cio non posso piu contrastare io;
ma che io v'ami esser non me pò tolto,
ne fia, mentre sarò in vita volto.'
[IX. lxxviii. 3–8]

['You alone shall be loved by me, nor shall Fortune ever alter my love. If the fates have chosen you for another, I cannot struggle against their decree; but that I love you cannot be taken from me, nor shall be while I live.']

It is the nature of things, as in Theseus' effort to help, that Nature cannot give everyone what he or she wants. Two of those three eagles (like two of Spenser's three suitors in his Squire's Tale) must ultimately 'go pipen in an ivy leef'. It is Nature's law—part of the harmonizing work of her who sees to it that all the universe proceeds in harmonious 'progressiouns and successiouns' rather than in wilful chaos—that the female eagle should not be immediately coerced, by a male eagle or any other being, into a hated union, even though her own nature, by another natural law, will in time ready her for the works of Venus and of Cupid. As Nature says in *The Parlement,*

Ye knowe wel how, Saint Valentines Day,
By my statut and thurgh my governaunce,
Ye come for to chese—and flee youre way—
Youre makes as I prike you with plesaunce.
[386–89]

For the female the most important point here is that Nature insists on freedom of choice. Spenser will make extensive use of this motif in *Faerie Queene* IV. I have already spoken of the appropriateness of the somewhat different speech of Theseus to Emelye on the subject of her marriage, when the equivalent period for her hesitation was long since past. His somewhat more hortatory tone is appropriate in another sense as well. He is a reasonable man expressing his own opinion and that of his 'parlement' (Knight's Tale, 2218; 3076). The members of the latter are presumably sage and sober men, who do not represent, like Nature's 'parlement', a colourful spectrum of all possible opinions. Theseus, then, can afford to give advice; Nature cannot, because she is not allowed to speak with Reason's voice. She can express only conditionally what, if she were Reason, she would wish to advise:

'But as for conseil for to chese a make,
If I were Reson, certes thanne wolde I
Conseile you the royal tercel take—
As saide the tercelet ful skilfully—
As for the gentileste and most worthy,
Which I have wrought so wel to my plesaunce
That to you oughte it been a suffisaunce.'
                    [631–37]

Nature's role is otherwise close to that of Theseus; equally the role of Venus in *The Parlement* is tyrannical and cruel like that of Cupid and the rest of the pagan pantheon in the Knight's Tale. Some of the words in which Love is described at the opening of this dream vision are reminiscent of what I have just been considering there:

The dredful joye alway that slit so yerne,
Al this mene I by Love, that my feelinge
Astonieth with his wonderful werkinge
So sore, ywis, that whan I on him thinke,
Nat woot I wel wher that I flete or sinke.

For al be that I knowe nat Love in deede,
Ne woot how that he quiteth folk hir hire,
Yit happeth me ful ofte in bookes rede
Of his miracles and his cruel ire;
That rede I wel, he wol be lord and sire:
I dar nat sayn—his strokes been so sore—
But 'God save swich a lord!'—I saye namore.
                    [3–14]

The 'two yonge folk' that 'ther cride / To been hir help, (278–79) in *The Parlement*'s Temple of Venus are receiving from the goddess none of the attention which Nature will give to the birds in the splendid *locus amoenus* outside. Chaucer added these lovers (who were not in the *Teseida*) presumably to stand in contrast with Nature's well-served followers. Here as well, it is to spite Venus' fellow goddess that the bows of Diana's virgin huntresses, who have now been seduced, were broken and have been hung up on the wall. All those in the list of worthies which follows have suffered by love, to an extent which matches both Theseus' description of the 'miracles' of the Love God and the parallel claim about that god's 'miracles' at the beginning of *The Parlement*.

The division in *The Parlement* between happy and unhappy lovers of which we are informed by the inscriptions on the portal as the dreamer enters the park may point in the same direction, although it may also be that a traditional subdivision is being made here which cuts across the area of Nature, if not that of Venus. Unhappiness in fact exists in Nature's camp, but what she can do for her votaries, she does. She proceeds in this task by 'evene numbres of accord' so that not only is she a harmonizing force, but as much harmony as the frame of reality will permit is produced in the relations of her followers with each other. These words over the portal of the gate in *The Parlement* relate, then, in part to her:

> 'Thurgh me men goon into that blisful place
> Of hertes hele and deedly woundes cure;
> Thurgh me men goon unto the welle of grace,
> Ther greene and lusty May shal evere endure:
> This is the way to al good aventure.'
> [127–31]

On the other hand the lovers who follow Venus are the servants of a deity who treats them as Cupid and the other gods had treated Arcite and Palamon. They are subjected by the dart of Love, yet even in subjection some of them are the victims of disdain and haughty denial ('Daunger') and thus meet the description of the remaining words on the portal:

> 'Thurgh me men goon', thanne spak that other side,
> 'Unto the mortal strokes of the spere
> Of which Desdain and Daunger is the gide,
> That nevere yit shal fruit ne leves bere;
> This streem you ledeth to the sorweful were
> Ther as the fissh in prison is al drye:
> Th'eschewing is only the remedye.'
> [134–40]

As he enters the Temple of Venus, the dreamer is met by fire-hot, desire-engendered sighs, providing a constant current to make all the flames upon the altars burn more intensely. They proceed, we are told, from the bitter goddess Jealousy (246–52), which, of course, is the quality we have found in the Love God's subjects in the Knight's Tale. Equally, the immediately preceding stanza seems to be concerned with love which is unsatisfied or is deceived:

Bifore the temple-dore ful sobrely
Dame Pees sat with a curtin in hir hond,
And by hir side, wonder discreetly,
Dame Pacience sitting ther I foond,
With face pale, upon an hil of sond;
And aldernext withinne and eek withoute
Biheeste and Art, and of hir folk a route.

[239–45]

Patience can remain here only if she is willing to build upon shaky and unjustified premises—upon a hill of sand. Promising—'byheste'—is undertaken with little expectation of keeping troth, for otherwise she would not be coupled with 'Art'—artful devices—or perhaps the two nouns are to be coupled (as Robinson suggests) as 'artful behests'. Like Patience, Dame Peace can remain here only if she hides the truth from herself with a curtain. Even if we can find no iconographical tradition for this interpretation of the curtain, the significance seems to be required in the context of lying promises and of artfulness, of a quatrain in which Peace is balanced against a deceived Patience, and of the following stanza on jealousy. Perhaps Chaucer's addition of the hill of sand (not in the *Teseida*) was intended to balance the parallel significance of the curtain as Chaucer understood it.

Hereafter some complications show that we are entering a somewhat different conceptual territory from that of the Cupid of the Knight's Tale, or, more likely, are covering the subject of the tyrannical kind of love more broadly. The party of Venus in *The Parlement* is not simply that of the Cupid of the Knight's Tale in another medium. One of the smaller problems, probably no more than an apparent one, is that in trying to be precise about *The Parlement* we ascribe significances to Chaucer's figures which are at variance with those ascribed to what are apparently the same figures in the *Teseida*. Attached to certain MSS of that work are Boccaccio's own glosses on the meaning; for this Temple they are particularly extensive. It is likely, however, that Chaucer was not acquainted with these *Chiose*, for if he had known them he would probably have written at certain points in the Knight's Tale something different from what we find. Also, there is reason to believe that Chaucer's MS belongs to a family which did not contain these glosses.[3] They

3. See R. A. Pratt, 'The Knight's Tale', in *Sources and Analogues of Chaucer's Canterbury Tales*, ed. W. F. Bryan and G. Dempster (Chicago, 1941), pp. 83–87; and R. A. Pratt, 'Conjectures Regarding Chaucer's Manuscript of the *Teseida*', *Studies in Philology*, 42 (1945), 745–63.

have some traditional interpretive weight, occurring as they do in a context which is specifically literary like Chaucer's, not encyclopedic or specifically homiletic; nevertheless there must be some doubt about how seriously even Boccaccio took them.[4] His own statement about Peace (VII. lviii) is curious, for it does not account for the curtain at all. He says only that Peace sits here because love must be embarked upon between lovers by peaceful consent, not by coercion. We may in any case dismiss this if we suppose that Chaucer did not read it.

A greater difficulty is that, while Desdain and Daunger are the qualities, supposedly, of Venus herself as a deity being unsuccessfully prayed to, these two qualities are not present in all the relationships among the lovers who are subject to her will, as is the case with the followers of Cupid in the Knight's Tale. Of the famous lovers listed here by Chaucer, not nearly all are thus victimized, although they all have sad ends. Canace, Tristram and Iseult, Paris and Helen, Cleopatra, and Rhea Silvia are all additions made by Chaucer himself to Boccaccio's original list, yet none of them suffered the disdain or repulse of the one loved. What they suffered were the blows of Fortune or the malice of third parties. Chaucer intends the list, then, to affirm the bad treatment of Venus' followers, not their own suffering from unrequited or deceptive love. How, then, reconcile their presence with the other evidence of the victimizing of lovers within or in the vicinity of the Temple?

It is of course possible that, charmed by Boccaccio's delectable description, Chaucer for once allowed his imitation to get out of hand, and produced an allegorical scene at war with itself. As Pratt points out,[5] the twelve stanzas (211–94), translated here more or less literally, constitute the longest passage from the Teseida used anywhere by Chaucer. He might even have regarded this particular translation as a kind of exercise. However, in adapting the Teseida and the Filostrato as wholes Chaucer displayed remarkable self-possession and independence, never arguing with his source like some other medieval poets, yet

4. The betrothal of Palemone and Emilia was solemnized in this Temple of Venus, from which Palemone's personified prayer had gone forth to the corresponding temple on Mount Cithaeron, belonging to the Venus of lascivious desire, not of the desire for marriage and children ('onesto e licito desiderio, si come e' desiderare d'avere moglie par avere figliuoli, e simili a questo', corresponding to VII. 1 ff.). Palemone did not, perhaps, have offspring in the forefront of his imagination at the time, but did Boccaccio mean, in this blissful finale, that Palemone's desires were illicit? If we are to imagine that the source of this supposed perception is the eye of Mediterranean man, directed unflinchingly at the putatively non-Christian character of the romance hero's desire for his lady, then we must posit a very mechanical two-facedness indeed. I prefer to think that Boccaccio was hasty and opportunistic in this gloss, and did not think through the position.

5. 'Chaucer's Use of the "Teseida"', PMLA, 62 (1947), 606.

reshaping it as with an iron hand in a velvet glove. I have already pointed out in these twelve stanzas several additions in the direction of his own plan: it is most difficult to imagine that he has left anything here which is not part of his own feeling of what is right. Boccaccio may have led him to elaborate beyond his wont, but not, probably, to accept an essentially indigestible motif or detail. A more attractive solution to the difficulty is that Chaucer is using a kind of scanning mechanism which passes gradually, by almost imperceptible degrees, from one region to another in this 'landscape'. Outside and just within the Temple, one finds the jealousy and deception which Venus (like the Love God of the Knight's Tale) glories in imposing upon her subjects; at the end of the description, on the other hand, one finds the disastrous fates of her lovers in the paintings on the wall. Both sets of matters are in contrast with the hopeful doings of Nature. In this sense, the hard words on the portal (134–40) actually cover the whole field of the Temple.

So may they as well cover a third category, the Temple's emphasized sensuality. Priapus, in a state of manly readiness, stands in sovereign place there:

In swich array as whan the asse him shente
With cry by night, and with his sceptre in honde;
Ful bisily men gonne assaye and fonde
Upon his heed to sette, of sondry hewe,
Gerlandes ful of flowres fresshe and newe.
[255–59]

The elevation of obscenity and the ridicule proceeding from undesired publicity seem to be elements of the scene; and Priapus is celebrated and perhaps encouraged to new feats by the flowers, in ever new garlands, pressed upon him. The appearance of Venus also suggests lasciviousness; the presence of Bacchus and Ceres—heartening drink and food—signifies that what is encouraged here is physical lovemaking. Probably because the latter needs to be accompanied by no mental sympathy, Richesse is here as well. It is true that Richesse is one of the inhabitants of the garden of happy and mutual love presented in the first part of the *Romaunt of the Rose*, but here, in the Temple, she is the porter, like Idelnesse in the *Romaunt*, through whom the lover gains entrance. (In Boccaccio, as well, Idelnesse, removed by Chaucer, was among the first figures we see, outside the Temple and in fellowship with Cupid.) In a later part of the *Romaunt* (5893–5952),[6] the God of Love

---

6. In Robinson's 2nd edition, p. 620.

criticizes his mother for her selling of lust for money, as a *meretrix*; and an overtone of that cold physicality is probably signified here by Richesse, just after the clinical obscenity of Priapus. No one may approach Venus who cannot pay. Perhaps in the glorification of pleasure at the expense of everything else lies one significance of the fish dying of drought in the prison of the weir, so different from the other fish which Chaucer adds to the park outside the Temple, and before that Temple is even brought into the scene:

> And colde welle-stremes no thing dede,
> That swimmen ful of smale fisshes lighte,
> With finnes rede and scales silver-brighte.
> [187–89]

The realms of Nature and Venus overlap widely, but with Nature there is a saving grace. Her kingdom is indeed concerned with sex; the power by which she works upon the birds is that 'pricking' (389), which she also employs in the General Prologue to *The Canterbury Tales*. They all seek to be released by mating from their anguished desire. Nevertheless, sexual pleasure under her rule is not associated with contrived exposure or with money. Those in Nature's realm also suffer from jealousy and grave disappointment: two eagles out of three are bound to suffer permanently. But the harmonizing power of Nature works for all birds as best she can manage:

> 'And as youre hap is shul ye winne or lese—
> But which of you that love most entriketh,
> God sende him hire that sorest for him siketh.'
> [402–4]

She is the vicar of the Almighty Lord (379), as Theseus is the representative of God in Athens. Venus, on the contrary, works for her own glory alone, and for disharmony.

The significance of the material concerned with the *Somnium Scipionis* in the beginning of *The Parlement* has proved one of the most troublesome problems of modern Chaucer criticism. The persona speaking in *The Parlement* tells us that he has been reading the *Somnium*. He tells us of the younger Scipio's dreamed star journey, which resembles the one at the end of the *Troilus*. We hear summarized Cicero's Platonically modelled myth, with its ascetic recognition of this world's vanity, its torment and hard grace, as opposed to the harmony that is the music of the spheres; we hear of the certainty that at the end of the Platonic Great Year man's doings will be forgotten. We learn of Cicero's doctrine of escape from this death-in-life into a place of bliss: to earn it we should serve the well-being—the 'commune profyt'—of our society. If, on the other hand, we give ourselves up to bodily pleasures, we shall in consequence suffer for many ages in the afterlife. As the *Somnium* has it:[7]

> Namque eorum animae, qui se corporis voluptatibus dediderunt earumque se quasi ministros praebuerunt impulsuque libidinum voluptatibus oboedientium deorum et hominum iure violaverunt, corporibus elapsi circum terram ipsam voluntantur nec hunc in locum nisi multis exagitati saeculis revertuntur. [*De re publica*, VI. xxvi. 29]

This emerges in *The Parlement* as:

> 'But brekeres of the lawe, sooth to sayne,
> And likerous folk, after that they been dede
> Shul whirle aboute th'erthe alway in paine,
> 'Til many a world be passed, out of drede.'
>   [78–81]

A connection between the body of *The Parlement* and this Ciceronian, and no doubt Macrobian, lore seems confirmed by Chaucer's opening his poem with talk of love; saying that one learns new knowledge out of old books; claiming at the end of the *Somnium* passage that he had from his reading what he did not want but lacked what he wanted; inventing the fiction that the revelation of his dream comes from the same guide—Scipio Africanus the Elder—who conducted Scipio himself; and finally returning to the question of reading at the end of the poem. To account for the connection, perhaps the most attractive theory is that the ascetic doctrine of the world's futility is affirmed here, as it is in one passage in the Knight's Tale and in another in the *Troilus*, but that to this position Africanus allows the dreamer to see by means of his dream a large qualification, according to which the service of pleasure in this world finds in Nature a validating principle, so that all is not, after all, vanity.

---

7. In Brewer's translation, in the cited edition, p. 137: 'For the souls of those who have given themselves up to the pleasures of the body, and have become as it were the slaves of the body, and who at the instigation of desires subservient to pleasure have broken the laws of gods and men, when they have left their bodies fly around the earth itself, and do not return to this place except after many ages of torment.'

As noticed in the last chapter, it is in Plato's *Timaeus* that we first find this qualifying doctrine. By 'progressiouns and successiouns' the cosmos and all nature, subject though they be to imperfection and death, participate in a kind of recirculating eternity. This doctrine, familiar in Boethius' *Consolation*, lives on, for our purposes, in the figure Natura, chiefly through Alanus de Insulis and Jean de Meun, to take form in Chaucer's and Spenser's works.

We have noticed how, in Theseus' last speech in the Knight's Tale, the doctrine of an ascetic rejection of the world finds a place beside this qualification. He tells his listeners of how Arcite has left the 'foule prison of this lif' and tells them as well of this 'wrecched world' which in its corruptible state has descended from something perfect, stable, eternal, and incorruptible (2145–52; 3003–10). The Boethian passage (III. Prosa 10, initial speech) upon which Chaucer builds here has a very direct relation to Cicero's words near the end of the *Somnium*, which Chaucer must have remembered at this point, and which read in D. S. Brewer's translation:[8]

> That alone, therefore, which moves itself, never ceases to be moved, because it is never deserted by itself: indeed it is the source and beginning of motion of all other things which are moved. The beginning itself has no origin; for all things arise from a beginning, but that beginning itself cannot be born from something else, for that would not be a beginning which originated from something else. And since it never had a beginning, then indeed it will never have an ending; for if a beginning were destroyed it could neither be reborn from anything else, nor could it create anything else from itself if, indeed, everything has to arise from a beginning. Thus it happens that the beginning of movement derives from that which is self-moved and that can neither be born nor die, otherwise the whole heaven must fall and all nature come to a standstill, finding no force to stir them to motion again.

Theseus immediately turns in his speech from the asceticism just cited to the incidental consideration of the 'progressiouns and successiouns' over which Nature presides, and which will presumably have effect in the marriage of Palamon and Emelye. In the *Troilus*, the Ciceronian ascetic rejection is located at the very end, and the Boethian qualification—the love within the universe that holds the whole creation of time

8. P. 37.

and space in harmony, and that ought to reign in nations, in friendships, and in marriages—is celebrated in the middle, at the high point of Troilus' earthly bliss.

There is good reason, then, to suppose that in *The Parlement* Chaucer begins by sounding as a kind of ground bass, at the beginning of this, his principal dream vision of love, the hatefulness of much in this world and the necessity of our devotion to a higher duty which is dictated, as Cicero says, by our immortal part. But having accepted this generalization, the poem goes on to qualify it by saying that Nature, as the vicar of the Lord, has given us in one form of earthly love something which is productive of the good and is conformable to his behests, although another kind of love is so false as to be suitably symbolized in terms of the rule of a self-serving and riggish planetary deity. It may even be possible to say, as Dr. Pamela Gradon has most recently pointed out,[9] that in *The Parlement* the first kind of love serves the common good in the sense of furthering the national interest, if this work was in fact written to celebrate a royal marriage.

9. *Form and Style in Early English Literature* (London, 1971), pp. 77, 78. I do not, however, understand why Dr. Gradon feels a need to follow Aldo S. Bernardo (*Petrarch, Scipio and the 'Africa'*, Baltimore, 1962, pp. 1, 25, 184, 185n.) in maintaining that Chaucer follows Petrarch's figural version of Scipio Africanus the Elder as a saviour of souls from sensuality (this Scipio having once saved Massinissa from it, and having thus benefited the state). Dr. Gradon and Professor Bernardo mean either that Chaucer read Petrarch's *Africa* or that he did not. There is no reason, except for apparent convenience in demonstrating one interpretation of *The Parlement*, to assume that Chaucer ever saw the *Africa* or is likely to have seen it. In attempting to show its influence on Chaucer in *The Parlement*, Bernardo points out that in all references to the *Somnium* in Chaucer's works, except for *The Parlement*, the name Scipioun is employed, and that, in *The Parlement*, the name Affrycan is employed. But in fact the name Scipioun is employed for the dreamer in *The Parlement*, 36. As for the use of 'Affrycan', the guide in the original dream is Scipio Africanus the Elder. He is referred to in the *Somnium* as 'Africanus'. Correspondingly, Chaucer refers to him (and only to him) as 'Affrycan': what does this have to do with Petrarch? On the other hand, whether or not Chaucer read the *Africa*, it may be asked why we need to raise in connection with the *Africa* the subject of the figural significance of Scipio Africanus the Elder as a saviour of souls from sensuality, when his opposition to sensuality is already emphatically given by the concluding words of the original dream, quoted above, as well as by evidence elsewhere in this dream.

5

On the Marriage Group

I have already touched on the Marriage Group in the context of the Boethian, Platonizing Chaucer of the Knight's Tale and *The Parlement*. The discussion continues here in much the same terms, because they are the ones which make clearest what Spenser found in these tales. Although it is obvious that as narrative this part of *The Canterbury Tales* breaks new ground, I am concerned with what should be an equally obvious continuity with Chaucer's earlier imaginative achievement.

It seems to have been generally accepted that at some point in the composition of *The Canterbury Tales* Chaucer decided to develop a series of its narratives in a roughly dialectic arrangement so as to present certain opposed positions on the question of love and marriage. This series runs through four groups of material—tales and linking matter—gathered around the Wife of Bath (and the two fabliaux appended to her tale), the Clerk, the Merchant (followed by the excursus of the incomplete Squire's Tale), and the Franklin. Although the notion of a Marriage Group has been with us for a long time and may be thought by some to require re-examination, there seems little need to revise it fundamentally or to discard the proposition associated with Kittredge's name that in the Franklin's Tale Chaucer does arrive at some kind of resolution of the dialectically presented positions.[1]

1. George Lyman Kittredge, *Chaucer and His Poetry* (Cambridge, Mass., 1915).

Even casual reflection on the contents of the Marriage Group rein-
forces the points that much of its material belongs to a different side of
Chaucer from the writer of philosophical and idealistic romance and
dream vision, but that much of that Chaucer survives. The Franklin's
Tale of Arveragus, Dorigen, and Aurelius is a romance of the shorter
kind with supernatural overtones which is called a Breton lai, and it is as
well an exemplary tale with an ostensibly idealistic outlook according
to which there is no such thing as too much *gentilesse*, and a contest
concerning who can display the greatest quantity of it is an improving
spectacle. In formal terms, the Wife of Bath's Tale of the young knight
and his aged wife, with its schematic *demande d'amour* ('What thing it
is that wommen most desiren'), is also much the same mixture: a short
romance with supernatural overtones, told to prove a point. Like the
interpolated matter of Pluto and Proserpina in the Merchant's Tale, it
begins with a classic act of male mastery (rape in the Wife of Bath's Tale,
raptus in the case of Pluto's abduction of Proserpina),[2] and ends in the
victory of female resourcefulness. The Clerk's Tale of patient Griselda,
on the other hand, is not really a romance in the medievalist's sense as
that sense holds for the Franklin's and the Wife's Tales, although partly
through Chaucer's additions to his source this tale has affinities with
that form. The Clerk's Tale is perhaps primarily an allegory, built on
characters whose actions have their premises in a numinous world; but
its quality is just as much defined by saying that the narrative mobilizes a
powerful late medieval sentiment, the admiring and sometime lach-
rymose contemplation of an innocence which is put to the test and
eventually receives divine vindication.

At the other end of the narrative spectrum from the Franklin's, Wife
of Bath's, and Clerk's Tales lie two of Chaucer's great fabliaux, those of
the Friar and the Summoner. They are enclosed within the bounds of the
Marriage Group, but fall most decisively outside the literary sphere
which I have been discussing. As Charles Muscatine long ago stated
with the clarity which this matter demands, what characterizes the
fabliau world is that in it the only acceptable motives are bluntly
material: sex, food, tangible possessions, the avoidance of pain.[3] In that
world only fools act on any other grounds.

The Merchant's Tale of old January, young May, and Damian is
something else again, and probably the most astonishing performance
of the whole group. It might be said to create a romance milieu in which

2. Cf. Claudian's *De raptu Proserpinae*, which Chaucer knew of.
3. *Chaucer and the French Tradition* (Berkeley, California, 1957), pp. 60–61.

the characters act for fabliau motives. It is impossible to say whether January or May is more dishonest in idealizing sordid motives, but January is at least less conscious of what he is doing. At the same time, all of the first section of the Merchant's Tale, much like the Prologue of the Wife of Bath's Tale, is given over to the ironic deployment of lore and exempla in the service of conceptual as well as fictionally framed satire on the self-deceptions and egotism relating to age, wealth, sex, marriage, and the male and female genders, but without the Wife of Bath's taking brand of carnality. The Merchant's Tale also deploys, most subtly, the moralized landscape of an actual, not visionary, garden in the service of a complexly symbolic structure of meaning.

Beyond these devices of the separate narratives are those now extremely familiar but still resonant shibboleths in the literary criticism of *The Canterbury Tales*, the characterization of the tellers by their tales and the interactions among the pilgrims. These matters are of less importance here than in other contexts. For my purposes the dialectic presentation of several attitudes towards love and marriage through successive narratives having complex relationships with each other—in other words, through a series of interlocking 'mythic' narratives—is more significant than the narrators' own depiction of themselves and their relationships. In *Faerie Queene* III and IV and associated passages Spenser is in a sense the first commentator on the dialectic of the Marriage Group. The continual reverberations of these matters are to be traced in following chapters, but we may remember here, for example, that in Book IV Spenser completed the Squire's Tale, which he would have thought of as introducing the Marriage Group (see chapter 2), and that his tale of Malbecco, Hellenore, and Paridell in *Faerie Queene*, III. ix–x, is modelled on the Merchant's Tale of January, May, and Damian.

The Merchant's and Franklin's Tales are in fact the important ones in bringing to completion my consideration of relevant matters connected with 'philosophical' or 'moral' Chaucer. The material attached to the Wife of Bath and the Clerk is not important in this connection. By any other criteria it is outstanding, but as part of a soberly conducted and convincing argument about love and marriage it does not amount to much, because it verges by turns on *jeu d'esprit*, hyperbolic satire, and the expression of a sensibility related to pity. The Merchant's and Franklin's Tales, on the other hand, envision respectively a very likely marriage and an entirely possible one, even though the Merchant's Tale begins with much satirical hyperbole and the Franklin's Tale consists, outside its marriage relationship, almost entirely of romantically improbable incident.

It is true that the Wife of Bath's Tale shows harmony achieved after the acceptance of female chieftainship in marriage, but as a practical proposition rather than as a piece of virtuosoship on the part of a self-fulfilling female imagination her case lacks statistical support. The mutual happiness which she and her fifth, younger husband finally found together, like that of the married pair in her tale, needs to be balanced by any levelheaded male reader against the hangdog state of her first four husbands (three older than she, one of her own age), hectored, bullyragged, and hornswoggled into surrender of their earthly goods and kept in uneasy, amply justified suspicion of their multiple cuckoldry. Furthermore, she is not only contentious but the cause of contention in other men. The argument which is started by the Summoner and the Friar over her right to speak at whatever length she pleases, escalates, step by step, to a climax in the Summoner's Tale, which presents an irritating friar whose sermon on anger (with many graphic examples) to a surly audience of one brings both that audience and the preacher into a state of prodigious wrath, only finally purged away by our laughter at the denouement.

The Clerk's Tale of a masterful husband and an obedient wife must likewise be left out of consideration in any dialectic of philosophically appreciable counterpositions. It is admirable as an allegory of the soul's proper relation to God and as an ironical rebuke to the Wife's position; but both in its telling and in its final comic reduction by its own teller it is recognized even by the Clerk as bearing only an inhuman relation, or no relation, to the problems of real marriage, touching as medieval listeners may have found the martyred and innocent selflessness of the wife of low degree in the face of the arbitrary behaviour of her noble husband.

The Merchant's Tale, however, is a picture of one of the real possibilities in the marriage of a wealthy sixty-year-old to a young woman from a family impressed by his money and influence. Similarly, the Franklin's Tale puts before us (if not so concretely, at least in terms that only idealize reality and do not contradict it) an enduring love match between a highly placed lady and a knight of somewhat lower degree.

One often hears that the success of the marriage in the Franklin's Tale is due to the compatibility of the prospective spouses, and their harmony of ages and interests is of course an important point. Their marriage is not a biologically unpropitious one of Spring and Winter like that in the Merchant's Tale. But the fundamental cause of the success of the marriage of Arveragus and Dorigen does not lie in their compatibility; it lies, rather, in the fact that both parties have really fallen in love and have chosen each other freely, without the pressure of some ulterior need. Had their worlds been farther apart, they would not, presumably, have so chosen, but the freedom of the choice, without deception and irrelevant pressures, is the point. The distinction is important here, and it will turn out to be important in *The Faerie Queene*.

There is in fact a social disparity between man and wife in the Franklin's Tale as there is in the cases of the other three couples in the Marriage Group, although it is of an opposite character to theirs. In the Wife of Bath's Tale the inequality between the young knight and his crone is so great as to be farcical. In the Clerk's Tale we accept the gulf between the status of the marquis and that of the peasant girl only because as readers we are temporarily in the world of romance. In the Merchant's Tale the power and wealth of the knight January enables him, in deed if not in word, to get his wife by barter from a family who can stomach the marriage for the sake of the alliance; May's real feelings about him either are not consulted or are dissembled. In the Franklin's Tale, on the other hand, the lady is not only so beautiful but also of so highly placed a family that the knight Arveragus scarcely dares to approach her. Yet since she at first both admired him for his worth and felt compassion for the wound which she had inflicted upon him, and then later began to love him, the path to a viable marriage was open.[4] As the Merchant's and Franklin's Tales take place in possible (although fictionally quite different) worlds, so the social differences between the spouses in these two tales, while of reverse nature, are smaller than in the two preceding tales in the Group. The worlds of the Wife of Bath's and Clerk's Tales are, in their two different ways, unrelated to any pragmatic social generalization about marriage in the real world of either the fourteenth or the twentieth century.

The Merchant's Tale traverses the same path from male mastery to female victory as the Wife of Bath's Tale and the story of Pluto and Proserpina, but in an institutionally recognizable and socially condoned form. In the Wife of Bath's Tale it had been appropriate for the aged, unnoble wife to lecture her knightly young husband on the superiority of personal *gentilesse* to gentility by inheritance because, having styled

4. Incidentally, in the case of an author whose own marriage is sometimes pessimistically speculated on, it is worth noting that in terms of comparative social positions this ultimately successful marriage in the Franklin's Tale is closer to Chaucer's own (and that of his son Thomas in 1394–1395) than is any of the satirically treated marriages in Chaucer's works.

Figure 1. Pluto Committing *Maistrye* upon Proserpina. From the *Emblemas morales de Don Sebastián de Covarrubias Orozco* (Madrid, 1610), Second Century, No. 39 (Leaf 139). The Latin on the scroll, 'Roganda non rapienda fuit' ('She should have been sued for, not abducted'), is from Ovid, *Metamorphoses*, V. The first four Spanish verses may be thus translated: 'To carry away the will of another by wooing her is valiant and courteous, but to compel her heart by carrying off her person is evil and tyrannical.'

himself a gentleman by birth, he had nevertheless begun the tale with the ungentlest *maistrye* of all: he had raped a woman. At the tale's end, however, his wife has gained the mastery over him. Correspondingly, Pluto begins his relationship with Proserpina by forcibly carrying her off in his chariot. (See the Spanish emblem of 1610 in figure 1, which represents, some two hundred years later, the moral truth that Spenser probably found in this episode.) At the last, of course, we see her winning the trick over him when he self-righteously reveals May *in flagrante* to January. In the story of May and January themselves, however, the transition from male to female mastery takes a more everyday character. Instead of casually raping her or carrying her off at the beginning of the action, January in effect buys physical possession of her with his position and money, but with as little consultation of her wishes as if he had been the young knight or Pluto. At the end, May reverses the situation by getting her husband's property into her own hands and embarking with impunity on a career of commonplace adultery.

The extreme wittiness with which Chaucer makes use of the enclosed garden, or *hortus conclusus*, in this story entails an innovation in moralized landscapes. At an advanced point in the action, January addresses May in the springtime, with maundering obscenity, when she has egged him on for her own purposes and he apparently feels in trim for yet one more sexual passage:

'Ris up, my wif, my love, my lady free;
The turtles vois is herd, my douve sweete;
The winter is goon with alle his raines wete.
Com forth now with thine yën columbin.
How fairer been thy brestes than is win!
The garden is enclosed al aboute:
Com forth, my white spouse! out of doute,
Thou hast me wounded in myn herte. O wif,
No spot of thee ne knew I al my lif.
Com forth and lat us taken oure disport—
I chees thee for my wif and my confort.'
 Swiche olde lewed wordes used he.
   [894–905; 2138–49]

His words are from the Song of Songs; and in particular the reference to the walled garden that is enclosed on all sides comes from chapter IV, where the lover addresses his beloved:

Quam pulchrae sunt mammae tuae, soror mea sponsa!
Pulchriora sunt ubera vino,
Et odor unguentorum tuorum super omnia aromata,
Favus distillans labia tua, sponsa;
Mel et lac sub lingua tua;
Et odor vestimentorum tuorum sicut odor thuris.
Hortus conclusus soror mea, sponsa,
Hortus conclusus, fons signatus.
Emissiones tuae paradisus malorum punicorum,
Cum pomorum fructibus, cypri cum nardo.
Nardus et crocus, fistula et cinnamomum,
Cum universis lignis libani;
Myrrha et aloe, cum omnibus primis unguentis.
Fons hortorum, puteus aquarum viventium,
Quae fluunt impetu de Libano.
                    [Canticum canticorum, IV. x–xv]

[How fair are thy breasts, my sister, my spouse! how much fairer
are thy breasts than wine! and the smell of thine ointments than all
spices! Thy lips, o my spouse, drop as the honeycomb: honey and
milk are under thy tongue; and the smell of thy garments is like the
smell of frankincense. A garden enclosed is my sister, my spouse; a
spring shut up, a fountain sealed. Thy shoots are an orchard of
pomegranates, with pleasant fruits; camphire, with spikenard,
spikenard and saffron; calamus and cinnamon, with all trees of
frankincense; myrrh and aloes, with all the chief spices: a fountain
of gardens, a well of living waters, which flow suddenly down
from Lebanon.   Song of Solomon, IV. x – xv]

In spite of the well-known Christian allegorization of this passage,
the primary reference of the metaphor of the enclosed garden, like that
of other metaphors here, is patently to the sexual parts of the beloved,
and old January's allusive use of this perfervid and beautiful love lyric
is, correspondingly, of a singular loathsomeness. Beyond this, however,
lies the narrative datum that January (with the sole motive of Epicurean
pleasure-seeking) has built himself an actual walled-in garden into
which only he and his wife may go, for he holds the only key to it, a small
'cliket'. Beyond this datum, in turn, we are told that in his earlier life he
had adventured in the sexual world at large as long as he was capable of
doing so, but that after he was sixty his horizons contracted; he had in
principle bought himself a small sexual preserve on which, by the

sacrament of marriage, he hoped to prevent the kind of trespass from without which he himself had previously commited so often. He 'wolde bothe assayen his corage / In libertee and eek in mariage' (481 – 82; 1725 – 26). In sum, he has built himself a *hortus conclusus*; May (appropriately named for this reason as well as for her youth) is his *hortus conclusus*; and she possesses a *hortus conclusus* which (calling herself 'a gentil womman and no wenche', 958; 2202) she claims to defend carefully. With her eager collusion, Damian fashions a key by which to trespass on all three of these enclosed gardens. (A very different mythic merging of the female genitalia and a walled garden reappears in the Garden of Adonis in *Faerie Queene*, III. vi.)

Concerning the moral posture of May herself, on which Spenser seems to have reached complete clarity, it is easiest to say something by way of a Chaucerian irony. At one point in the narrative of the Merchant's Tale she retires to the privy, reads her future lover Damian's *billet-doux* and drops it appropriately in the place of excrement, and retires as previously directed to January's bed. His afternoon nap is then interrupted by his cough, and he proceeds to take his pleasure of her until again interrupted by the bell for evensong.[5] The net result of these, and earlier, combined experiences is that she decides to bestow her favour on Damian, and we hear from the narrator:

Lo, pitee renneth soone in gentil herte!
[742; 1986]

The use of the same words which had been applied to Theseus and to the flower-lady Alceste need cause no confusion, for Chaucer had already set forth discursively the distinction between the mercy which is the better part of justice and another mercy which is mere frivolity.

In the Prologue to *The Legend of Good Women* there is a pleasing, if somewhat arch, development of Chaucer's device of bird allegory, no doubt connected in his imagination both with the events of *The Parlement* and with the villainous tercelet of the Squire's Tale, who was guilty of the sin of 'newefangelnesse' (610, Robinson) against his faithful ladylove. In this passage in the Prologue Chaucer speaks first of the birds whose love is entire and perfect, next of those male birds who have been guilty of frivolous unfaithfulness towards their mates, and last of how some are forgiven. It is in connection with this last subject, which is covered in the latter part of the following quotation, that he makes the distinction which he would surely have us make in the case of May:

5. It is difficult to make anything of the possible verbal recall of this bell image in the interpolation discussed at the end of chapter 2.

And therwithalle hire bekes gonnen meete,
Yeldyng honour and humble obeysaunces
To love, and diden hire other observaunces
That longeth onto love and to nature;
Construeth that as yow lyst, I do no cure.
And thoo that hadde doon unkyndenesse—
As dooth the tydif, for newfangelnesse—
Besoghte mercy of hir trespassynge,
And humblely songen hire repentynge,
And sworen on the blosmes to be trewe,
So that hire makes wolde upon hem rewe,
And at the laste maden hire acord.
Al founde they Daunger for a tyme a lord,
Yet Pitee, thurgh his stronge gentil myght,
Forgaf, and made Mercy passen Ryght,
Thurgh innocence and ruled Curtesye.
But I ne clepe nat innocence folye,
Ne fals pitee, for vertu is the mene,
As Etik seith; in swich maner I mene.

[F 148–66, Robinson]

One extreme, then—that of tyranny and arbitrary force—has as its opposite the other extreme of folly and betrayal of undertaken troth; between them, in the familiar Aristotelian pattern of the mean, lies true mercy, which in its *gentilesse* is greater than justice. Whatever May's provocation may have been in the enormities perpetrated by her old husband, her reaction to Damian is a superficial folly because her nature is capable of nothing else. It is difficult to imagine a more unsavoury object to have committed oneself to, but, whatever the object, she would presumably not have been capable of reaching out towards the sober commitment of a Griselda. What she says is 'I rekke nat.' (A Victorian novelist would have had her accompany this with a toss of her curls.) It was on precisely this basis that Spenser created his Hellenore.

The culmination of the Marriage Group in the Franklin's Tale has traditionally been discussed in terms of a key concept—*gentilesse* —which Chaucer shares with Dante and the latter's fellow poets of the *dolce stil nuovo*, and also with earlier poets of French chivalric romance and with a number of writers in Latin.[6] What had originally been

---

6. See Ernst Robert Curtius, *European Literature and the Latin Middle Ages* (New York, 1953; paperback, 1963) (or the later editions of the original German *Europäische Literatur und lateinisches Mittelalter*, or later editions of the French translation), chap. IX ('Heroes and Rulers'), sec. vii ('Nobility of Soul').

a notion of hereditary gentility became in the hands of vernacular writers like Guillaume de Lorris a *topos* of élitist altruism according to which love, particularly sexual love, reaches its finest flower, as we have said, in the interplay of exquisite considerateness between lovers: love is most generously given and returned where it is a communion of free spirits, freely choosing each other and attuned to each other's wishes.

Recent thinking,[7] however, has called into question the premise that the Franklin knew what he was talking about. Chiefly, his fulsome compliments to the preceding storyteller, the young Squire, on the score of the latter's abundance of *gentilesse*, seem to betray lack of discrimination, and his expressed wish that his son should associate with the right people so as to go about learning his *gentilesse* on the approved model has seemed to smack of an arriviste's etiquette book rather than of an aristocratic ideal of conduct, particularly since the Franklin weighs the possibility of implementing this wish against another possibility of gaining twenty pounds' worth of land. Many modern readers sympathize with the instant reaction of the Host: 'Straw for youre gentilesse!'

We are not constrained to sift this question here. Spenser apparently did not read this conversation between the Franklin and the Host, because in his edition of Chaucer the words of the Franklin praising the Squire for his *gentilesse* are put in the mouth of the Merchant, who, consequently, is the one to be scoffed at by the Host. In this edition the Merchant's Tale then immediately follows that of the Squire (see chapter 2). Also, it may be more profitable to discuss the Franklin's Tale itself primarily in terms, not of *gentilesse*, but of the allied concept of friendship in love and in other relationships—a concept nearly or completely identical, in fact, with the Boethian one in the Knight's Tale. Concerning friendship, the Franklin makes a preliminary speech which seems to have made the strongest kind of impression on Spenser:

> For oo thing, sires, saufly dar I saye:
> That freendes everich other moot obeye,
> If they wol longe holden compaignye.
> Love wol nat be constrained by maistrye:
> Whan maistrye comth, the God of Love anoon
> Beteth his winges and farewel, he is goon!
> Love is a thing as any spirit free;

7. See the review of this matter in John H. Fisher, 'Chaucer's Last Revision of the "Canterbury Tales"', *The Modern Language Review*, 67 (1972), 250.

Wommen of kinde desiren libertee,
And nat to been constrained as a thral—
And so doon men, if I sooth sayen shal.
Looke who that is most pacient in love,
He is at his avantage al above.
Pacience is an heigh vertu, certain,
For it venquissheth, as thise clerkes sayn,
Thinges that rigour sholde nevere attaine.
For every word men may nat chide or plaine:
Lerneth to suffre, or elles, so mote I goon,
Ye shul it lerne, wherso ye wol or noon.
For in this world, certain, ther no wight is
That he ne dooth or saith somtime amis:
Ire, silknesse, or constellacioun,
Win, wo, or chaunging of complexioun
Causeth ful ofte to doon amis or speken.
On every wrong a man may nat be wreken:
After the time moste be temperaunce
To every wight that can on governaunce.
            [53–78; 761–86]

The speech pursues one theme up to its eleventh line. We are told that by
nature women (and men) desire freedom; consequently any attempt of
one party in a sexual union or in any other kind of 'felaweshipe' to
dominate another can only end love: when mastery comes, the God of
Love takes flight. A close paraphrase of Chaucer's words embodying
this last idea constitutes the first words that we hear from Spenser's
Britomart, near the beginning of *Faerie Queene* III. Because Arveragus
and Dorigen have chosen each other freely and have promised perfect
freedom to each other, the life of their marriage is unaffected by a strong
temptation put before the wife. A parallel but weaker form of the same
temptation brings the unfree marriage of May to January to what in
principle is collapse. The happy harmony and concord based on freedom of both parties to the marriage in the Franklin's Tale is an implicit
criticism of the Wife of Bath's premise of happy harmony and concord
based on female mastery in her fifth marriage and in her tale, and it is an
implicit affirmation of the Boethian myth-making on the theme of love
and friendship in the Knight's Tale.

Beginning with the eleventh line of the Franklin's speech just quoted,
however, our attention is turned from freedom to its apparent opposite,

the patience and *suffrance*—the endurance of the other party's faulty words and actions—which, he says, are also necessary in friendship and in marriage. One may not take vengeance for every wrong. A temperate response is what every man who is capable of self-control ought to give to his fellow's offending speech and deeds, for each of us, being no more than human, may err through any of the many factors that bend or weaken our reason, and each of us is in need of forbearance. The symptoms, or the causes, of these errors may be anger, sickness, temporary malign influences, a drop too much, or some physiological disturbance. Tolerance, not striving contentiousness, is the proper reaction to all this in one's companion or spouse.

Some may consider that these latter reflections of the Franklin constitute a pedestrian vulgarization of the doctrine of freedom in our relationship with others. Yet they are near to a definition of Theseus' necessary frame of mind when he controlled his ire and offered his friendship to the two young fools of Love fighting each other in violation of his authority in the forest, and these words are, as well, the key to much of the behaviour of Arveragus to Dorigen in the ensuing tale.

It is without a word of recrimination that Arveragus suffers his wife's announcement of her indiscreet and (to Aurelius) thoughtlessly cruel promise. Arveragus no doubt reflects, in the same reasonable, mitigating way as Theseus with two young men on his hands, that his wife has given this promise partly because of her love for him and her regard for his safety. On this same occasion, after his return from his temporary absence, he makes up his wife's mind for her, briskly, decisively, and without any display of male complacency, after she has dithered for two days (749–51; 1457–59) over Aurelius' suggestion that she should fulfil her promise now that he had fulfilled its apparently impossible condition. During this time her mind has weltered in a plethora of heroic exempla of self-immolating females, but to no effect: nothing emerges. Arveragus saves the situation by his patience, even though his passions involve him to the point of tears (772; 1480). In his firm marriage it may not even occur to him that there is anything unusual about his distinctively male variety of self-control: "'ye, wif,'" quod he, "lat sleepen that is stille''" (764; 1472).

The chief display of *suffrance* in the tale is from the husband, as might be expected from a male narrator who sees the problem in terms of how a husband may best behave so as to hold his wife. Yet Dorigen as well never reminded her husband earlier that she was stepping down the social ladder when she married him, as she would apparently not have been doing, later, if she had had an affair with Aurelius. The words which are applied ironically to May in the Merchant's Tale concerning her ready extension of mercy to her lover instead of murdering him with chastity can be applied in all seriousness to Dorigen, who, reinforced by her high position, might easily have scorned Arveragus. It is an earnest of the strength of her marriage compared with that of May that May surrenders at the first opportunity to a mere page, while Dorigen cannot even entertain the possibility of a liaison with someone who is described thus:

> He singeth, daunceth, passing any man
> That is or was sith that the world bigan.
> Therwith he was, if men him sholde descrive,
> Oon of the beste-faring man on live:
> Yong, strong, right vertuous, and riche and wis,
> And wel-biloved, and holden in greet pris.
> [221–26; 929–34]

In relation to her husband Arveragus, on the other hand, Dorigen is said to 'come of so heigh kinrede / That wel unnethes dorste this knight for drede / Telle hire his wo' (27–29; 735–37)—a reason which is not given in connection with Aurelius' similar, but merely 'courtly', reluctance to divulge his love.

The complementary notions of the uncoerced sexual choice and of charitable self-control in a sexual relationship as we have found them at the end of the Marriage Group reappear in *Faerie Queene* IV in various guises. Their contexts there indicate that Spenser was transforming material which had entered his imagination from the Chaucerian direction.

Aside from the matters of freedom and of patience, the Franklin's Tale stands in a counterrelationship to the Merchant's Tale in many other respects. Perhaps the most obvious is the matter of the garden in each tale. Both gardens relate to love: Aurelius makes his plea to Dorigen in one garden; Damian the page attains his physical goal in the other garden when May climbs to where he sits in the tree above her husband's head. Asked where she is going when she is dispatched to fill her promise, Dorigen answers, 'Unto the gardin as myn housbonde bad!' With symbolic propriety *Le Roman de la rose* and Priapus are evoked in connection with the garden of the Merchant's Tale (788–90; 2032–34), and that of the Franklin's Tale is compared to Paradise (204; 912).

Yet in spite of the closeness of these parallels and contrasts, we need to hold in mind that the Franklin's Tale has another, perhaps more important, affinity with the Knight's Tale. Like the Knight's Tale, as we know, the Franklin's Tale is a romance of idealist character with an ending consolatory to human sentiment, and treats the concepts of friendship, love, and *gentilesse* very much as does the Knight's Tale. Dorigen questions the powers that rule this universe very much as Palamon had done before her, in connection with the absence of her lover:

> 'Eterne God that thurgh thy purveyaunce
> Ledest the world by certain governaunce,
> In idel, as men sayn, ye nothing make:
> But Lord, thise grisly feendly rokkes blake,
> That seemen rather a foul confusioun
> Of werk, than any fair creacioun
> Of swich a parfit wis God and a stable,
> Why han ye wrought this werk unresonable?
> For by this werk south, north, ne west ne eest,
> Ther nis yfostred man ne brid ne beest:
> It dooth no good, to my wit, but anoyeth.
> See ye nat, Lord, how mankinde it destroyeth?'
>   [157–68; 865–76]

Although when her eyes are later opened by the granting of her wish, she says that what she had desired 'is agains the proces of nature', nevertheless at the point in the story represented by the quotation just cited she resembles Palamon in leaving the problem to the experts (177–82; 885–90). Aurelius of the Franklin's Tale appeals to a pagan divinity for help in his love very much as do the two desperate young lovers in the Knight's Tale, and gets as short shrift: he implores Apollo to persuade the latter's sister, the moon, to raise the tides so as to fulfil the condition with which Dorigen has hedged her promise, and Apollo gives him no answer.

6

Spenser's Squire's Tale and Four-Groups; Libido and Its Limitation

In *Faerie Queene*, IV. ii. 30, four riders journey in a rectangular formation. They are the knights Cambell and Triamond and their loves
Cambina and Canacee, of whom the first and last are borrowed by
Spenser from Chaucer's Squire's Tale. Riding in the lead, the two
knights are in absorbed conversation. They are bosom friends. Their
two loves, no less absorbed in friendly exchanges, ride side by side, each
behind her spouse. This rectangular relationship is supplemented by
two diagonal lines of consanguinity, for each lady is the sister of her
lover's friend.

In the same stanza of this scene of chivalric adventure these four
encounter four more identically deployed riders—Paridell, Blandamour, Duessa, and false Florimell—who are unstably linked by
feigned friendship and opportunistic sexual attraction.[1] At just this
point Spenser says that the soul of Chaucer, the well of English
undefiled, has been transfused into him (see the epigraph of the present
book), unworthy vessel though he is, and that he will now complete the
Squire's Tale, of which he believes the conclusion to have been lost

---

1. Ate, temporarily transformed into a beautiful woman and, a few stanzas before this,
having filled the role of Blandamour's lady, has been replaced in this position in the inner
group by false Florimell (whom Paridell also covets), but she still accompanies the two
couples. Scudamour, Glauce, and the Squire of Dames have also joined them.

through the depredations of cursed Eld (ii. 33). In completing it, Spenser was naturally both limited and guided by what he found in Chaucer's incomplete tale: a milieu of magic and the miraculous, a magical ring, a king's chaste daughter, Canacee, who possesses magical insight, and her brother Cambalo who (a little oddly) 'faught in lystes with the brotheren two / For Canacee er that he myghte hire wynne' (668–69, Robinson). Neglecting other elements, Spenser makes free with these particular ones and contrives a tale of initially intimate friendship, which is interrupted by temporary discord for the sake of love, which in turn is replaced by friendship and harmonious love at the end. The pattern, then, is that of the Knight's Tale; but without more to go on, we could not deduce that Spenser borrowed that pattern there, for he could have found it in many another romance.

We need to recollect here the arrangement in which Spenser found *The Canterbury Tales,* down through what we now call the Marriage Group, and beginning immediately after the General Prologue: Knight, Miller, Reeve, Cook, Man of Law, Squire, Merchant, Wife of Bath, Friar, Summoner, Clerk, Franklin. Spenser's notion of the sequence thus starts with the Knight's Tale, which is followed by two short fabliaux in which two young lovers have designs upon a young woman guarded by an older man and/or upon the older man's wife. Perhaps these fabliaux struck Spenser, as they do many modern readers, as low-life parodies of, or at least pendants to, the Knight's Tale. The third fabliau, the Cook's, is only a fragment. Spenser next finds the tale of the Man of Law concerning Constance and her terrible mothers-in-law, which probably has to be thought of here as an excursus. Thereafter, however, except for the incomplete Squire's Tale, he finds the run of tales which we have examined as the Marriage Group, having to do with mastery and harmony in marriage. As modern readers of Chaucer, we are accustomed to seeing the Squire's Tale in a radically different position from the one in which Spenser saw it. Depending on which of only two possible present-day arrangements we follow for this part of *The Canterbury Tales,* the Squire's Tale is either six tales from the end of the entire work, removed by nearly the full length of *The Canterbury Tales* from the Knight's Tale (in Skeat's edition, for instance), or it follows four large groups of material (Man of Law, Wife of Bath, Clerk, Merchant), plus four complete fabliaux and one incomplete one, between it and the Knight's Tale (in Robinson's edition, for instance). For any reader of one of Thynne's family of editions, who, like Spenser, was thinking of completing the Squire's Tale, its position at the beginning of the series of tales about love and discord in marriage might well suggest that this tale should somehow be related to those others, and should perhaps introduce them with a fine embodiment of discord and ensuing concord, so as to look forward to the conclusion of the series in the Franklin's Tale. The Squire's Tale might also be related to the tale of his father, the Knight, only a little before it, in reorchestrating its elements of friendship, love, exclusivity, and hate. It is true that the atmosphere of the Squire's Tale contains more of the exotic and the magical than does the Knight's Tale, but there is an obvious exotic element in the latter in its Greek funeral habits and the curiously described visitors to its tournament; the alarmingly supernatural also has its place in that tournament. Both tales are also thoroughgoing romances, about a world where characters act for exalted motives. The Squire even begins his tale as his father had done: he summarizes what the listener needs to know before the story proper begins, and then returns us momentarily to the pilgrimage: 'I wol nat taryen yow, for it is pryme, / And for it is no fruyt, but los of tyme; / Unto my firste I wole have my recours' (73–75 Robinson). (For his father's corresponding words, see the Knight's Tale, 31–34; 889–92.)

The resemblance of the plot of Spenser's continued Squire's Tale to that of the Knight's Tale goes further than a general pattern. The initial stage of harmony which we have posited in Chaucer's tale concerns two men, born of two sisters, and bound by oath in brotherhood and in an apparently indissoluble friendship. Spenser, in turn, gives us three men who are brothers by blood, born of one mother and bound even more emphatically in friendship:

> These three did love each other dearely well,
>   And with so firme affection were allyde,
>   As if but one soule in them all did dwell,
>   Which did her powre into three parts divyde;
>   Like three faire branches budding farre and wide,
>   That from one roote deriv'd their vitall sap.
>   [IV. ii. 43]

All three brothers (like Arcite and Palamon with Emelye) fall in love with Canacee, whose protector is her brother Cambell (like Emelye's brother-in-law Theseus). 'To prevent . . . peril' of more extended strife (Theseus, too, was trying to end strife), this brother provides (a little strangely, but corresponding to Chaucer's formula) that he will engage in formal, public battle with the three stoutest of her many contentious suitors, the winner being the one to take her.

In terms of their literary and imaginative descent, then, these events constitute the stage of discord and the attempt to institutionalize a solution for it, which we have already seen in the Knight's Tale. Two of the brothers die in battle with Cambell, and all three of their souls are supernaturally combined in the third, Triamond, who may be said to occupy the same final role as Palamon. The grudging supernatural agents in this case are the Fates, who behave nearly as cruelly as, and more churlishly (49–51) than, any of the pagan pantheon in the Knight's Tale. The battle is concluded by a miraculous event of exactly opposite bearing from the one at the end of the battle in the Knight's Tale. The hitherto unknown sister of Triamond, a second magically endowed female who bears a harmonizing wand with intertwined snakes and a circular wreath, touches the two weary combatants with it and sprinkles them with Nepenthe; they are then transformed from enemies to fast friends. She is Cambina (from the Italian *cambiare*, 'to transform', 'exchange', but also no doubt related to the English 'to combine'). In the Knight's Tale the survivor of two sworn brothers had become the friend of his former enemy, and in the finale that new friend and he had been shown married to two sisters; in the new Squire's Tale the survivor of three brothers correspondingly becomes the friend of his former enemy and each marries the sister of the other.

It seems plain, then, that in composing his new Squire's Tale Spenser rearranged the themes and narrative materials of the Knight's Tale. He was probably encouraged to do so by the accident of the position of the original Squire's Tale in his edition of Chaucer's works. An interesting corollary is that Spenser's continuation of the Squire's Tale ought now to be put beside the fifteenth-century *Kingis Quair* as one of the chief products of imaginations set into action by the Knight's Tale, although the difference between these two offshoots is as instructive in its way as that between the two chief descendants, in part, of Chaucer's *Troilus*, that is, Henryson's *Testament of Cresseid* and Shakespeare's *Troilus and Cressida*.

The grouping of four as the final tableau of the Squire's Tale, and in the riding formation when we first meet these characters, embodies both love and friendship, just as the opposed precarious sodality of four —Blandamour and his companions—falsifies both kinds of relationship. The motifs of the combination of love and friendship, and of serpents related to a circle, reappear in the most important moralized landscape of Book IV, the Isle of Venus (see next chapter. Spenser's Venus is generally a more exalted figure than Chaucer's).

More immediately, this Chaucerian tale of the harmonization of four individuals in love and friendship is the chief model for a number of similarly significant groups of four throughout *Faerie Queene* IV.[2] The pattern of two men and two women associated variously in love and friendship was no doubt familiar to Spenser from other sources, but the primacy of the Chaucerian model in his imagination is suggested by the matching or contiguity of this motif with the other Chaucerian ones of the set battle to terminate dangerous strife among sexual competitors, of a Theseus figure, of the female's ultimate freedom of choice among suitors, and of the addition of steadfastness and *suffrance* to love. The most obvious four-group in the latter half of Book IV is a highly evolved one without a fixed combat. Aemylia and Poeana, two daughters who oppose their powerful fathers, finally marry two squires of low degree, Amyas and Placidas, who are knit in a friendship so powerful that they look exactly alike.

As the story opens, Aemylia plans a tryst with her lover Amyas so that they may flee from her father. At the meeting place, however, she finds, not Amyas, but Lust himself, who carries her off to his cave. There it is his custom to rape and eat one woman after another. Aemylia temporarily escapes this fate because a hag is prepared to offer herself instead to the monster in his dark lair (lust—including her lover's—is concerned with consummation, not individuality). Aemylia is finally released from lust itself, presumably when Belphoebe as the virgin huntress kills Lust at the portal of his cave.

The plain allegorical sense of the substituted partner in the lovers' tryst is that Amyas was lustful, but Aemylia's role in subjection to lust had not been simply passive. Her own description of her prospective lover is suspect in Spenserian terms:

> It was my lot to love a gentle swaine,
> Yet was he but a Squire of low degree;
> Yet was he meet, unlesse mine eye did faine,
> By any Ladies side for Leman to have laine.
> [IV. vii. 15]

---

2. These four-groups correspond to Alastair Fowler's 'tetrads', for which see his *Spenser and the Numbers of Time* (London, 1964), chaps. 4 and 11. See the Preface of the present book.

She has not chosen rightly among the hierarchy of characteristics that belong primarily to a lover in the language of romance. His nature-given ability to make physical love is important in the context of Books III and IV, but it ought not to be singled out in that context by one damsel telling her story to another, as Aemylia is doing here. Like the Squire of Dames (that captivator of the bodies of many hundred women) when he was carried off by the Argante who is an embodiment of lust, Aemylia herself is subjected to carnality.

Aemylia's lover Amyas tells his side of the story later. Arriving at the same tryst where his lady had fallen prey to Lust, he relates how he himself was captured by Corflambo, or 'burning heart'. The sharp eye beams of this being had a basilisk-like strength: they filled men and women alike with sexual passion. Having subjected them, he would then shut them up in his castle, as he proceeded to do with Amyas. There Corflambo's daughter Poeana was accustomed to fall into carnal liaisons with her father's male prisoners, and has attempted to seduce Amyas.

No one can really follow the opportunistic twists and turns of late medieval and Tudor allegory unless he accepts a departure here from the principle with which the moral meaning of the narrative began.[3] Although Amyas himself is lustful, he does not surrender to Corflambo's daughter (any more than, at the allegorical level, the carnally minded Aemylia had done to Lust). Instead he now becomes an ordinary romance hero rejecting the blandishments of a woman who is trying to supplant his true love. Poeana on her side is given to passion because she is the daughter of this principle; yet she is also human, and later opposes her father for the sake of love in the same perfectly human way as Aemylia has opposed hers. In this Poeana belongs to the same class as Tasso's Armida, who is a principle of seduction but is finally herself seduced by her love for Rinaldo.

Amyas' friend Placidas secretly arranges to take Amyas' place temporarily in prison (one is reminded of Palamon's escape from prison through the help of a friend). Appearing to Poeana to be Amyas, and having no former love of his own, Placidas willingly succumbs to her.

It is given to Arthur, the hero of The Faerie Queene, to destroy Corflambo as it had been given to Belphoebe to destroy Lust. Having done so, he performs the Thesean function: he reunites Amyas and

---

3. Probably the most illuminating modern book on the subject of medieval and Tudor allegory is Rosemond Tuve, *Allegorical Imagery: Some Mediaeval Books and Their Posterity* (Princeton, 1966).

Aemylia; and in order 'to shut up all in friendly love' (ix. 15), he frees Poeana and accomplishes a reformation of her nature so that she repudiates her evil father and marries his enemy Placidas, who will rule Corflambo's lands and riches. The continuing friendship of Amyas and Placidas is complemented by joining each of them to his beloved.[4] What Arthur achieves with Poeana (and what by implication is achieved with the other personnel) is that to her natural endowment as a woman something else is added:

> He with good thewes and speaches will applyde,
> Did mollifie, and calme her raging heat.
> For though she were most faire, and goodly dyde,
> Yet she it all did mar with cruelty and pride.
> [ix. 14]

What was given to her by Nature—the same component that was given to Edmund in *Lear*—was complemented by something else added to it from the time of her marriage:

> From that day forth in peace and joyous blis,
> They liv'd together long without debate,
> Ne private jarre, ne spite of enemis
> Could shake the safe assuraunce of their state.
> And she whom Nature did so faire create,
> That she mote match the fairest of her daies,
> Yet with lewd loves and lust intemperate
> Had it defaste; thenceforth reformed her waies,
> That all men much admyrde her change, and spake her praise.
> [ix. 16]

What must be added to the inherent principle of Nature in us, for the sake of enduring marriage, is an acquired art of friendship, which means, as the Franklin would have said, an end of cruelty and pride. As pointed out before, the motif of the combination of nature (in the sense of either physical or competitive love) and this art reappears in the moralized landscape of the Isle of Venus, which, in fact, occupies the canto following the story of Amyas and his companions.

Two other four-groups in Book IV depend upon the motif of a fruitful confusion concerning the sex of Britomart (the heroine of Books III and

---

4. Preoccupation with Book IV's general notion of the complementary nature of love and friendship is likely to have been Spenser's reason for saying improbably that the three brothers in his Squire's Tale added their mutual love of and desire for one woman to their friendship among themselves in order to increase the total of affection (IV. ii. 54).

IV of *The Faerie Queene*) or, rather, concerning her fulfilling simultaneously the male role of a knight and the female one of a beauty. Such a double role is, in turn, a quality of the central figure, the hermaphroditic Venus, in this moralized landscape (see next chapter). The hermaphrodite is well known as having been a popular Renaissance symbol of concord, friendship, and marriage.[5] Confusion about Britomart's sex is natural but is emphasized on only a few occasions. In the first canto of Book III, Malecasta, the unchaste chatelaine, mistakes her for a man and tries to arouse her carnally. In the first canto of Book IV, Amoret, the constant lover of the knight Scudamour, fears the apparent maleness of her friendly companion Britomart for opposite reasons, and Britomart plays lightly on this fear by making ambiguous speeches. A situation involving a four-group of the kind already described follows immediately upon this, and immediately precedes the appearance of the false and the true four-groups led respectively by Blandamour and Cambell. The members of Britomart's four-group number only three because Britomart takes two of the roles.

She and Amoret come at the end of a day of travel to a castle where they seek shelter. It is the custom of this castle that, in order to gain lodging, any male visitor must either be accompanied by his lady or win a lady on the spot; the alternative is exclusion for the night. A young knight who also seeks shelter, and who is not otherwise provided, lays claim to Amoret. Britomart immediately gives battle and overcomes him. But because she is 'courteous' as well as a 'stout' fighter, she carries through a scheme to satisfy all three parties: the custom will be kept, but the young knight will not be excluded although it 'seem'd full hard t'accord two things so far in doubt' (i.11). She first requests lodging for herself and Amoret on the grounds that as a knight she has won Amoret and set her free from challenge. This being granted, she takes off her helmet, letting her golden hair fall about her, and claims that she may now gain entry for the young knight. This granted, 'so did they all their former strife accord.' Concord reigns. All three gain lodging through this friendly gesture; Amoret's doubts about Britomart's intentions towards her are laid to rest, and these two are bound in greater amity than before (stanza 15); the young knight is bound to them in fellowship.

A more significant four-group is modelled in one respect upon this one and depends likewise on the same confusion about Britomart's sex,

5. See Donald Cheney, 'Spenser's Hermaphrodite and the 1590 *Faerie Queene*', *PMLA*, 87 (1972), 192–200.

or about her double role. Much more drastically than Amoret, Scudamour fears Britomart's supposed maleness. Duessa and Ate had told him, in Book IV, canto i, that Britomart and his Amoret were in company and were sleeping together—a literal truth since Britomart and her friend share the same bed. Scudamour then suffers extraordinary jealousy and anguish in the House of Care. Later, he meets Artegall, the knight who, in disguise, had been humiliatingly unhorsed by Britomart in the central tournament of Book IV and had lost, as he considered, the chance to gain the prize of the companionship of Florimell. Both he and Scudamour are ready to avenge themselves upon what they take to be their male enemy. Britomart appears, defeats Scudamour, unhorses Artegall again, but is then unhorsed by him. In the ensuing sword-fight with Artegall, she is for the first time about to be defeated. When, however, his final blow shears away the ventail of her helmet, her face appears, framed in her golden hair. The result of this revelation, as before, is good fortune for all three parties. Artegall and she find their eternal love in each other, as had been predicted; and Scudamour, like Amoret in the previous sequence, is released from all his fears. Another four-group of three is cemented.

Yet another likely, but never completed, four-group may have been intended to lead to a climactic four-group for Book IV. In canto ix Arthur re-enacts the role of Britomart with Amoret. He now rides with Amoret under his protection, as his lady. As Britomart had been doing, he is seeking his true love, and as Britomart was feared by Amoret, so is Arthur now, and with as little cause: his chastity is as strong a safeguard as was Britomart's sex. In their travels they come upon a battle among six knights, four against two. Four inconstant friends—Blandamour, Paridell, Claribell, and Druon—had first started fighting jealously among themselves, two against two, concerning the results of the great tournament. When, however, the two now friendly knights Britomart and Scudamour had happened upon them, the four had turned against these two in spite of Britomart's attempt to pacify them. They hate her because she had previously overcome them in the tourney and (as they suppose) had won the prize of Florimell herself. When Arthur separates the two groups and tries in turn to pacify the group of four, these turn against him. He quells them, and, now thoroughly aroused, would have done more if the friendly two had not in turn pacified him (the incident has common features with the one of Theseus' separating the two young knights in the forest and being in turn pacified by his womenfolk).

Arthur hears the complaints of the four, who say that they have fought against Britomart because she has taken Florimell from them. In fact, Britomart points out, this lady had simply been given freedom to choose whatever knight she wished. Arthur then reproaches the four for renewing troubles which the tourney had already adjudicated, and for infringing upon woman's liberty of choice. Britomart broaches a new subject by saying that, under the heading of lady consorts won by valour, an even greater wrong remains, namely, that she no longer had under her care the lady whom she had won (meaning Amoret). Britomart adds that as a protector she had been accompanying this lady and, while sleeping exhaustedly after the tournament, had lost her. Scudamour complains, in the third place, that his loss of Amoret (whom he had won by valour) is the greatest sorrow of all.

What the plot cries out for at this point is that Arthur should produce Amoret, from behind a nearby bush or a convenient disguise, for it now lies within Spenser's control to come full circle. In the first place, Arthur by so doing would re-enact Britomart's role in delighting the members of a four-group through a friendly gesture concerning Amoret: that is, he would content Britomart by producing her former charge, content Scudamour by returning to him his long-lost wife, and content Amoret by restoring her to her beloved husband. In the second place, he would make possible the re-enactment, on the moral plane of friendship, of what had happened physically to three other friends bound by the physical tie of brotherhood: Priamond, Diamond, and Triamond had all loved one woman, yet the souls of the first two had passed into the third, who became her sole lover and husband. Similarly, Scudamour had first married Amoret but had lost her to the House of Busirane, Britomart had saved her from that House but had lost her to Lust, and Arthur had thereafter obtained her as his lady and had been her protector. Yet Arthur and Britomart would have willingly resigned her to her true love Scudamour, and would thus have performed an act of signal friendship. In the third place, the behaviour of these three in the case of Amoret, who had been the lady of each of them, would have formed an ideal contrast to the behaviour of the other four—the unworthy friends who had been fighting among themselves over the false Florimell, wishing to constrain her freedom and causing discord where concord had already been established. In the fourth place, Scudamour and Amoret, reunited, and Marinell and Florimell, brought together as a preparation for the friendly marriage in the last canto of Book IV as it now stands, could have ridden off together into the sunset, the four-group to end all such groups (in fact there are none in *The Faerie*

Queene outside this book). Of these two pairs of lovers, the first one, who had been married at the beginning of the book, in canto i, had been separated, as it seems, by a defect in Scudamour (see chapters 7 and 8), with the result that Amoret had been imprisoned for seven months by Busirane and released only by the friendly, indeed heroically magnanimous, efforts of Britomart. The other pair, who finally meet at the end of the book, in canto xii, had been kept apart by an opposite defect in Marinell (see chapter 7), with the result that Florimell, after undergoing much other cruelty, has been imprisoned for seven months by Proteus, although Marinell had already been drastically chastened by Britomart. Having learned their lessons, these four, joined in friendship, would have constituted an exemplary achievement of the quest of the Book of Friendship for both Britomart and Arthur, although these latter two friends, on their side, would have noted with sadness that their final unions with their own loves lay in the future. Britomart had still before her the tortures of Artegall's involvement with Radigund in Book V, and Arthur had to face we know not what mutations before attaining his Gloriana. The situation of these two friends, then, would have resembled, and replaced, that of the single knight Britomart in the conclusion of Book III in its first published version, later radically revised: as she had observed, meanwhile longing for her own love, the hermaphroditic embrace of Scudamour and Amoret which she had made possible, so Britomart and Arthur together at the end of Book IV might have looked with unfulfilled anguish on the fourfold bliss that was their handiwork.

But Spenser does none of these four things. Instead, Amoret, having accompanied Arthur as far as the battle of the six knights, seems to evaporate. In what is probably the most scandalous loose end in the whole *Faerie Queene*, neither Britomart nor Scudamour sees any trace of her (except for a single, half-line indication of an aborted amendment at IV. x. 4. 8), nor is anything seen of her in the remainder of the book. Scudamour enlarges upon his sorrow at her absence by relating in canto x how he had won her long before from the Isle of Venus, and the last two cantos are occupied with the marriage feast of the rivers and with the release of Florimell from Proteus, after Marinell has learned to love her.

What may have happened to Spenser's plans at this point is sufficiently important, in recognizing both the nature of his art and his response to the imaginative stimulus of Chaucer, to justify an excursus.

It now seems clear that in his first, three-book edition of *The Faerie*

Queene Spenser took care to arrange each of the first three books around a centre point, fixed with arithmetical precision by stanza count, and indicating matter that is symbolically central in that book.[6] The scene of each centre point is a *locus amoenus*, and its verbal signal consists of the words 'in the midst (middest)'. The most startlingly obvious of these centre points is the arithmetically central stanza in the first edition of Book III, for this stanza corresponds also to the geographically central point, the mount or hill, in the (in turn) symbolically central Garden of Adonis (and Venus), and to the sexually central point of the female anatomy, the *mons veneris*. Beneath this mount, Venus preserves her Adonis and enjoys him at her will:

> Right in the middest of that Paradise,
>> There stood a stately Mount, on whose round top
>> A gloomy grove of mirtle trees did rise,
>> Whose shadie boughes sharpe steele did never lop,
>> Nor wicked beasts their tender buds did crop,
>> But like a girlond compassed the hight,
>> And from their fruitfull sides sweet gum did drop,
>> That all the ground with precious deaw bedight,
> Threw forth most dainty odours, and most sweet delight.
>> [III. vi. 43]

The centric quality of the phrase 'Right in the middest' is seconded by the sense of a circular enclosure which is given by 'garland' and 'compassed'.

A source of confusion about the function of these centre points is, however, that Spenser does not continue to establish them in the second edition of *The Faerie Queene*. Changes which affected the number of stanzas moved the arithmetical centre points in Books I and III to symbolically insignificant positions, and centre points of the described character do not appear at all in the later books. Yet there is a striking resemblance between the just mentioned centre point in Book III and the stanzas (not forming an arithmetical centre point) in Book IV, indicating the central and symbolically most important object in the Temple of Venus. Venus placed the growing Amoret in the Garden of Adonis in III; Amoret sits at the foot of the statue of Venus in the Temple in IV. As in the centre point of Book II (see chapter 12), it may be that we should take into account three stanzas instead of only one:

6. See M. Baybak, P. Delany, A. K. Hieatt, 'Placement "In the Middest" in *The Faerie Queene*', *Papers on Language & Literature*, 5 (1969), 227–34, rpt. in *Silent Poetry*, ed. A. Fowler (London, 1970), pp. 141–52. See also pp. 200–202 and chap. 12, n. 3.

Right in the midst the Goddesse selfe did stand
  Upon an altar of some costly masse,
  Whose substance was uneath to understand:
  For neither pretious stone, nor durefull brasse,
  Nor shining gold, nor mouldring clay it was;
  But much more rare and pretious to esteeme,
  Pure in aspect, and like to christall glasse,
  Yet glasse was not, if one did rightly deeme,
But being faire and brickle, likest glasse did seeme.

But it in shape and beautie did excell
  All other Idoles, which the heathen adore,
  Farre passing that, which by surpassing skill
  Phidias did make in *Paphos* Isle of yore,
  With which that wretched Greeke, that life forelore,
  Did fall in love: yet this much fairer shined,
  But covered with a slender veile afore;
  And both her feete and legs together twyned
Were with a snake, whose head and tail were fast combyned.

The cause why she was covered with a vele,
  Was hard to know, for that her Priests the same
  From peoples knowledge labour'd to concele.
  But sooth it was not sure for womanish shame,
  Nor any blemish, which the worke mote blame;
  But for, they say, she hath both kinds in one,
  Both male and female, both under one name:
  She syre and mother is her selfe alone,
Begets and eke conceives, ne needeth other none.
                [IV. x. 39–41]

Both passages—the central stanza of Book III and this one—start with
the 'signal phrase' preceded by the word 'Right'; and the serpent encircling Venus' legs and having its tail in its mouth suggests a circular
enclosure as do the 'garland' and the 'compassed' of the first passage. In
addition, the hermaphroditic character of this Venus, both male and
female, is symbolically as central to Book IV as is the reproductive
character of the *mons veneris* to III. Yet the Isle and Temple of Venus are
described in canto x, far from the centre point of its own Book IV. It
now seems likely that in some earlier plan Spenser had intended this
material to occupy the centre point of its book, but that he found it

necessary to move the material to its present position because he needed the central position for other matter.

Two of the centre points of the originally published Books I, II, and III were in the seventh cantos, one in the sixth. In Book IV the latter part of canto vii (and part of viii) is occupied by the material concerning Amoret's capture by Lust, Timias' attempt to rescue her, Timias' love Belphoebe's killing of Lust, Belphoebe's return to find Timias fondling Amoret, the alienation of Belphoebe from Timias, his life as a hermit, and his reconciliation with her through the offices of the friendly and loving turtledove which bears around its neck a piece of jewelry known to Belphoebe. All of this material is grafted onto the story of the four-group Amyas-Placidas-Aemylia-Poeana by the device of Lust's imprisoning Amoret and Aemylia together in his cave. The material does not contribute to that story, and it does not, apparently, advance the main story of Amoret, except to cause her transfer to her third protector, Arthur—and this could have been otherwise arranged with less trouble.

It has in fact been generally accepted that Spenser inserted the material concerning Timias, Amoret, and Belphoebe because of the misfortune of his friend and benefactor Sir Walter Ralegh. In 1592, Ralegh, who was on the officially semi-amorous terms with Elizabeth that were customary among her favourites, became the lover of, and subsequently married, Elizabeth Throgmorton, one of the Queen's maids of honour. The Queen imprisoned both of them in the Tower. Although Ralegh was released later in the year, he apparently did not regain the Queen's favour for a long time.[7] It may well be that his piteous *XIth and Last Books of the Ocean to Scinthia* was written to appease the Queen and that it contained the verses which, as we hear in *Colin Clouts Come Home Againe*, Ralegh recited to Spenser:

His song was all a lamentable lay,
Of great unkindnesse, and of usage hard,
Of *Cynthia* the Ladie of the sea,
Which from her presence faultlesse him debard.
And ever and anon with singulfs rife,
He cryed out, to make his undersong
Ah my loves queene, and goddesse of my life,
Who shall me pittie, when thou doest me wrong?
[164–71]

7. See K. Koller, 'Spenser and Ralegh', *ELH*, 1 (1934), 37–59; and Fred Sorenson, 'Sir Walter Ralegh's Marriage', *Studies in Philology*, 33 (1936), 182–202. The most recent

We now generally believe that the material concerning Timias, Amoret, and Belphoebe in Book IV, cantos vii–viii, alludes to the same situation and was Spenser's emergency measure to put Ralegh's actions in the best possible light and to elicit the Queen's sympathy. Spenser apparently alludes to Ralegh's difficulty again in the treatment of Timias in VI. v. 39–41, vi. 1–15. Allegorically, Ralegh is Timias, and, in IV. vii, seems to the Queen as Belphoebe to be offering comfort of ambiguous character to Elizabeth Throgmorton as Amoret. Belphoebe then flees afar, and Timias lives inconsolably as a hermit until allegorically (or, as Spenser and Ralegh would have hoped, in actuality) a final reconciliation takes place.

Having to place this new material at the centre of the book where it could be connected with the story of Amyas and Placidas, in which Lust plays a part, Spenser may have been compelled to move his formerly composed centrepiece to a later position. The result would have been that the whole conception of centre points in each of the books of *The Faerie Queene* would become inconsistent and would no longer be worth preserving. Also, since the formerly central canto would now have to be placed near the end of the book, there would no longer be room there, within the fixed limit of twelve cantos, for the finale which I have outlined; and the embarrassment of the disappearing Amoret, poised for discovery but never revealed, may have been impossible to adjust suitably. Having to give up his centre point in Book IV, Spenser would then have been uninterested in maintaining it in all of the other books.[8]

It is necessary to assume here that the inconsistency about the presence or absence of Amoret in one episode may have stood in manuscript as early as 1592 and was not eliminated by the time of publication in 1596. This is not a difficult assumption, considering, for instance, Spenser's failure to correct in the edition of 1596 such an obvious inconsistency as the name 'Palladine' for Britomart (III. vii. 52. 6) in the edition of 1590. We know nothing of his conditions of work in 1592–96

---

and interesting study of this matter is contained in Walter Oakeshott, *The Queen and the Poet* (London, 1960).

8. At the present stage of speculation concerning Spenser's numerical patterning in *The Faerie Queene*, no clear picture emerges of his frame of mind at the time when he may have changed his plan. He might have had the additional motive that numerical structuring had been seriously reducing his other, more purely expressive options, although that motive was certainly not at work when he composed *Epithalamion* in or shortly before 1594. On the other hand, he might, as Professor Alastair Fowler would probably claim, have decided to make his planning more complex and subtle in ways that I have not detected.

except that he was under pressure. In that period he wooed and won Elizabeth Boyle; composed *Amoretti and Epithalamion*, at least parts of the *Foure Hymnes*, and *Prothalamion*; managed a large and troublesome estate in an alien land; sat as Justice of the Queen for the County of Cork; and frequently went to law with his neighbour Lord Roche. The embarrassment about Amoret may, in any case, have arisen later than 1592.

If it was for the reasons given that Spenser abandoned a supposed earlier and much more coherent plan for Book IV, and numerical centre points in *The Faerie Queene*, then the abandonment began in the Book of Friendship and was caused by Spenser's probably real friendship for Ralegh.

Beyond four-groups, another motif borrowed from Chaucer in Book IV is that of the institutionalized, once-and-for-all fight which is designed to end competition by giving it a public, terminal expression. In the Knight's Tale this was the tournament proposed by Theseus to end strife over his sister-in-law. Spenser takes over this motif in Cambell's decision to stop strife among his sister's unruly suitors by himself fighting each of the three sturdiest in a fixed, public battle. The main tournament in Book IV is designed with the sole object of similarly restraining strife and is Spenser's chief instance of the motif. Satyrane holds the girdle of Florimell, who is thought to be dead:

> Full many knights, that loved her like deare,
> Thereat did greatly grudge, that he alone
> That lost faire Ladies ornament should weare,
> And gan therefore close spight to him to beare:
> Which he to shun, and stop vile envies sting,
> Hath lately caus'd to be proclaim'd each where
> A solemne feast, with publike turneying,
> To which all knights with them their Ladies are to bring.
> [IV. ii. 26]

(Significantly, the motive for the tournament in Book V is not the same. There, as is often the case with tournaments, the idea is simply to memorialize a great occasion.) When, in IV. ii, Blandamour and Paridell are fighting jealously over the false Florimell, the Squire of Dames pacifically describes to them the projected adjudicative tourney. He points out that their difficulty will be solved in open fight if they attend. They are then 'well accorded' (ii. 29), even though their accord is hypocritical. Similarly, a little later, when Cambell sees the possibility of renewed strife over the false Florimell because Braggadocchio has appeared on the scene, he half-jokingly re-evokes the same motif (iv. 12). And, at the other end of the book, the four unstable knights who have renewed their fight for the false Florimell, even though the tournament had long before produced a decision, are reproached by Arthur for opening up troubles which had been definitely adjudged (ix. 37). Theseus had also gone to some lengths (Knight's Tale, 1857–80; 2715–38) to restrain jealousy, and the outbreak of further discord after his tourney had produced a decisive result.

Obviously there can be no sensible objection to the discord of the competitive fixed battle itself. Where there is competition for a prize, some way must be found for one of the competitors plainly to win, although if the prize is a woman, it ought to be left to her to accept or to reject what looks like a winner, or to investigate further the feelings of one or both parties by the device of procrastination. If the initial competition is not somehow formalized, it will express itself chaotically and violently. Like the other motifs discussed above, this culling of the candidates finds its way into Book IV's moralized landscape, the Isle of Venus. Before entering the Isle, Scudamour worthily defeats a score of knights in fixed battle. He is then in a position to take the shield of Love, of which it is said, '*Whose ever be the shield, faire Amoret be his.*' There is never a question about Scudamour's natural endowments, in terms of either combat or maleness. His difficulty lies in allowing for the additional necessary step (see chapters 7 and 8).

A final motif, intertwined with this one, and directly related to Scudamour's difficulty, goes back to the beginning of the Franklin's speech on friendship, where he tells us 'Wommen of kinde desiren libertee,' and to Nature's insistence in *The Parlement of Foules* that the tercel eagle under her protection should be allowed to choose her mate or even entirely to put off her decision for a year. Britomart's first speech in *The Faerie Queene* is her paraphrase of the Franklin's words condemning mastery in love:

> Ne may love be compeld by maisterie;
> For soone as maisterie comes, sweet love anone
> Taketh his nimble wings, and soone away is gone.
> [III. i. 25]

In the corresponding canto of Book IV Duessa mockingly echoes this sentiment in deceiving Scudamour about Amoret's true feelings for him:

> For Love is free, and led with selfe delight,
> Ne will enforced be with maisterdome or might.
>> [IV. i. 46]

Arthur returns to the same notion at the point where he is reproaching
the unstable knights on the grounds already mentioned. He says that to
ladies

> the world this franchise ever yeelded,
> That of their loves choise they might freedom clame,
> And in that right should by all knights be shielded.
>> [IV. ix. 37]

In fact, Satyrane had already yielded precisely this franchise. He had not
only tried to stop discord over ownership of the girdle of Florimell by
instituting the tournament; at its conclusion he made false Florimell
choose for herself, as Nature had made the tercel do in *The Parlement*.
Strong emphasis is put on love's liberty at this point:

> Which troublous stirre when *Satyrane* aviz'd,
>> He gan to cast how to appease the same
>> And to accord them all, this meanes deviz'd:
>> First in the midst to set that fayrest Dame,
>> To whom each one his chalenge should disclame,
>> And he himselfe his right would eke releasse:
>> Then looke to whom she voluntarie came,
>> He should without disturbance her possesse:
> Sweete is the love that comes alone with willingnesse.
>> [IV. v. 25]

The emptiness of false Florimell's nature, and the futility of confronting
the spiritually unfree with the freedom to choose, are elegantly revealed
in her choice of Braggadocchio.

Nothing is more despicable in the inglorious career of the unstable
four-group led by Blandamour in Book IV than its members' fighting
for, and exchanging, females as booty. Travelling with Ate as his lady
(who has been given a false beauty by magic arts), Blandamour repudiates her instantly and without a word as soon as he has captured
false Florimell from another knight. False Florimell is not consulted on
that occasion, nor when, correspondingly, Paridell fights Blandamour
for her, with the expectation of giving up his own Duessa without
explanation. Braggadocchio in turn would have taken false Florimell

away by force, and without speech with her, if he had not been so vile as to be unable to get his courage to the sticking point.

The same dichotomy of liberty-mastery turns up at many points in the action of Book IV, as when Arthur, instead of keeping Poeana imprisoned, frees her so that she may freely choose to marry Placidas (ix. 13–15), and as when Proteus is forced finally to give the true Florimell her liberty so that she may be united with her own love Marinell. The blandishment and persuasions in Artegall's gradual, successful wooing of Britomart contrast with the constraint which Scudamour exercises upon Amoret in extracting her from the Temple and Isle of Venus—a constraint which is the beginning of all his troubles.

It is the association of such Chaucerian motifs as the female's right to freedom with Spenser's four-groups that gives the latter their flavour. Renaissance literature otherwise shows many four-groups of non-Chaucerian provenance. The plot of Sidney's *Arcadia* is built on one. They are basic ingredients of Shakespearean comedy. But in Spenser's case the associated motifs of the formal battle to end sexual strife is plain in the completed Squire's Tale and the main tournament of Book IV, and is likely elsewhere. Participation in a Theseus role seems plainly intended in the cases of Cambell and Satyrane, and also likely elsewhere. The motifs of the justly decisive female choice among suitors as in *The Parlement of Foules* and of constancy and *suffrance* in love and friendship have just been shown to be represented in various episodes of Book IV. In addition to these matters of what are called here mythic embodiments of moral ideas, Spenser's imagination has long been known to have been engaged with Chaucer's works at a more superficial and formal level. In *Faerie Queene* IV it is the Squire's Tale which Spenser completes; in III it is the Merchant's Tale that provides the framework for the story of Malbecco; and it is the words of the Franklin that are Britomart's first utterance in *The Faerie Queene*. All of this is part of a mass of formal and motival influences of Chaucer from the very beginning of Spenser's career in *The Shepheardes Calender* to its end in *Mutabilitie*.

Before entering a new division of the subject, we may pause to consider the care that Spenser lavished on the names of his characters. Many of his lovers and friends have names which are phonetically related: 'Amyas' and 'Placidas' have common suffixes; 'Amyas' and 'Aemylia', and 'Placidas' and 'Poeana', have identical initial sounds. The last two syllables of 'Scudamour' are the first two of 'Amoret', and 'Britomart' and 'Artegall' share a syllable; the names of Florimell and

Marinell end with the same sound; even the false lovers Paridell and Hellenore have the beginning of one name in the ending of the other. The ladies named Aemylia and Amoret may well abide together in a cave or elsewhere. The etymology of Amoret's name is plain; Scudamour's name signifies 'shield of love'; the shield which he has captured in gaining Amoret bears a picture of the masterful Love God. Britomart and Artegall, each being the hero of a book, share a syllable with Arthur. Britomart is a martial Briton and is related to Tasso's lady knight Bradamante and to the virgin goddess of classical Crete, Britomartis. Placidas is so-called because he is pleasing but also because he says 'Placet': he readily says yes to Poeana, whereas Amyas does not. Amyas is so-called partly to remind us of the medieval story of the two inseparable friends Amyas and Amiloun. Two more reasons for Artegall's name are that a knightly hero bears this name in the *Historia Regum Britanniae* of Geoffrey of Monmouth, and that, as the hero of the Book of Justice and Equity, he deserves a name of which the latter part signifies equal treatment. Marinell is so-called not only because he is connected with and descended from the sea, but also because in Middle English and Early Modern English 'He nill marrye' means 'He doesn't want to get married.'[9] Paridell is so-called because he re-enacts the role of Paris in seducing Helen-Hellenore, but also because he accomplishes this deed in idleness (Idelnesse being the porter of the garden of love in the *Romaunt of the Rose* and Ease being the introducer of the Masque of Cupid in Book III): instead of continuing the quest with other knights, he remains behind so that, in days of *dolce far niente*, he may achieve his amatory exploit. Such examples of Spenser's significant namings can be easily multiplied.[10]

9. Mr. James D. Redwine, now a professor of English in Bowdoin College, once confronted me with this interpretation when I was trying to extract the marine significance of Marinell's name from a graduate pro-seminar group. I was amused at the time (I hope without offense to him), but I now think that Mr. Redwine was right.

10. Information and conjecture on Spenser's names are widespread. An unpublished Columbia University doctoral dissertation must be mentioned: Joel J. Belson, 'The Names in *The Faerie Queene*' (1964).

7

Garden of Adonis, Bower of Bliss, Isle of Venus: Amoret and Scudamour

Of the two principal pairs of lovers whose paths intersect with Britomart's and Arthur's, Florimell and Marinell offer fewer puzzles than Amoret and Scudamour. Florimell had been reared among the attendant Graces of Venus in the goddess's retreat on Mount Acidale (in Book VI we see these same Graces dancing about Colin Clout's lass). Florimell, loved by all of Gloriana's court, loves none but Marinell, but Marinell has denied himself to love. His mother had learned from the sea god Proteus that her son would be destroyed or done much ill by a woman. A *topos* of the divine augury then unrolled. Unaware of the true meaning of the prophecy, his mother persuaded him to avoid all women, not out of a devotion to purity like Belphoebe's, but as a self-serving precaution. The prophecy fulfills itself inexorably, and at two symbolic levels. The wound of love is first executed upon him allegorically when Britomart, with all her maiden force, transfixes him with her resistless spear and leaves him half-dead upon his Rich Strond, in III. iv. Barely cured of the one wound, he sickens, apparently hopelessly, when he finally falls in love with the by then apparently unattainable Florimell, in IV. xii. (This variety of conceit is a familiar sonneteering one, also used, for instance, for Belphoebe's curing of Timias' physical wound at the same time that she makes him sick with love.)

Florimell's experience in the interim has been similarly clear. Deprived of her proper complement and protector, she was pursued and importuned by a wide spectrum of uncouth lovers, for the consolation of one of whom his mother fabricated the snowy False Florimell. Eventually, given up for dead by all, Florimell fell into the hands of Proteus. He imprisoned her for seven months, torturing her spirit to make her love him. But she will not give up her chaste constancy to Marinell even to be the consort of a god (IV. xii. 16. 9). It is the discovery of this which causes Marinell first to pity her and then to love her. United at the end of Book IV by the efforts of his now repentant mother, they will celebrate their marriage in Book V with a splendid tournament.

All this being true, it seems that in the case of Amoret and Scudamour a symbolic progression of a parallel nature ought to be observed: as the sufferings of Florimell, culminating in a seven-month imprisonment beneath the sea at the hands of a being who was trying to make her love him, had been precipitated by the watery and cold defectiveness in love of the sea-descended coast-dweller Marinell, so the seven-month imprisonment of Amoret, by a being making an identical demand, in a house whose portal was filled with sulphurous fire, ought to proceed from an opposite defect in Scudamour: his fiery and demanding quality as a lover, bolder than he ought to be.

It is a measure of Spenser's power as a narrative poet that readers who see Scudamour's and Amoret's position in this light, and other readers of quite contrary conviction, like Professor Thomas P. Roche, Jr.,[1] still bear united witness to the power of the allegorical process that Spenser set going in the House of Busirane. The story of Amoret and Scudamour is among Spenser's most powerful and enigmatic allegorical sequences. Its implications are elaborated in a series of carefully related and counterpointed moralized landscapes and chivalric adventures: Garden of Adonis, tapestry of Malecasta, Bower of Bliss, Isle of Venus, Castle Joyous, House of Malbecco, House of Busirane, and Isis Church. Chaucer is at the beginning of the story and at its end.

Amoret, like her sister Belphoebe, was engendered by the sun in his role as 'great father of generation' in the moistened flesh of the sleeping Chrysogone ('gold-engendered' or possibly 'gold-inseminated'), daughter of Amphisa ('on both sides').

---

1. *The Kindly Flame: A Study of the Third and Fourth Books of Spenser's 'Faerie Queene'* (Princeton, 1964).

> Miraculous may seeme to him, that reades
>   So straunge ensample of conception;
>   But reason teacheth that the fruitfull seades
>   Of all things living, through impression
>   Of the sunbeames in moyst complexion,
>   Doe life conceive and quickned are by kynd.
>   [III. vi. 8]

In this role the sun begets, for instance, in the mud left by the Nile, 'infinite shapes' which are 'informed in the mud, on which the Sunne hath shynd'. As the father of shapes and forms, the sun cooperates with the moon, who provides matter to fill these forms. (Traditionally the moon governed the growth of plants in an astrological sense through her phases, and, as Lucina, presided over the parturition of women, with whom she shares a cycle.) Of the sun and the moon Spenser says here:

> Great father he of generation
>   Is rightly cald, th'author of life and light;
>   And his faire sister for creation
>   Ministreth matter fit, which tempred right
>   With heate and humour, breedes the living wight.
>   [vi. 9]

Spenser will bring us back to the communion of sun and moon, but with moral, not physical, application in the Temple of Isis (see chapter 9).

Venus, hunting in company with Belphoebe for her son Cupid, or *Amor*, finds instead the two newly born infants. She takes one and names her 'Amoret'. This child is then raised in Venus' Garden of Adonis in companionship with physical Pleasure—*voluptas*—daughter of Cupid and Psyche. Amoret is thus made ready to get and give sexual pleasure as a woman; it is in this physical sense that here she absorbs 'the lore of love, and goodly womanhood'.

In the Garden of Adonis is repeated the pattern described for the sun and the moon in connection with the episode of Amoret's birth. Adonis is for Spenser (as for Sir James Frazer) a dying god, killed by the boar but annually reborn in the cycle of the year along with the vegetation and other life that renews itself with the sun. In the Garden he is preserved eternally and enjoyed at wish by Venus in a cave beneath the central mount. This mount, in the central stanza of this Book of Love, is the *mons veneris*, the focus of sexual pleasure, as previously described (see chapter 6). Within it lies the source of human life by means of which,

individually mortal and subject to alteration though we are, we attain a
kind of immortality and changeless persistence through the procreation
of descendants, by Nature's direction to us and all other life. Adonis is
said, like the sun, to be the father of all forms:

> And sooth it seemes they say: for he may not
>> For ever die, and ever buried bee
>> In balefull night, where all things are forgot;
>> All be he subject to mortalite,
>> Yet is eterne in mutabilitie,
>> And by succession made perpetuall,
>> Transformed oft, and chaunged diverslie:
>> For him the Father of all formes they call;
> Therefore needs mote he live, that living gives to all.
>> [vi. 47]

As the moon ministers 'matter fit' for the sun, so in the Garden surrounding the mount, matter is provided and the same process goes forward.
Genius, the Garden's porter, lets out new souls clothed with flesh and
lets back in the old:

> Daily they grow, and daily forth are sent
>> Into the world, it to replenish more;
>> Yet is the stocke not lessened, nor spent,
>> But still remaines in everlasting store,
>> As it at first created was of yore.
>> For in the wide wombe of the world there lyes,
>> In hatefull darkenesse and in deepe horrore,
>> An huge eternal *Chaos*, which supplyes
> The substances of natures fruitfull progenyes.

> All things from thence doe their first being fetch,
>> And borrow matter, whereof they are made,
>> Which when as forme and feature it does ketch,
>> Becomes a bodie, and doth then invade
>> The state of life, out of the griesly shade.
>> That substance is eterne, and bideth so,
>> Ne when the life decayes, and forme does fade,
>> Doth it consume, and into nothing go,
> But chaunged is, and often altred to and fro.
>> [vi. 36–37]

The material of living bodies remains the same; but new forms, of new individuals, are continually being imposed upon it. Exuberant vegetation continually springs up in the Garden, corresponding to Adonis' function as a god of fertility, and is as continually mowed down by Time with his scythe. The form of the fertility myth according to which the dead Adonis is transformed to a flower is only briefly touched on here, and is qualified by the notion of immortality through poetry, analogous to the main idea here of immortality through procreation:

> Sad *Amaranthus,* in whose purple gore
> Me seemes I see *Amintas* wretched fate,
> To whom sweet Poets verse hath given endlesse date.
> [vi. 45]

With Genius and cyclic regeneration this main idea has returned us to a Platonizing milieu familiar from Theseus' 'progressiouns and successiouns' and *The Parlement.* The Demiurge of the *Timaeus* institutes cyclical return in accordance with numerical pattern, as the provision nearest to eternal perfection in the universe of temporal and spatial change. Alanus de Insulis, and Jean de Meun following him (and translated by Chaucer), give us a Nature, or 'Kynde', who regulates the perpetual orbiting of the heavens and the perpetual regenerations of the biological world; her priest is Genius, concerned with generation. This macrocosmic-microcosmic notion is a favourite one of Spenser's which he most obviously relates to Chaucer's mythic world in the plainest Spenserian imitation of *The Parlement,* which is the latter part of *Mutabilitie.* He celebrates it as well in the numerical patterning and symbolism of the sun's daily and annual motion in *Epithalamion.*[2] Genius is found there (398–404), as well as in the Garden of Adonis.

Thus, although this Garden is an abode of Venus in her procreative aspect, it is Nature who is its dame in a more profound sense. Her Genius is its porter, and all that occurs within it is by course of Kynde (38. 7, 30. 6, 44. 2), although 'dame Nature' herself is mentioned but once (30. 2). In a usefully connected sense Spenser makes plain that everything here, including human physical love, functions naturally, innocently, ingenuously:

> For here all plentie, and all pleasure flowes,
> And sweet love gentle fits emongst them throwes,

2. See A. Kent Hieatt, *Short Time's Endless Monument: The Symbolism of the Numbers in Edmund Spenser's 'Epithalamion'* (New York, 1960; rpt. Port Washington, N. Y., 1972).

> Without fell rancor, or fond gealosie;
> Franckly each paramour his leman knowes,
> Each bird his mate, ne any does envie
> Their goodly meriment, and gay felicitie.

> . . . .
> The whiles the joyous birdes make their pastime
> Emongst the shadie leaves, their sweet abode,
> And their true loves without suspition tell abrode.
>   [vi. 41, 42]

The startlingly physical symbol of the female pudendum as the mount in the centre of the Garden is of a piece with this frankness about sexual pleasure, like that of Reason in robustly naming the male member in *Le Roman de la rose*. The description of the mount bears some resemblance to the passage from the Song of Solomon (quoted in chapter 5), which is the exalted source of January's debased injunction to May to enter his garden. Spenser is at pains to show that the central feature itself is a work of nature and not of artifice or imitation—of 'art' in the pejorative sense:

> And in the thickest covert of the shade,
>   There was a pleasant arbour, not by art,
> .But of the trees owne inclination made.
>   [vi. 44]

In what is in an essential sense Nature's garden, the mention of her only in connection with flowers may seem a curious emphasis:

> In that same Gardin all the goodly flowres,
>   Wherewith dame Nature doth her beautifie,
> And decks the girlonds of her paramoures,
>   Are fetcht. . . .
>   [vi. 30]

Yet an image system of flowers, as a synedoche for vegetation in general, extends through at least two other landscapes, the tapestry in the Castle of Malecasta, and the Bower of Bliss. These two clarify the significance of the Garden of Adonis.

In the tapestry, in that House of overmastering pleasure in the first canto of Book III, is depicted a radically different enactment of the Garden's myth. On flowers there is much verbal parallelism to what has already appeared:

> The love of *Venus* and her Paramoure
> The faire *Adonis*, turned to a flowre.
>> [i. 34]

She

> wooed him her Paramoure to be:
> Now making girlonds of each flowre that grew,
> To crowne his golden lockes with honour dew.
>> [i. 35]

When he bathes, she throws into the water 'sweet Rosemaryes, / And fragrant violets, and Pances trim, / And ever with sweet Nectar she did sprinkle him' (i. 36). But the course of love here is far removed from that in the Garden. Venus herself is first mastered in 'her tender hart' with fervent passion, like Malecasta. She then seductively masters Adonis in turn, leading him away from his normal companions and from the eye of Heaven,[3] to lay him to sleep in the guilty secrecy of a dark glade. She peers at him with lewd interest as he bathes:[4] 'And whilest he bath'd, with her two crafty spyes, / She secretly would search each daintie lim.' For a time she 'joyed his love in secret unespyde', as the other Venus enjoyed him in the Garden; the significant difference, however, is that, in the tapestry, after Adonis is killed by the boar, there follows no great fable of recurrence and persistence in and through mutability. Sexual pleasure here has no complement in generation and offspring, and the sense of the myth is lost in the self-indulgent picturesqueness of Ovidian pathos. Venus is left grovelling; Adonis is transformed to a flower and nothing more:

> Hym to a daintie flowre she did transmew,
> Which in that cloth was wrought, as if it lively grew.
>> [i. 38]

'As if' is the operative word: the flower seems alive, but is only worked by artifice in a tapestry.

One of the main features of the Bower of Bliss, the garden of irresponsible pleasure in the last canto of Book II, is that it is the work, not of Nature herself, but of an art which deceptively imitates nature. The establishment of Nature's role in the Garden of Adonis is partly accomplished by counterpointing, in detail after detail, the natural effects of the Garden against the meretricious art of the Bower. In it Art is the mother of Flora, the ornaments of whose pride mantle the grass (II. xii.

---

3. The opposed role of the sun is worth noting.
4. Like Cymochles in the Bower, II. v. 34.

50). The Bower has been created by a technical virtuosity of those most gifted at imitating nature's work by art (xii. 42), although the art is carefully hidden (58). Art and Nature are in competition (59). Whereas the arbour of Adonis is made 'not by art, / But of the trees owne inclination' (III. vi. 44), and true fruit burden the branches (42), the vines of the Bower are 'beautified' by artful grapes of gold 'lurking from the view', which by their dead mineral weight 'over-burden' the boughs that bear them (II. xii. 55). The centrepiece of the Bower, corresponding to the centrepieces of Spenser's other moralized landscapes, is a crystalline work of art and, in place of the true 'wanton' ivy of the *mons veneris* (III. vi. 44–45), is covered with a delicious trail of tremulous ivy made of gold carefully coloured green and *seeming* to weep crystal drops 'for wantones' (II. xii. 61).[5] In the Bower a cold-bloodedly egotistical hedonism is the moral coefficient of the notion of love without recurrence. This is most pointedly voiced in the perversion of the truism of the song of the once beautiful rose which is 'deflowered' and 'no more doth flourish after first decay'. The song is sung in the presence of the substitute Venus figure here, who is Acrasia. She seems to preserve an artfully insulated environment of Bliss, but she is the destroyer of that possibility of true human growth which is symbolized vegetatively in the name Verdant of her misled lover. He is led from honour and true companions as is the Adonis of the tapestry. She has brought her former lover, Mordant, to death.[6] Her Circean reduction of men to beasts will occupy us in part II of the present book.

As the Bower of Bliss of II stands in contrast with the Garden of Adonis of III in counterfeiting nature by a false art, so it stands in contrast with the Isle of Venus of IV in counterfeiting the true art of the Isle by the art of apparent love. This island is the second moralized landscape in which Amoret is found. Here she takes upon herself the role of Womanhood in a moral and social sense (IV. x. 49–52). Placed in the tenth canto of the Book of Friendship, it is the stage upon which nature and art—the latter in the sense of an acquired accomplishment rather than a natural endowment—are brought into a complementary relationship, not into antipathy. The principle of this moralized landscape is familiar to readers of the Merchant's and Franklin's Tales: if a relationship of love is to become humanly responsible and constant in a real and social sense, nature must not be negated and betrayed by an art of falsification, but nature must nevertheless be completed by an art of friendship. The symbolic arrangements in this landscape

5. Cf. the samy ivy over Cymochles in II. v. 29.
6. On the deaths of Mordant and Amavia through the agency of Acrasia, see chapter 12.

are more complex than any described so far.

Scudamour penetrates to this island and on it obtains his Amoret forcibly. To do so, he must pass through the two distinct sublandscapes into which the total area is divided, both of them presided over by the Venus who is mounted on an altar at the centre point of the Temple. The first of these two divisions is populated by symbolic figures who test and restrain intending lovers in the fashion of the *Romaunt of the Rose*. For these, Scudamour is admirably equipped: he is boldly competitive and ready to hazard all on fortune. Only just arrived at manhood, he has heard of the enterprise of the shield of Love through which Amoret is to be gained. He viewed the adventure as a way of gaining honour, much as the contenders for false Florimell view their own efforts in neighbouring cantos. He has thus readily undertaken it, although he has been disappointed in the sequel:

> Then hearke ye gentle knights and Ladies free,
> My hard mishaps, that ye may learne to shonne;
> For though sweet love to conquer glorious bee,
> Yet is the paine thereof much greater then the fee.

> What time the fame of this renowned prise
> Flew first abroad, and all mens eares possest,
> I having armes then taken, gan avise
> To winne me honour by some noble gest,
> And purchase me some place amongst the best.
> I boldly thought (so young mens thoughts are bold)
> That this same brave emprize for me did rest,
> And that both shield and she whom I behold,
> Might be my lucky lot; sith all by lot we hold.
>   [IV. x. 3, 4]

In a castle guarding the bridge to the island live a score of knights, duty-bound to defend the approach. He encounters the first 'boldly' and unseats him 'by good fortune' (10). He succeeds in the same way with the rest (in a process at one with the set battles of chivalric adventure in other parts of Book IV) and then takes from its pillar a shield, beneath which is the inscription

> *Blessed the man that well can use his blis:*
> *Whose ever be the shield, faire Amoret be his.*
>   [IV. x. 8]

That is, because Scudamour is suitably bold, he obtains the shield and will obtain his Amoret; the question is whether he will be able to use the

ensuing bliss as he should. Meanwhile, having eliminated the competition for the lady, he now suitably overcomes in the castle itself the
qualities of the female temperament itself when wooed: Doubt and
Delay, sitting on either side of the gate. At the next gate he is faced by
Daunger, who opposes to his boldness a 'countenance bold', and who in
the *Romaunt* and other medieval allegories is the aroused and temperamental, angry response of a woman of spirit to any attempt to win
her precipitately.[7] Daunger is immediately overcome by being shown
the shield, on which the Love God is displayed in his masterful
masculinity.

Scudamour next enters the landscape of the island proper, where such
competitive and hindering figures as we have just seen have no place,
with the one exception of the totally regulated and counterpoised figure
of Hate. Love and friendship reign, as in the benign four-groups of Book
IV at large. On the one side, pairs of lovers sport 'Their spotlesse
pleasures, and sweet loves content' (26) without rebuke or blame, as in
the Garden of Adonis. On the other side, however, are pairs of friends
who 'love not as these, for like intent, / But on chast vertue grounded
their desire' (26). Famous friendships of the past continue here, among
them that of Theseus and Pirithous. Scudamour longs for these couples'
blissful freedom from fear and jealousy (Britomart's friendly revelation
had released him from such suffering only shortly before he tells his
tale).

As a physical landscape the Isle is also the work of Nature and Art in
cooperation:[8]

> For all that nature by her mother wit
> Could frame in earth, and forme of substance base,
> Was there, and all that nature did omit,
> Art playing second natures part, supplyed it.
>
> [x. 21]

Even on the bridge crossing to the island, Scudamour had noticed the

---

7. So Daunger seems to be here, according to his behaviour and to the various described
responses to him, as well as by association with Doubt and Delay. Yet when he is viewed
from the back, 'hatred, murther, treason, and despight' are his qualities, which would
more likely proceed from the 'danger' of jealous competitors rather than from the
'daunger' of a lady. Perhaps this is another aspect of Daunger here, and not his whole
meaning. By Daunger in the Masque of Cupid the dangers arising from jealousy are surely
signified.

8. Such definite statements are found in connection with other moralized landscapes in
The Faerie Queene apart from the ones discussed here. The mention of Nature only,
without Art, in connection with Venus' retreat on Mount Acidale (VI. x. 5) puts in some
doubt much modern speculation about the primary bearing of the subsequent scene
among Colin Clout, Calidore, and the Graces upon the theoretical nature of poetry.

ideal symbiosis of the artisan's bridgework and the stream passing beneath it, impelled by nature. He beheld

> The goodly workes, and stones of rich assay,
> Cast into sundry shapes by wondrous skill,
> That like on earth no where I recken may:
> And underneath, the river rolling still
> With murmure soft, that seem'd to serve the workmans will.
>
> [x. 15]

On the Isle the vegetation that nature brings forth is arranged with the artful care of a formal garden. The landscape:

> Fresh shadowes, fit to shroud from sunny ray;
> Faire lawnds, to take the sunne in season dew;
> Sweet springs, in which a thousand Nymphs did play;
> Soft rombling brookes, that gentle slomber drew;
> High reared mounts, the lands about to vew;
> Low looking dales, disloignd from common gaze;
> Delightfull bowres, to solace lovers trew;
> False Labyrinthes, fond runners eyes to daze;
> All which by nature made did nature selfe amaze.
>
> [x. 24]

The garden:

> And all without were walkes and alleyes dight,
> With divers trees, enrang'd in even rankes;
> And here and there were pleasant arbors pight,
> And shadie seates, and sundry flowring bankes,
> To sit and rest the walkers wearie shankes.
>
> [x. 25]

Through landscape is signified here what in chivalric adventure Arthur, for instance, achieved in transforming Poeana. To her physical endowment was added the acquired skill or art of friendly selflessness, and, in the Franklin's terms, 'patience' and 'suffrance' replaced her fell cruelty. On the Isle, love in Nature's sense of the Garden of Adonis is complemented by the art of friendship. This is the significance, for marriage, of the womanly virtues seated with Amoret and Womanhood herself in the Temple. In addition to *Shamefastnesse*,[9]

9. Women may be slightly better than men at achieving the following list of virtues, but surely Spenser would assert that both men and women ought to practise all these virtues in many contexts and some of them in all contexts. He says that these virtues are for saints, without distinction of gender. The male Guyon is said in II. ix. 43 to possess shamefastness (*Verecundia*) in particular. Radigund is considered in chapter 12.

her against sweet *Cherefulnesse* was placed,
  Whose eyes like twinkling stars in evening cleare,
  Were deckt with smyles, that all sad humours chaced,
And darted forth delights, the which her goodly graced.

And next to her sate sober *Modestie*,
  Holding her hand upon her gentle hart;
  And her against sate comely *Curtesie*,
  That unto every person knew her part;
  And her before was seated overthwart
  Soft *Silence*, and submisse *Obedience*,
  Both linckt together never to dispart,
  Both gifts of God not gotten but from thence,
Both girlonds of his Saints against their foes offence.
  [x. 50, 51]

Upon the harmonious scene of the Isle Scudamour is an interloper.
Full of his enterprise, he advances determinedly upon the Temple of
Venus. He is admitted by Concord, who is in the noble Boethian
tradition which Chaucer put into English verse in Theseus' reference to
the Prince and First Mover of the universe: 'For with that faire chaine of
love he boond / The fir, the air, the water, and the lond / In certain
boundes that they may nat flee' (2133–35; 2991–93), and in his
reference to other categories in *The Parlement*, 'Nature, vicarye of the
Almighty Lord / That hoot, cold, hevy, light, and moist, and dreye /
Hath knit with evene nombres of accord' (379–81). Spenser's Concord:

By her the heaven is in his course contained,
  And all the world in state unmoved stands,
  As their Almightie maker first ordained,
  And bound them with inviolable bands;
  Else would the waters overflow the lands,
  And fire devoure the ayre, and hell them quight,
  But that she holds them with her blessed hands.
  [x. 35]

She restrains by the powers of attraction and repulsion the tendency of
the elements of the universe to fall into a warring chaos, as does the
Ovidian creator-Love in *An Hymne in Honour of Love*:

The earth, the ayre, the water, and the fyre,
  Then gan to raunge them selves in huge array,
  And with contrary forces to conspyre

Each against other, by all meanes they may,
Threatning their owne confusion and decay:
Ayre hated earth, and water hated fyre,
Till love relented their rebellious yre.

He then them tooke, and tempering goodly well
Their contrary dislikes with loved meanes,
Did place them all in order, and compell
To keepe them selves within their sundrie raines,
Together linkt with Adamantine chaines;
Yet so, as that in every living wight
They mixe themselves, and shew their kindly might.

[78–91]

It is in this sense that Concord joins together the brothers Love and Hate sitting on either side of her. As the mother of Peace and Friendship (34), she is the opposite of the Ate who holds the House of Discord (i. 20–26). The combination of a crown containing white ('Poudred with pearle and stone') with a gown woven with gold appears to refer to the same harmonization of the male and female principles which we shall see more clearly, in Isis Temple, in the sun and moon representing Osiris and Isis, and in the unorthodox golden crown with orthodox white linen garment of Isis herself. Such a combination has already been touched on in the relation of the sun and the moon in providing form and matter in the passage introducing the Garden of Adonis.[10]

10. An allusion to Elizabeth I seems likely in this figure, as the Variorum note, IV, 226, suggests. Her female character is stressed by saying that she showed 'great womanhood', which incidentally relates her to the figure Womanhood within the Temple. As I try to show in chapter 9, there is reason to believe that the crown of Isis, and her white gown, signify one hierarchy of, respectively, male 'solar' and female 'lunar' values. In Concord's gown what may be called the female moon symbol is placed above what may be called the golden, male sun symbol, reversing the order of colours in the figure of Isis and suggesting the particular monarchical situation in which the female element takes the upper position in the hierarchy. Her divinity is stressed in a way familiar in Spenser's treatment of the Queen, but hardly necessary in the case of a straightforward personification of a divinity Concordia. Her political role is also stressed: 'And she her selfe likewise divinely grew; / The which right well her workes divine did shew: / For strength, and wealth, and happiness she lends, / And strife, and warre, and anger does subdew' (IV.x. 34).
    What Spenser meant by saying that Concord's crown was like a 'Danisk hood' (31. 7) is not known. The usual books of reference offer no help. I am much indebted for aid and suggestions in this connection to Mrs. Madeline Ginsburg of the Victoria and Albert Museum's Department of Textiles, to Mrs. Fritze Lindalhl, Assistant Curator of the Danish Collection's Historical Section to 1600, of Nationalmuseet, Copenhagen, and to Dr. Roy Strong of the National Portrait Gallery. Their scrupulous reflection and research produced no answer. I have followed up all their kind suggestions without gaining further light. Possibly Spenser was using the name of some variety of man's hood to describe what he meant, or wished to avoid a more usual name (e.g., 'French hood') for fear of a political allusion, or (as several have suggested to me) wrote initially 'damask hood'.

Concord is 'the nourse of pleasure and delight, / And unto *Venus* grace the gate doth open right' (x. 3 5). She is the porter to love, because, without friendship and cherishing, love is not given willingly, and when affection is demanded without the accompanying grant of freedom to accept or reject, 'sweet love anone / Taketh his nimble wings, and soone away is gone' (III. i. 25). Because it is her role, Concord helps Scudamour past her in friendly fashion, on the side of Love, not Hate, who, like Daunger, would have expelled him.

Within, a hundred altars send forth from their sacrificial fires the frankincense-like odours, not of lovers' sighs, as in *The Parlement*, but, very similarly, of such true lovers' vows as are fully committed ones—'entire'. A like number of brazen cauldrons are there, 'To bath in joy and amorous desire' (IV. x. 38); these are tended by priestesses, all dressed in white linen, again like the moon priests of the Temple of Isis, and again probably representative of the female principle. The usual centrepiece, 'Right in the midst', is a crystalline altar, like the artful central fountain of the Bower of Bliss, but 'purer'. On it stands the hermaphroditic Venus, symbolizing in her self-sufficiency true love in friendship and the marriage of true minds. The serpent, or ouroboros, encircling her legs and having its tail in its mouth, relates to the inter-twined serpents and circular garland on the shield of Cambina as she helps to join four in love and friendship in Spenser's Squire's Tale. This Venus, however, is not simply a duplicate of her own porter Concord. She is indeed, as a planet, a pacifying *stella maris*:

> That with thy smyling looke doest pacifie
> The raging seas, and makst the stormes to flie;
> Thee goddesse, thee the winds, the clouds doe feare,
> And when thou spredst thy mantle forth on hie,
> The waters play and pleasant lands appeare,
> And heavens laugh, and al the world shews joyous cheare.
>   [x. 44]

But she is also being importuned by all kinds of unfortunate and unhappy lovers, like the Venus of *The Parlement of Foules*. Some have lost their loves and some are caught in delay; some have prideful loves and some disdain their lovers; some fear that they are being deceived and others deceive. From the second and third stanzas of a petitioner's song in her praise, it appears that she, much like Nature, with whom she is partly synonymous as in the Garden, is necessarily the cause of much agonized searching and strife. She inspires animal natures with 'fury' to quench their inward fire 'in generation'. Having caused the earth to send forth its flowers, she first 'pricks' (the Chaucerian word for the action of Nature in the General Prologue to *The Canterbury Tales* and *The Parlement of Foules*) the birds 'to coole their kindly rages', that is, to cool the loving fury associated with each species and with Dame Kynde. She then arouses the other animals sexually, to the point where they all go off their feed. First the birds chirp, then lions roar, tigers bray, bulls rebellow through the wood. All such dare to cross the deepest flood (as Scudamour has indeed done) to come where Venus draws them. The description of her powers modulates from the peace of concording harmony to the sexual violence that aspires towards that harmony.

She is, then, not simply a bland yoker together of things, but also the ruler of the landscape beyond the Isle and its bridge, and the cause of Scudamour's fighting twenty knights, of his taking the shield, not of harmony, but of the masterful Cupid, and of his pressing on deterninedly past the figures in the successive portals. She inspires the raging and fiery boldness which is in search of a cooling of 'kindly rages' (x. 45) and a quenching of 'inward fire' (46). Because she is a bold goddess, she will laugh with favour upon Scudamour and his bold act.

The singer closes with a forlorn plea to have his love, and Scudamour adds a private prayer in his own interest. He instantly sights the group of female figures among whom Amoret sits.

> The which was all in lilly white arayd,
> With silver streames amongst the linnen stray'd;
> Like to the Morne, when first her shyning face
> Hath to the gloomy world it selfe bewray'd,
> That same was fayrest *Amoret* in place,
> Shyning with beauties light, and heavenly vertues grace.[11]
>
> [x. 52]

The premise of Scudamour's reaction to all this betrays a certain callowness. He knows no better than to apply in and out of season a hearsay truism:

> Tho shaking off all doubt and shamefast feare,
> Which Ladies love I heard had never wonne
> Mongst men of worth, I to her stepped neare,
> And by the lilly hand her labour'd up to reare.
>
> [x. 53]

11. As will be shown in chapter 9, a series of descriptions of females (this one, and others of Concord, Britomart, and Radigund) seem to relate either to the whiteness of the moon or the gold and red of the sun in connection with the symbolism of the Temple of Isis and the name Chrysogone. The combination of pure white with silver in this description agrees with the garment and with the material of the statue of Isis in V. vii. 6.

Womanhood then sharply rebukes him for being 'overbold'; as we shall see, the reiterations of 'bold' in this canto, and now the word 'overbold', play into the hands of the successive adjurations in the House of Busirane: *'Be bold,' 'Be hold,' 'Be not too bold.'* Also, the sense of sacrilege to the Temple (53), and of a male irruption of violence in peacefully ordered surroundings, resembles the chthonic violence which, in Britomart's dream, we shall see arising in the Temple of Isis. Against it Isis herself will be helpless, and it will be absorbed by a suddenly male crocodile, so as to arouse his libido. When Scudamour grasps Amoret's hand:

> Thereat that formost matrone me did blame,
>   And sharpe rebuke, for being over bold;
>   Saying it was to Knight unseemely shame,
>   Upon a recluse Virgin to lay hold,
>   That unto *Venus* services was sold.
>   To whom I thus, Nay but it fitteth best,
>   For *Cupids* man with *Venus* mayd to hold,
>   For ill your goddesse services are drest
> By virgins, and her sacrifices let to rest.
>
> With that my shield I forth to her did show,
>   Which all that while I closely had conceld;
>   On which when *Cupid* with his killing bow
>   And cruell shafts emblazond she beheld,
>   At sight thereof she was with terror queld,
>   And said no more; but I which all that while
>   The pledge of faith, her hand engaged held,
>   Like warie Hynd within the weedie soyle,
> For no intreatie would forgoe so glorious spoyle.
>   [x. 54–55]

Significantly, the figure of a deer unwilling to be held is discordant with Spenser's idealization of the course of his own wooing, in *Amoretti*. Only after much persuasion and many blandishments does he get his prey within his dominion, and he gets her only by her own good will and free choice:

> Lyke as a huntsman after weary chace,
>   Seeing the game from him escapt away,
>   sits downe to rest him in some shady place
>   with panting hounds beguiled of their pray:

So after long pursuit and vaine assay,
> when I all weary had the chace forsooke,
> the gentle deare returnd the selfe-same way,
> thinking to quench her thirst at the next brooke.
There she beholding me with mylder looke,
> sought not to fly, but fearelesse still did bide:
> till I in hand her yet halfe trembling tooke,
> and with her owne goodwill hir fyrmely tyde.
Strange thing me seemd to see a beast so wyld,
> so goodly wonne with her owne will beguyld.
>> [67]

It is not so with Scudamour. Holding Amoret firmly by the hand, he takes her past the helpless personifications of the qualities of woman-hood, as Amoret implores him with both tears and 'witching smyles',

> but yet for nought,
That ever she to me could say or doe,
Could she her wished freedome fro me wooe.
>> [x. 57]

'Wished freedome' is here the key concept, one of the great themes of Books III and IV. Just before the opening of this canto it had been pregnantly reaffirmed by Arthur, in relation to the foolish foursome, who

> the love of Ladies foule defame;
To whom the world this franchise ever yeelded,
That of their loves choise they might freedom clame.
>> [IV. ix. 37]

The great difference between Venus and Nature, the otherwise similar figures here, is that Venus encourages in such a contingency the boldness which is a necessary aspect of the attainment of union; but that in the greater tolerance of Nature in her truest sense,[12] and of natural law, that boldness must be restrained from mastery over an unwilling partner. Venus:

Whom when I saw with amiable grace
To laugh at me, and favour my pretence,

---

12. Nature in a 'less true' sense—that is, the nature of Lear's Edmund—is blurred into a poetic ambiguity with this one in, for instance, the nature of Poeana before she was redeemed.

I was emboldned with more confidence,
And nought for nicenesse nor for envy sparing,
In presence of them all forth led her thence.

[x. 56]

The Nature of *The Parlement of Foules* speaks thus of the formel eagle: 'she hirself shal han the eleccioun / Of whom hire list' (620–21). The formel replies, with dread and piety: 'unto this yeer be goon, / I axe respit for to avise me. . . . I wol nat serve Venus ne Cupide / Forsoothe, as yit' (647–48, 652–53).

Amoret's situation is in one way comparable to the formel's. Although she is already well and truly Scudamour's in the most important sense (as Britomart is Artegall's before she admits it), so that Scudamour's behaviour is not so culpable as that unsteady foursome's reproved by Arthur, yet as a virgin of the Temple Amoret seeks leisure, 'To avise me', if only in the hope of being gently convinced. She wants to take the matter under advisement. Whatever may be objected here on the score of Doubt and Delay, Scudamour has carried boldness beyond the region where it properly applies—the approaches to the Isle—into the Temple where friendly persuasion is the proper technique, that is, a willed behaviour which is finally an art. The hermaphroditic state, suggested in the conclusion of Book III in 1590,[13] and symbolized by this Venus herself, is not to be attained in the human and social order solely by the boldness and bull-like rebellowing which the generative aspect of Venus herself encourages among both her animal and human subjects. It is no wonder, then, that Concord befriends Scudamour in his retreat from the Temple, for he does not belong there.[14] Perhaps significantly, he had not in the first place understood the harmonization of the male and female principles in her attire.[15] Amoret is his, but he does not know how to use his bliss. Ahead of him is a flawed marriage day and no quenching or cooling, but only the sulphurous flames of the House of Busirane, until Britomart gives him and Amoret the friendship of which self-control is the *sine qua non*. It is an ominous presage at the

13. I am indebted to Dr. Judith Anderson for reminding me that here the deer image again reappears (Variorum, III, 181, 2nd stanza), applied this time to Scudamour.

14. As Concord is the nurse of pleasure, Venus is finally the preparer of all that serves it. Concord, while superintending the powers of attraction, is mainly concerned with friendly harmony; Venus, while harmonious in her planetary and hermaphroditic blissfulness, is concerned, as a goddess and a planet, to engender the attraction which with sexual fury breaks down the barriers. The progress towards harmony is for her accompanied by the rages of Mother Kynde; for Concord that harmonious interaction is closer to the music of the spheres.

15. See chapter 9.

end of the episode of the Isle of Venus that Scudamour compares his carrying off of Amoret to the recovery of Eurydice by Orpheus from the Underworld. He forgets the last-minute failure of that boldly executed enterprise. He could more aptly have compared his action to Pluto's forcible abduction of Proserpina in the opposite direction, down to Tartarus, as recalled by Chaucer in the Merchant's Tale (see figure 1).

8

Amoret and Scudamour Continued: Malecasta, Malbecco, Busirane

The next step in the careers of Amoret and Scudamour is their marriage, described in two stanzas at the opening of IV. i, where Busirane abducts Amoret in the midst of the Masque of Cupid. This Masque is no doubt to be imagined as marching into, and then out of, the hall of 'the bridale feast, whilest every man / Surcharg'd with wine, were heedlesse and ill heded'. Chronologically, we next find Scudamour without, and Amoret within, the House of Busirane, in the conclusion of Book III.

Each of the three books of *Faerie Queene* 1590 has within its first canto an episode which states the nature of the problem and of the ultimate accomplishment in that book. At the beginning of Book I, Redcross's defeat of Error, only to be himself deceived, looks forward to his problem with Duessa and Orgoglio in the middle of that book, and to his final victory over the dragon, father of lies. In II, the pathetic ends of Mordant and Amavia, and Guyon's and the Palmer's ensuing definitions of intemperance and temperance, point forward to Guyon's overcoming of the House of Mammon in the midst of the book and of the Bower of Bliss at the end (see part II of the present book). Even in the 1596 edition, the theme and the problem of IV, of how to graft an art of friendly understanding on the libidinal drive, are embodied in its first canto, along with a possible foretaste of its perhaps intended (but aborted) conclusion in a four-group embodying both friendship and the sexual relation. In that canto, Britomart forms the preliminary friendly and loving four-group by showing herself to Amoret as a friend whose sex is not an issue, so as to assuage her fears, and by putting herself forward at the same time as a lady for the young knight at the castle so that he may gain lodging. Contrariwise, in the same canto, Scudamour's remaining trust in Britomart and Amoret is destroyed by Ate, or Discord, in a false four-group.

Much as in these other books, the first canto of Book III, concerning Britomart's overcoming of the Castle of Malecasta, states the problem and anticipates her victory over the House of Busirane in the last canto. The episode of Malecasta, we are told, concerns mastery, the opposite of friendship in the Chaucerian sense. Except for the central section on love in the Garden of Adonis, most of this Book of Chastity, or true love, is devoted to the compulsions imposed upon the human will by sexual attraction or repulsion, and to ensuing masterful action—compulsive or deceptive—without regard for the will and liberty of its object.

The first canto of Book III is mainly taken up with the episode of Malecasta, but a bridging episode, and something more, also precede this. Without having recognized each other, the knight of Temperance, hero of the preceding book, who at its conclusion had destroyed the Bower of Bliss, meets Britomart, the knight of chaste love, the positive side of which concept in this Book of Chastity will be epitomized in the grass and herbs of the Garden of Adonis. They run a course together, his horse's hooves burning 'the verdant grass'; she unseats him, so that he is stretched upon 'the green', yet the two are immediately reconciled, as Guyon is persuaded to control his irascibility with reason. Thus far the bridging episode, looking back to the power of natural love and growth, as in the green herbage of the Garden of Adonis. Immediately after this episode, we are given a foretaste of male mastery in sexual passion, as drastic as the opening of the Wife of Bath's Tale, when a churlish forester is discovered in rapid pursuit of a terrified Florimell, the lady whose proper sexual complement has shut her out of his universe. Britomart, unlike one of her temporary companions, does not follow this quarry, and travels on to the adventure of Castle Joyous.

The pursuit of Florimell in canto i prefigures the physical, compulsive kind of sexual mastery which is followed up later in the book in Florimell's experiences with the witch's son, with the fisherman, and with Proteus, and in the examples of the insatiable, incestuous twins Argante and Ollyphant. Britomart's experience of Castle Joyous in the same canto prefigures the mental mastery which victimizes Amoret.

Within this episode lies the description of the tapestry of Venus and Adonis, played off against the Garden of Adonis and in many ways parallel to the Bower of Bliss. The 'Joy' of Castle Joyous is synonymous with the 'Bliss' of the Bower. Both are the instruments of sensual egotists who destroy the lives of their paramours instead of creating new life, and who thus act contrary to Nature's plan. The episode of this castle begins the series of episodes in which there is significant confusion about Britomart's sex, pointing symbolically to an opposed ideal of sexual cooperativeness. The most startling features of the episode of the castle are that it re-enacts at different levels the operation of masterly wiles in a love situation and that much of it runs in parallel, both verbally and symbolically, as Alastair Fowler has perceived,[1] with the story of Malbecco, Hellenore, and Paridell, and then with the moralized landscape within the House of Busirane, most specifically with the Masque of Cupid within that House. The three episodes thus in a sense stand together.

Before Malecasta's castle Britomart rescues a knight who is heroically resisting its six knightly guardians. These are attempting to enforce the castle's noxious custom: that anyone who passes must serve its lady Malecasta, the damsel of Delight, either simply, if he has no former commitment, or by transferring his fealty from his former love to her. Britomart conquers all six, who are Gardante, an archer, the darting power of the female eye to pierce to the heart, the arrows of Cupid; Parlante, the affective power of talk; Jocante, enlivening games and joyful devices; Basciante, the power of delectable lips; Bacchante, drink and banqueting; and Noctante, lovers' activities associated with night. It is in her preliminary parley with these knights that Britomart paraphrases Chaucer's Franklin concerning the incompatibility of mastery and love (III. i. 25. 5–9).

Inside the castle, the devices of these six are re-enacted in terms of courtly behaviour and especially of Malecasta's frenzied campaign against the fortress of Britomart's affections and heart. It is in this scene that the episode of Malecasta begins to exhibit parallels with that of Malbecco. In the latter tale, Paridell, on the first night of his stay and on

---

1. 'Six Knights at Castle Joyous', *Studies in Philology*, 56 (1959), 583–99. My material in this chapter traces a different conceptual pattern from his, but Fowler anticipated in this too little read article the parallels between the courting of Britomart by Malecasta and the courting of Hellenore by Paridell, in terms of six operations, and the role of 'mastery' in both. He also noted the relation of the wounding of Britomart by Gardante to her falling in love through a mirror, and a connection between this wound and the one given by Busirane.

later occasions (remaining behind in idleness at Malbecco's castle while the other knights pursue their quest), suffers and acts almost precisely, in his male role, as Malecasta has done before him. Because of the difference between the briskly dismissive Britomart and the licentious Hellenore, already smarting under the uncongenial mastery of an aged husband, Paridell is successful where Malecasta is not. Both of them immediately fall prey themselves to the Love God, for they are both much practised in falling. Malecasta is mastered by this imperious deity in this way:

> Her fickle hart conceived hasty fire,
> Like sparkes of fire, which fall in sclender flex,
> That shortly brent into extreme desire,
> And ransackt all her veines with passion entire.
> . . . .
> Nought so of love this looser Dame did skill,
> But as a coale to kindle fleshly flame,
> Giving the bridle to her wanton will,
> And treading under foote her honest name:
> Such love is hate, and such desire is shame.
> . . . .
> But yet her wound still inward freshly bled,
> And through her bones the false instilled fire
> Did spred it selfe, and venime close inspire.
>   [i. 47, 50, 56]

And in the night, in a scene that strongly impressed the author of 'The Eve of Saint Agnes', her 'engrieved spright / could find no rest in such perplexed plight' so that 'panting soft, and trembling everie joynt / Her fearful feete towards the bowre she moved' and 'Of every finest fingers touch affrayd', she slipped into Britomart's bed and 'inly sigh'd'. Paridell, equally susceptible, is mastered in the same way, by a dart from Hellenore's eye. He

> to the wound his weake hart opened wyde;
> The wicked engine through false influence,
> Past through his eyes, and secretly did glyde
> Into his hart, which it did sorely gryde.
> But nothing new to him was that same paine,
> Ne paine at all; for he so oft had tryde
> The powre thereof, and lov'd so oft in vaine,
> That thing of course he counted, love to entertaine.
>   [ix. 29]

His heart is indisposed to suffer only a superficial wound of the kind that Britomart receives from Gardante's arrow.

Chiefly, however, in both scenes Malecasta and Paridell show their own masterful devices. Mastered by love, they attempt to overpower their love objects with deceitful sleights. Making use of the power represented by Gardante, Malecasta behaves thus to Britomart:

> Still did she rove at her with crafty glaunce
> Of her false eyes, that at her hart did ayme.
> [i. 50]

And Paridell, with 'his inward griefe' (ix. 30):

> With speaking lookes, that close embassage bore,
> He rov'd at her, and told his secret care,
> [ix. 28]

in which he is answered:

> She sent at him one firie dart, whose hed
> Empoisned was with privy lust, and gealous dred.
> [ix. 28]

Thereafter he at her 'many belgardes let fly' (ix. 52). The gazing motif is complicated in this case by the fact that Malbecco throughout the tale strikes the averages between January's two successive conditions of perfect physical sight and complete blindness by being blind in one eye only, so that he misses everything significant that passes, and sees everything else. Paridell

> *Malbeccoes* halfen eye did wyle,
> His halfen eye he wiled wondrous well,
> And *Hellenors* both eyes did eke beguyle,
> Both eyes and hart attonce. . . .
> [x. 5]

The mastery of Paridell, a bold and disrespectful guest, extends even to his host: Malbecco must go in dread of 'That fierce youngmans unruly maistery'. As for Parlante, Malecasta

> all attonce discovered her desire
> With sighes, and sobs, and plaints and piteous griefe,
> The outward sparkes of her in burning fire;
> Which spent in vaine, at last she told her briefe,

That but if she did lend her short reliefe,
And do her comfort, she mote algates dye.
[i. 53]

Paridell:

He sigh'd, he sobd, he swownd, he perdy dyde,
And cast himselfe on ground her fast besyde:
Tho when againe he him bethought to live,
He wept, and wayld, and false laments belyde,
Saying, but if she Mercie would him give
That he mote algates dye, yet did his death forgive.
[x. 7]

And, as well, he re-enacts Aeneas' stealing away of Dido's heart as he recounts Trojan history at a banquet (ix. 32 ff.), for in Paridell abounded 'a kindly pride of gracious speech' (ix. 32).

In connection with Jocante, in Castle Joyous:

Some fell to daunce, some fell to hazardry,
Some to make love, some to make meriment,
As diverse wits to divers things apply;
And all the while faire *Malecasta* bent
Her crafty engins to her close intent.
[i. 57]

Paridell:

And otherwhiles with amorous delights,
And pleasing toyes he would her entertaine,
Now singing sweetly, to surprise her sprights,
Now making layes of love and lovers paine,
Bransles, Ballads, virelayes, and verses vaine;
Oft purposes, oft riddles he devysd,
And thousands like, which flowed in his braine,
With which he fed her fancie, and entysd
To take to his new love, and leave her old despysd.
[x. 8]

Basciante does not have much opportunity in either scene. In Castle Joyous:

Tho were the tables taken all away,

> And every knight, and every gentle Squire
> Gan choose his dame with *Basciomani* gay,
> With whom he meant to make his sport and courtly play.
> [i. 56]

As Paridell speaks,

> Upon his lips hong faire Dame *Hellenore*,
> With vigilant regard, and dew attent,
> Fashioning worlds of fancies evermore
> In her fraile wit, that now her quite forlore.
> [ix. 52]

Bacchante is more interesting. The knights received by Malecasta are immediately cheered with wine and spicery (i. 42). At supper Malecasta makes use of the same stimulation for the continuance of amorous battling:

> Whiles fruitfull *Ceres,* and *Lyæus* fat
> Pourd out their plenty, without spight or spare:
> Nought wanted there, that dainty was and rare;
> And aye the cups their bancks did overflow,
> And aye betweene the cups, she did prepare
> Way to her love, and secret darts did throw.
> [i. 51]

Similarly Paridell at supper:

> Thenceforth to her he sought to intimate
> His inward griefe, by meanes to him well knowne,
> Now *Bacchus* fruit out of the silver plate
> He on the table dasht, as overthrowne,
> Or of the fruitfull liquor overflowne,
> And by the dauncing bubbles did divine,
> Or therein write to let his love be showne;
> Which well she red out of the learned line,
> A sacrament prophane in mistery of wine.
> [ix. 30]

Hellenore answers him:

> And when so of his hand the pledge she raught,
> The guilty cup she fained to mistake,

> And in her lap did shed her idle draught,
> Shewing desire her inward flame to slake.
>
> [ix. 31]

The time for rest comes similarly in both scenes:

> By this th'eternall lampes, wherewith high *Jove*
> Doth light the lower world, were halfe yspent,
> And the moist daughters of huge *Atlas* strove
> Into the *Ocean* deepe to drive their weary drove.
>
> [i. 57]

And

> now the humid night was farforth spent,
> And heavenly lampes were halfendeale ybrent.
>
> [ix. 53]

As for Noctante, it is 'under the black vele of guilty Night' that Malecasta goes to enter the bed of Britomart. Paridell and Hellenore use their time in a way similarly described:

> And Night, the patronesse of love-stealth faire
> Gave them safe conduct, till to end they came.
>
> [x. 16]

Both Malecasta's and Malbecco's stories contain many Chaucerian reminiscences. In the latter case, of course, the Merchant's Tale is re-enacted. The rich old man and the enslaved young wife, the motif of blindness (even the sharp-sighted cannot always watch lovers), the unavailing walled-in area, and the irrelevance of the lover's motives to any moral world are all common to both stories. In the episode of Malecasta's castle, apart from the paraphrase from the Franklin's Tale, there are traces, perhaps, of Dido's reception of Aeneas in *The Legend of Good Women* (III. 1106–12). Also the 'damzels and Squires' who rejoice in Malecasta's castle suggest the same immaturity as characterizes May and her lover, the squire of January in the Merchant's Tale. More decisively, there is a reawakening of Chaucer's irony at May's all-too-ready *gentilesse* upon Damian's piteous disclosure of his love:

> Lo, pitee renneth soone in gentil herte!
>   Here may ye see how excellent franchise
> In wommen is whan they hem narwe avise.
> Som tyrant is, as ther be many oon,

That hath an herte as hard as is a stoon,
Which wolde han lete him sterven in the place,
Wel rather than han graunted him hir grace,
And hem rejoisen in hir cruel pride,
And rekke nat to been an homicide.
[Merchant's Tale, 742–50; 1986–94]

That Britomart thinks Malecasta's complaint that she is dying of love to be genuine is natural, and the following reflection on Britomart's frame of mind is seriously intended, particularly since it points forward to Marinell's attitude to Florimell. Yet Malecasta's heart is no more gentle than May's:

For great rebuke it is, love to despise,
Or rudely sdeigne a gentle harts request.
[i. 55]

The scenes in Malecasta's and Malbecco's castles are, then, structurally and verbally similar to the point of being mated. In the third place, the Masque of Cupid, and all that depends upon it in the House of Busirane, have strong affinities with these scenes. Scudamour's infringement upon Amoret's liberty through his masterful propensities produces a situation related to those of Malecasta and Paridell, mastered by the imperious Love God and in their turns craftily masterful: Amoret's plight is to be tempted through the jealous imperiousness of her husband-lover to be unfaithful to him and to join the throng of the frivolously and sordidly sensual adulterers. It does not fall to Amoret to occupy either Hellenore's role, confined by a jealous husband and then blissfully subject to male seduction, or the role of Malecasta, mastered by love and practising seduction upon others. Her sexual constancy was intended by Spenser to receive its reward in a reunion with Scudamour, once (or perhaps twice) postponed, and never written into *The Faerie Queene* as we know it. If the story of Malbecco is in some fashion the Merchant's Tale, then the stories of Amoret and Florimell are stepchildren of the Franklin's Tale. What threatens the constancy of Amoret and Florimell is an imperfection in each of the lovers (unlike Arveragus) to whom they (like Dorigen) are essentially well matched.

A difficulty lies in understanding how Amoret can be imagined to love and yet to resist Scudamour. Is there really a psychologically appreciable object for our attention in the House of Busirane? It has long been obvious that the difficulty symbolized by that House has something to do with Scudamour's attitude towards Amoret and Amoret's response to this attitude. The Cupid upon the shield of Scudamour is the same as the one represented upon the altar in the House and as the one in action in the Masque. We have already seen, as well, what the balance of episodes and of symbols seems to require here. On the one hand, Marinell has unfeelingly turned his back on a fellow being, and has insulated himself against Florimell's emotions as though she were an inanimate object, subject to discard. He has not given her feelings a chance to affect him because he himself was not willing to take a chance. On the other hand, we are to imagine in Scudamour a lover who through his masterfulness and forcefulness in laying his hands upon Amoret has kept her in some sense from giving herself to him, *even though she loves him with constancy.*

To what psychological and physical reality can we suppose this paradox to correspond? To overpudicity, as Professor Roche proposes? Probably not. We have already noticed that she had grown up in the Garden of Adonis, with Pleasure, and had become learned in the lore of womanhood in the sense that she is in a state of biological readiness. Also, the balance of the fable requires that as the fault lies with Marinell, not Florimell, so it must lie with Scudamour, not Amoret. And another reason for rejecting the motive of virginal shame will arise in the course of discussion.

Must we then suppose that Spenser is indicating symbolically a primitively physical literal level at which a man has physically captured a woman and is bending her to his will? Certainly this would have little to do with the social world to which Spenser addresses his book. Are we, on the other hand, to imagine a psychological drama of seven months' duration during which the feelings of a new wife remain painfully ambivalent, as her masterful husband, whom she loves, repels her by the brutality which is an aspect of the fine boldness with which he first won her? Perhaps something like that is possible; certainly we as moderns have no difficulty in imagining it. But would Spenser have done so? Something like that on a shorter time scale, perhaps, but as an extended psychodrama it does not really seem to belong to his kind of narrative. Or are we to suppose something more clinical—a sexual frigidity induced by clumsily brutal marital efforts on that vinous wedding night which is indicated at the beginning of Book IV? Something like that, too, perhaps; but the full dimension of what is being examined here can really be appreciated only in terms of a defined area of behaviour, not of a single instance or point upon it. Scudamour's efforts, embodied in

Busirane, 'to make her love the worker of her smart' (xii. 31) have imposed upon Amoret a martyrdom in which her heart was riven from her body. Her lover insists on a relation conceived in terms of the jealous domination by which he had won her rather than in terms of harmonious trustfulness. He treats her as though she were nothing but the prize which he had initially won the right to woo, and not also as a separate, free ego whose consent must be sought by gentle parley. 'Jalousie and teene' like Malbecco's and January's, even though Scudamour is not given real occasion to undergo them, are his unsuitable continuation by the same means of his initially appropriate amorous warfare (compare the Justinus-like speech on this subject by Sir Satyrane, III. ix. 6, 7). He tries to confine her straitly because he does not realize that he has won her; he pays no attention to her mind and will, and aims only at her heart. Until friendship is added unto him by the principle and activity of Britomart, he cannot conceive of a relationship with Amoret except in terms of the overcoming of resistance. Britomart can reach Amoret when Scudamour cannot, because she stands for a relationship that includes the dimension of trust and hearts' consent; she can also help Scudamour because friendship removes distrust. In the corresponding sense, Ate hinders him.

Canto xi of Book III opens with the condemnation of jealousy that turns 'love divine / To joylesse dread'. The condemnation points back to the drastic case of Malbecco at the end of the previous canto, but also forward to the episode of Scudamour and the House of Busirane. As jealousy, self-proclaimed, is what keeps Scudamour in the House of Care in Book IV, so jealousy is at the basis of his concern here, reflected in the Masque of Cupid. In this canto Satyrane and Britomart are discovered riding on their quest, having left Paridell behind to initiate in Malbecco's castle the happenings which have just reached their conclusion in canto x. The knights break into pursuit of Argante, an embodiment of male lust, as they[2] had long before fought against Ollyphant, his sister, for the Squire of Dames. Satyrane continues the chase in a direction which takes him out of the episode; Britomart finds no monster but only Scudamour, flat on his face beside a fountain. Here again, in the figure of Argante, we have a projection of one aspect of the difficulties of Scudamour. In the next book, Amoret will again run afoul

---

2. Britomart bearing the name 'Palladine', vii. 52. 6. Conceivably 'Palladine' was Spenser's original choice for Britomart's name. The nearby passage in the 1590 edition on 'Chylde Thopas' as the conquerer of Ollyphant (stanza 48) was held by J. W. Bennett to be among the earliest in the poem. See chap. 1, pp. 20–24.

of Lust, a mastering figure of libidinousness. Scudamour's disregard for Amoret's 'wished freedome' in the Temple of Venus contains this aspect as well.

His tearful attitude when Britomart finds him has moved through 180 degrees from the one with which he entered the Temple of Venus. There he was willing to take his chances on Dame Fortune, 'sith all by lot we hold'; now, like some Chaucerian youthful figure, he breaks out against the injustice of the heavens. His former boldness, which compassed a deed, as he described it, like that of Orpheus leading Eurydice forth from the Lower Regions, has been replaced by feelings thus expressed:

> What boots it plaine, that cannot be redrest,
>   And sow vaine sorrow in a fruitlesse eare,
>   Sith powre of hand, nor skill of learned brest,
>   Ne wordly price cannot redeeme my deare,
>   Out of her thraldome and continuall feare?
>   [III. xi. 16]

His earlier attitude now becomes in part that of Britomart herself—'bold Virgin'—who refuses to surrender so easily, but who also mixes her boldness with discretion.

What she discovers guarding the porch of Busirane's House is 'A flaming fire ymixt with smouldry smoke, / And stinking Sulphure, that with griesly hate / And dreadful horrour did all entrance choke' (xi. 21). 'Hate' is curious in this context. It is in fact part of the picture that Spenser is building of jealousy and masterful love: in Malecasta's castle, 'such love is hate.' Where Scudamour's shield of the mastering Cupid had carried all before it in the Isle of Venus, it has no power here; Britomart, however, advancing her shield and sword, pierces through the portal like a thunderbolt that transforms soaring clouds into rain. Like Concord of III. x, she can truly link Love and Hate—selfless *gentilesse* and bold aggressiveness. Scudamour, with a resumption of the competitiveness which has formerly been his strong point, now seeks to follow 'with greedy will, and envious desire'; his 'threatful pride', however, is met by a stronger degree of the same: the 'mighty rage' and 'imperious sway' of Mulciber (xi. 26).

The arrangements of the two successive rooms of the House of Busirane through which Britomart now passes carry through the theme of Cupid's imperious mastery, and of the mastering lust which it inspires in his servants. In the tapestry of the first room, Cupid conquers Jove and occupies that god's heavenly throne, so that Jove goes to the earth and, in turn, like the other gods, works his own masteries there in promiscuous love. As in the Bower of Bliss, the gold of the tapestry here lurks 'privily' (xi. 28), revealing yet concealing itself for deceitful ends, and as Cymochles there feigns himself 'to sleepe / Whiles through their lids his wanton eies do peepe' (II. v. 34) at loose ladies and lascivious boys, and as Venus 'with her two crafty spyes' searched every limb of Adonis as he bathed in the tapestry of Malecasta, so here, Leda, watching Jove as a swan closing on her, 'slept, yet twixt her eyelids closely spyde, / How towards her he rusht, and smiled at his pryde' (III. xi. 32). As Malbecco's one eye could not guard his wife from her lover, so the guard at the door of Danae's tower watches in vain (xi. 31) while Jove descends from above into her lap in a 'honydew' of gold.

The golden image of Cupid upon an altar is the lordly, great winged Love God of medieval tradition. In place of the ultimately benign crocodile of Isis and the serpent of Venus, encircling each main figure, a dragon lies beneath the feet of Cupid. Both of its eyes are pierced by darts, and its tail rises no higher than his left foot. This is the dragon-guard of chastity (see figure 2), hopelessly *hors de combat*; and with its defenceless blindness we come to the end of Book III's symbolism of eye beams, darts, and sightlessness which began with Gardante in canto i. Over the door of the first room, and in all but one place in the second (into which Britomart presses 'with bold steps', xi. 50) is inscribed '*Be Bold*'; over the door communicating with the third room stands '*Be not too bold*' (xi. 54). These words correspond to those describing Scudamour's behaviour in the Isle of Venus. Upon the walls of the first and second rooms hang Cupid's spoils, including the broken bows and arrows of the huntresses of Diana (xi. 46), as in the Temple of Venus in *The Parlement*.

The Masque of Cupid emerges at night from the third room with another whiff of sulphur and smoke, along with a storm and an earth-quake like the eruption of force in the Temple of Isis. The Masque shows much in common with Chaucer's description of the approach to that Temple of Venus, but also, as indicated, with the two sequences of Malecasta and Malbecco. In Malecasta's chamber, many beds are at hand for 'untimely ease' (i. 39), and in Malbecco's castle Paridell stays behind in unseemly sloth while the other knights continue their laborious quests. In the Masque, accordingly, the name of the Prologue is Ease. The 'Lydian harmony' which follows in the next stanza of the scene in Malecasta's chamber is equivalent to the 'delitious harmony' that follows directly after Ease in the Masque. The amorous Desire of that

Figure 2. Pallas and the Dragon-Guard of Chastity. From Andreas Alciati, *Emblemata* (Antwerp, 1581), p. 104. The verses: 'This is a true image of the virgin Pallas. Hers is this dragon, which remains forever at the feet of his mistress. Why is this creature attendant upon the goddess? The care of her affairs is given to him. Thus he watches over sacred woods and holy temples; his task is to maintain virgins by a careful vigil. Love lays his snares on all sides.' At some point in the composition of *The Faerie Queene* Spenser had apparently intended to call Britomart 'Palladine'. See chapter 8, note 2.

Cuſtodiendas virgines.

EMBLEMA XXII.

VERA hæc effigies innupta eſt Palladis: eius
  Hic Draco, qui domina conſtitit ante pedes.
Cur Diua comes hoc animal ? cuſtodia rerum
  ✱ Huic data: ſic lucos, ſacraq́ templa colit.
Innuptas opus eſt cura aſſeruare puellas
  Peruigili. laqueos vndique tendit amor.

Masque is equivalent to the fancy of Malecasta, who began 'with vaine thoughts her falsed fancy vex' in a passage which continues with the image of quick fire in flax (i. 47). Desire in the Masque:

> Twixt both his hands few sparkes he close did straine,
> Which still he blew, and kindled busily,
> That soone they life conceiv'd, and forth in flames did fly.
> [xii. 9]

The Fancy of the Masque, bearing a 'windy fan . . . That in the idle aire he moved here and there', is also equivalent to the same faculty in Hellenore, listening to Paridell's story and 'Fashioning worlds of fancies evermore' (ix. 52). Likewise the Feare who always keeps his eyes on his companion Daunger (that is, mischief and mishap, not the 'daunger' of the lady) was on the head of the eye-dart which Hellenore sent to Paridell (ix. 28), and the same Feare inspires Malecasta as she goes towards Britomart's bed in the night (i. 60, 61). The reference to 'sad lovers nightly theeveryes' in the House of Busirane (xi. 45) is at one with the instances of the power of Noctante in both Malecasta's and Malbecco's castles.

Most centrally, however, this Masque of Cupid as it relates to Amoret marshals the temptations and horrors of the life of loose sexual commitments, of frequent passion, and of angling for domination of a lover and for deception of a husband or other lovers, as these activities would be seen by a chaste woman, fully committed to one man but tortured by his jealous and insistent dominance over her, as over a sexual prize—a woman, that is, with whom he should have gently and gradually created an entirely different kind of relationship. Such love, we have heard, is really hate, close to the state of the Knight's Tale's Cupid, 'out of alle charitee'. The adulterous temptations begin for Amoret in the fancy and the artificially stoked desire of a life of ease and leisure. They progress through the doubt, dangers, and fearful delights of secret assignations and amours. Such love dangles hopes, but less often satisfactions, before its victims. All of these concepts, personified, pass before us in turn in the Masque of Cupid. Dissemblance and Suspect, Grief and Fury, Displeasure and Pleasure, attend on an unfaithful beloved and a jealous lover. Despite and Cruelty are the lot of an unfaithful wife as conceived by Amoret but also of Amoret herself, a chaste woman, who insists on maintaining her chastity in spite of all temptations and the provocations of a jealous and dominating lover: her heart is taken from her body and bedevilled, yet she will not surrender her love. Like Florimell, she remains love's martyr. As for the remaining figures of the Masque, a woman's ultimate fate in a life of superficial adultery, is, in Amoret's vision, not orgasmic bliss among lusty satyrs but rather something belonging to middle-class ideas, like the final stages of Hogarth's 'Marriage à la Mode', or, less familiarly but more accurately, like what is warned against in certain Continental and English morality plays and interludes:[3] Reproach, Repentance, Shame, Strife, Anger, Care, Unthriftihead, Loss of Time, Sorrow, Change, Disloyalty, Riotise, Dread, Infirmity, Poverty, and Death with Infamy.

All, or almost all, the figures in the Masque exist in Amoret's imagination, but this imagination is one that bodies forth the real consequences of a certain course of action for a chaste woman to whom frivolous surrender has for the first time become a live option, so that she knows what it is to waver ('wavering' being equivocally applied to both 'wemen' and 'wit'):

> There were full many moe like maladies,
>> Whose names and natures I note readen well;
>> So many moe, as there be phantasies
>> In wavering wemens wit, that none can tell,
>> Or paines in love, or punishments in hell.
>> [xii. 26]

These are quite different from the images of Hellenore's mind, facilely submitting to the Love God's pains and fashioning worlds of fancies 'In her fraile wit' (ix. 52). They are also different from the counterfeits which are the stock-in-trade of the spirit who had fallen with the Prince of Darkness and who animates the body of the false Florimell: he 'all the wyles of wemens wits knew passing well' (viii. 8).

Amoret's torturer, an element in Scudamour himself, is a destroyer of the concord between man and wife. The most advanced embodiment of this concord in *The Faerie Queene* is the relation in V. ii between Britomart-Isis-moon and Artegall-Osiris-crocodile-sun in the Temple of Isis, running 'in equal justice' and achieving a freely offered and freely accepted love and friendship (see next chapter). Certainly then, the explanation of this torturer's name—Busirane—suggested by Professor

---

3. John Rastell's *Calisto and Melebea* is an English example. Jean Bretog, *Tragedie françoise à huict personnages: traictant de l'amour d'un serviteur envers sa maitress, et de tout ce qui en advint* (Lyon, 1571; Chartres, 1831) is closer to what is meant here, although of little literary significance. Less to the point but far better than either of these, and well worth translating into English, is the work published as *De Spiegel der Minnen door Colijn van Rijssele*, ed. Margaretha W. Immink (Utrecht, 1913).

Roche,[4] is the most apposite one. The key to Roche's etymological explanation is the association of 'Busiris' with the death of Osiris. In the light of Spenser's usual masterful way with mythology, the partly contradictory late Classical and post-Classical lore concerning these two figures, the town of Busiris, and Typhon (see next chapter and appendices A and B) would have easily permitted him to identify the murderer of Osiris as Busiris. 'Busiris' in this sense, then, furnishes the root of the name 'Busirane', although this name no doubt embodies other phonetic felicities.

The harmonious relationship between Isis and Osiris has its antithesis in the House of Busirane. The similar concept of harmony, orchestrated in the Temple of Venus but not in this case defended by an aggressive, wand-bearing Britomart-Isis, is likewise violated in this House, extending as it does to fill the canto immediately before the Book of Friendship. We have yet one more reason, then, for supposing that the episode of the Isle of Venus was at an earlier point intended to lie at the centre of Book IV: as the natural love and generation of the Garden of Adonis at the centre of Book III stands in detailed contrast with the sterile appetite of the Bower of Bliss at the end of Book II, so the harmonious love and friendship of the Isle of Venus in Book IV stand directly opposed to the hateful mastery of the House of Busirane at the end of Book III. The equation asks for an Isle of Venus in canto vi or vii of Book IV, in its midst.

One further reason for believing that in the House of Busirane Amoret is being importuned unintentionally by the masterful practices of her husband to turn from her constant love of him to the life of sexual adventurism is that a kind of reduplicative allegory overtakes Amoret in Book IV. While Britomart sleeps, Amoret is captured by Lust himself—Lust who 'could awhape an hardy hart' (vii. 5): that is, who ostensibly is powerful enough to stupefy a strong hart with fear but in fact (considering the singularity of this image) is strong enough to snatch the strongest hearts, just as the Love God joys to see Amoret's heart removed from her bosom and carried before her in the Masque of Cupid. We have already seen that Amoret, like Aemylia, is not simply preyed on by a lustful being, but is herself in some fashion invaded by desire, although she will not perform the acts which desire calls for. She successfully resists both importunities—those of Busirane and Lust—and is finally rescued by the chaste amity of Britomart in the one

4. Thomas P. Roche, Jr., *The Kindly Flame* (Princeton, 1964), p. 81.

case and by Belphoebe's virginity in the other.

As discussed in chapter 6, it is probably true that this episode of Amoret, Timias, and Belphoebe in Book IV is required by Spenser's emergency measures in squaring the accounts of his friend Ralegh with the Queen after the revelation of Ralegh's relations with Elizabeth Throgmorton, but it is equally true that Spenser would not have chosen Amoret for this ambiguous role unless she had been suitable for it. She is readied for pleasure, not overpudicity. Spenser is apparently saying to the Queen that her maid of honour and her favourite Ralegh were touched, but not dominated by, Lust. So with Amoret. In the House of Busirane she is being driven by her lover to become part of the usual courtly round of love that Spenser so strongly condemns elsewhere:

> And is love then (said *Corylas*) once knowne
> In Court, and his sweet lore professed there?
> I weened sure he was our God alone:
> And only woond in fields and forests here,
>   Not so (quoth he) love most aboundeth there.
> For all the walls and windows there are writ,
> All full of love, and love, and love my deare,
> And all their talke and studie is of it,
> Ne any there doth brave or valiant seeme,
> Unlesse that some gay Mistresse badge he beares:
> Ne any one himselfe doth ought esteeme,
> Unlesse he swim in love up to the eares.
> But they of love and of his sacred lere,
> (As it should be) all otherwise devise,
> Then we poore shepheards are accustomd here,
> And him do sue and serve all otherwise,
> For with lewd speeches and licentious deeds,
> His mightie mysteries they do prophane,
> And use his ydle name to other needs,
> But as a complement for courting vaine,
> So him they do not serve as they professe,
> But make him serve to them for sordid uses,
> Ah my dread Lord, that doest liege hearts possesse,
> Avenge thy selfe on them for their abuses.
>   [*Colin Clouts Come Home Againe*, 771–94]

The allegory of Lust in Book IV is simply an intensification of what we have already seen in the House of Busirane. For purposes of Spenser's defending his friend and patron, and Elizabeth Throgmorton, and of maintaining the allegorical locus of Amoret, it was not intended that Timias and Amoret should be punished, but that the unclean cleaving thing, amorous desire without constancy to one lover, should be extirpated.

The friendship which Britomart brings to Amoret is what reverses the charms of Busirane, so that Amoret's wound becomes whole and the chains drop from her body, in the inner room where the magician had held her in thrall. Busirane must not be destroyed (III. xii. 34) because he is a part of Scudamour. As a masterful principle of hate, he is ready to destroy Amoret finally (xii. 32), and he wounds Britomart superficially as the masterful principle of Malecasta had done in canto i. In Book IV Britomart and Amoret now go forth in amity, in spite of Amoret's suspicions of what she takes to be a male's intentions—suspicions which are soon allayed in the formation of the first four-group of that book, with Britomart as knight to Amoret and as lady to another knight, so that they may all be lodged in a castle with a custom. And with that we are brought full circle back to our beginning in the Squire's Tale of Spenser and Chaucer.

9

Isis and Osiris

Isis's Temple (V. vii) and the events connected with it form the last link in the chain of moralized landscapes and chivalric adventures discussed here. I am concerned to show what Spenser would have known of Osiris, Isis, Horus, Typhon, and Busiris, and what he created by modifying this traditional material freely, and how a set of related images extend through Books III and IV and culminate in Book V in certain images in the Temple of Isis. This moralized landscape is replete with historical, national, and political allegory, for which one should consult particularly the works of Professors Graziani and Aptekar.[1] Insofar as Professor Aptekar concerns herself with the allegory of love and marriage in this episode, the general drift of my interpretation follows hers.

What Spenser would have known of Isis and Osiris he would have been likely to find, mainly and in the first place, in Plutarch, Diodorus Siculus, Macrobius (the *Saturnalia*), Natalis Comes, Cartari, and, perhaps, the *Dictionarium* of Robertus Stephanus—that is, in certain

1. René Graziani, 'Elizabeth at Isis Church', *PMLA*, 79 (1964), 376–89; Jane Aptekar, *Icons of Justice: Iconography and Thematic Imagery in Book V of 'The Faerie Queene'* New York, 1969), pp. 87–107. For a systematic interpretation of the love allegory of Books IV and V, see also Mark Rose, *Heroic Love: Studies in Sidney and Spenser* (Cambridge, Mass., 1968), pp. 77–134. Many of the points in the interpretation of Isis Temple which follows are anticipated in Elizabeth Bieman, 'Britomart in Book V of *The Faerie Queene*', *University of Toronto Quarterly*, 37 (1967–68), 156–74.

Figure 3. Two Figures of Isis. From Vincenzo Cartari, *Le imagini de i dei de gli antichi* (Venice, 1580), p. 120. The two figures show a selection of features from authorities cited in Cartari's text. Isis carries a ship (thus she entered Egypt, and she has care for sailors and sailing). On her head is a crescent moon or two small cow's horns and encircling serpent(s). On her head and in one hand is wormwood *(Artemisia absinthium? Artemisia maritima?)*. She has developed breasts because she is the earth or Nature, subject to the sun. She emerges from the sea and carries cymbals (to correspond to the sound of the Nile throughout Egypt, or to the sound made by the ancients to revive the moon when she was in eclipse) and a vase with a serpent handle. She wears the shining disk or sphere of the moon on her head, with sheaves of wheat and flowers. Flowers and fruit are in the border of her robe. Her white robe changes sometimes to yellow, gold, flame-colour, and red. She has a black robe as well (the dark of the moon, unilluminated by the sun) which shows the heavenly bodies with the moon in the centre.

Figure 4. Osiris, Horus, Typhon. From Vincenzo Cartari, *Le imagini de i dei de gli antichi* (Venice, 1580), p. 440. This reproduction incorporates features mentioned in Cartari's text. *Right:* Osiris with his symbol the sparrow hawk (in flying rapidly it is like the sun). Osiris (a fertility god) is shown with an erection: he appears as Priapus because Isis, having found all parts of his dismembered body but the male member, would have it so. As a sparrow hawk, Osiris battles with Typhon as a hippopotamus. *Centre:* Typhon with flames issuing from his mouth. *Left:* Horus (who is like Osiris in that he is mourned and sought by Isis, and found anew as a child; sometimes identified with Osiris, with the sun, and with Bacchus) battles with Typhon as a crocodile and removes his male member (and thus Typhon's power as well).

syncretizing Classical authors and, generally, in the mythographic and mythological lore of the Middle Ages and the Renaissance. The details in which we are interested (recorded in the Variorum notes, and in the captions of figures 3 and 4 of this book, as well as in appendices A and B) are that Isis represents the moon and Osiris the sun; that they are concerned with the various aspects of fertility and reproduction; that Osiris is a dying god, often compared with Adonis, from whose death new life is born; that he is in some sense form and Isis matter. He is attired in red. Isis is typically attired in white, for the moon, but this turns to other colours, including red (good weather is expected when the moon has a reddish tinge). She may wear black, signifying the dark of the moon, unilluminated by the sun.

Typhon killed Osiris, who was buried in the city of Busiris in Egypt. After Isis had discovered the body, Typhon dismembered it. Typhon is identified with fiery, scorching barrenness; flames shoot from his mouth and eyes. He was born from Earth, to avenge the rebellious giants after their defeat by the celestial gods. He is associated with their violence and with their blood which sank into the earth and returns as wine. For this reason priests associated with the cult of Isis are abstemious. Paradoxically, however, almost all sources except Plutarch say, and most emphasize, that Osiris is, or is equated with, Bacchus, and as such introduced men to the vine and the use of wine.[2] As Bacchus, Osiris was said to have been cut into pieces, cooked, and then reassembled and dyed a new colour so as not to be recognized, the meaning being that the grapes are thus treated by countryfolk to make wine, but that grapes later return to the denuded vines. Also, in connection with this identification with Osiris, Bacchus was said to be the secret virtue which gives life to plants; as such he is often associated with Ceres and Proserpina.

Typhon is identified with the crocodile; Horus, son or brother or new form of Osiris, attacked Typhon, and, either before or after Typhon metamorphosed himself into a crocodile, removed his male member. The aspect of fertility in Osiris-Horus appears in his erection; he is imaged as Priapus because Isis would have it so after having found all of his dismembered parts except the penis.

In R. Stephanus and elsewhere Typhon is identified as a cruel king of Egypt who sacrificed visitors on the tomb of Osiris in order to end a dearth. A king Busiris is often similarly described, although, except by

2. See Isabel Rathborne, *The Meaning of Spenser's Fairyland* (New York, 1937), pp. 88–89.

Spenser, Typhon and Busiris (the burial city as well as the king) are apparently never identified with each other.

As usual Spenser has preserved some of these mythological data without alteration, but he has also fused and modified other parts of the tradition, and has found ambiguities in it, to suit his own vision. At the beginning of the episode of the Temple of Isis, we are given the routine identification of Osiris and Isis with the sun and the moon. We are then told that the race run by the sun and the moon (that is, by the loving husband and wife Osiris and Isis) is symbolic of justice. Harmony rules between the god and the goddess. Another of Spenser's myths of concord and free interplay is in progress.

The priests of his Temple of Isis are clothed in linen, hemmed with silver; each wears a headdress shaped like the moon. This is to be expected, because Isis traditionally bears on her head an image of the moon as crescent, disk, or sphere (see figure 3). The statue of the goddess herself, however, departs from this tradition. Although she, too, is dressed in white linen trimmed with silver, her crown is of gold (said, with probably intentional obscurity, 'To shew that she had powre in things divine', vii. 6).[3] Also the pillars and arches overhead are covered with gold. When Britomart dreams in the Temple during the following night, she appears to herself first to be a priest of Isis, properly equipped with linen stole and moon headdress. Then, however, she is transformed into Isis herself, with golden crown and (now) scarlet robes. At the end of her stay in the Temple, she gives presents 'of gold and silver wroght' (vii. 24), no doubt continuing the symbolism of gold and silver introduced in connection with the statue of the goddess.

This central statue dominates beneath one foot the earth, which is 'open force', and, beneath the other foot, the crocodile, which is (initially) 'forged guile' (vii. 7). The crocodile's tail wreathes upward and encircles the waist of Isis. At the same time that she lords it over the beast beneath her foot, the position of that beast's tail signifies the other kind of control which the male principle may exert over the female. Isis' other foot upon the ground holds, in the sequel, a somewhat uncertain control over the anarchic forces of the giants who live beneath. Much is made by the priests of the Temple of the need to quell the giants'

3. The French version of Cartari translates Ovid, *Metamorphoses*, IX. 688–90, so as to give Isis a golden crown (not shown in the illustration from Cartari presented here as figure 3, or in the illustration in the French translation). Neither the original Latin nor the Italian translation says this: 'Inerant lunaria fronti / cornua cum spicis nitido flaventibus auro / et regale decus'; 'Di due corna la fronte havea signata, / La qual di bianche, e di mature spiche / Con vaghezza mirabile era ornata'.

rebellion against the gods. Related to the notion of the quelling of force, or of violence, is the refusal of these ascetic priests to drink wine, because they consider it to be violent giant-blood from the earth.

The significance of this emphasized point (vii. 10. 3–9, 11) seems plain. Anyone who had taken the trouble to find out as much about Osiris as Spenser needed for this scene would have read that Osiris was equated with the Egyptian Bacchus. The violence, then, which arises from the ground in the dream of Britomart-Isis during Britomart's nocturnal stay in the Temple, and which (in terms of historical and political allegory of violence) is devoured by the crocodile, but which in turn incites the crocodile (formerly she, now he) to dominate the goddess, is connected with Osiris himself,[4] and hence the male, solar principle. This is all the more surely Artegall as well, because Artegall has already been associated with Bacchus in a typically Spenserian equivocation (V. i. 1). The uncontrolled extreme of this principle has already been observed in Busirane.

In Britomart's dream, then, those anarchic, destructive forces suddenly rise and invade the Temple. The crocodile, who (we are not told until later) is Artegall in his historical role as saviour of the nation, destroys these flames by devouring them. He immediately turns from his historical role, however, to that of the male libido. He grows tumescent with these forces—'swolne with pride of his owne peerelesse powre' (vii. 15)[5] and threatens to consume the goddess, that is, Britomart herself. The response of Isis-Britomart to this aggression is to beat him down with the white wand of Isis, transparently an equivalent of the magic spear of Britomart, capable of laying any male opponent by the heels.[6] Surely this repulse by the wand corresponds to the situation of Artegall's being unhorsed by Britomart's lance on the last day of Satyrane's tourney (IV. iv. 44), and unhorsed as well as in the ensuing battle between them when Artegall is moved by envious, discordant

---

4. Unlike Professor Aptekar, I think that the identification of Osiris with the crocodile is more Spenser's summary dealing with the tradition than it is a part of the tradition itself. He wished to associate violence ambiguously with the male principle. If Professor Aptekar is right at this point, then Spenser's imagination has worked slightly differently from the way that I have imagined. Her and my interpretations remain similar.

5. Cf. Leda, observing Jove approaching her as a swan: 'She slept, yet twixt her eyelids closely spyde, / How towards her he rusht, and smiled at his pryde' (III. xi. 32). A phallic significance seems to be suggested in both cases. In the case of the crocodile the motif may have come to Spenser from that part of the tradition represented in figure 4.

6. It is probably relevant to remember here that Busirane and the Masque of Cupid get power over Amoret, and are *not* quelled, when everyone is heedless and ill-headed with wine at her marriage feast. Perhaps we should think of Spenser's Bacchante, rather than Bacchus, in this connection, when we consider what Scudamour's literal part in the affair may have been.

wrath to revenge himself upon her (IV. vi. 11). Just as she has struck him on his umbrere, or visor, with her spear, so on that occasion she wounds him in the eye with her beauty when her face is revealed by a stroke of his sword.

Frustrated in his direct attack, the crocodile now tries an alternative:

Tho turning all his pride to humblesse meeke,
    Him selfe before her feete he lowly threw,
    And gan for grace and love of her to seeke:
    Which she accepting, he so neare her drew,
    That of his game she soone enwombed grew,
    And forth did bring a Lion of great might;
    That shortly did all other beasts subdew.
                    [V. vii. 16]

Clearly this is a re-enactment of the artful and gentle courtship pursued by Artegall, formerly the 'salvage knight' (IV. vi. 31), by which he won Britomart, and from which a measure of amiable 'forged guile' was not absent (so extreme a pun as 'artful guile' cannot be excluded). In the dream, the crocodile is at least as successful as Artegall had been *in propria persona*: Britomart-Isis receives him; the royal line of Britain is conceived. As the head priest later tells Britomart, Artegall will actually beget on her a son of great power. The lion appears to be another male solar image, for the lion is associated with the sun by Macrobius in the *Saturnalia* in a passage in which the sun is also identified with Osiris;[7] and the sign of the lion in the zodiac is called 'the House of the Sun' 'because a lion seems to derive its essential qualities from the heat of the sun' (see appendix B). Merlin's prediction concerning Artegall is that he will be killed by a plot but that his and Britomart's son will punish the plotters and recover the rule of the kingdom (III. iii. 28, 29). Similarly, Osiris was killed by Typhon (Set), but the posthumous son of Osiris, who was born to Isis, destroyed Typhon and recovered the power.

The allegorical events just described form the final step in Spenser's progression through the stories of the three pairs of lovers, Scudamour and Amoret, Marinell and Florimell, and Artegall and Britomart. Only the last pair of these had assuaged the tyranny of the Love God without misstep or error so as to arrive at the sphere of love in friendship which Chaucer had represented in the Franklin's Tale, the Knight's Tale, and *The Parlement of Foules*. From the Temple of Isis, Britomart goes

7. Editions of the *Saturnalia* were numerous in the sixteenth century. The Bodleian possesses examples of eighteen such editions variously dated between 1472 and 1585.

directly to conquer Radigund and free her beloved from the unjust mastery which the Amazonian female principle had temporarily imposed upon him. She will restore to their proper male estate all the other knights who have been subjugated to this tyrannical Omphale figure. Doing so, she will be regarded as a 'goddess' (V. vii. 42). The sun and moon then run their race in equal justice, and the solitary and self-defeating dominance of the moon is ended.

It is feasible to identify Radigund with the moon in this way and, as well, to associate the act of begetting by Artegall-crocodile-Osiris-sun upon Britomart-Isis-moon with the begetting by the sun upon Chrysogone,[8] where the sun is associated with Adonis, in III. vi. For one thing, the late Classical syncretic notion found in the *Saturnalia* (appendix B), that sun, Adonis, and Osiris are one and the same, is likely to have been known to Spenser. More interestingly, a number of images of like intent, running from Book III through to the Temple of Isis in Book V, concur so as to form a family.

At the beginning of this series, the sun is presented as the creator of forms and his sister the moon as the provider of matter (III. vi. 8–9); associated with them in the same roles are Adonis and his mate Venus. At the end of the series, Osiris and his sister-spouse Isis are shown as sun and moon in 'equal race'. At the beginning of the series the sun begets two offspring upon Chrysogone, 'gold-engendered' or 'gold-inseminated'. At the end, Osiris-Artegall-crocodile-sun begets a lion (that is, a powerful son) upon Isis-Britomart-moon, untraditionally gold-crowned and robed in red instead of white and silver. In leaving Isis' Temple, Britomart bestows gifts of gold and silver (V. vii. 24). What these events seem to have in common is the complementing of the female principle by the male principle, by means of the addition of the golden refulgence and redness of the sun to the white and silver of the moon.

This is supported by the images applied to Britomart and Radigund when their countenances are initially revealed to Artegall in battle. Britomart's appearance suggests her role in supporting friendly and harmonious male-female combinations against the intransigence of Marinell, Scudamour, Artegall, and Radigund. She displays metaphorically the gold and solar red associated with Osiris, with the sun, and with the ideally mated Britomart-Isis. Radigund's appearance, on the other hand, is lunar, uncrowned with the sun, because she will not

---

8. The name of the mother of Chrysogone, 'Amphisa', reflects the notion of mutuality in its Greek root, meaning 'on both sides', 'on either hand', 'to each party'.

accept the traditionally feasible relationship between male and female. Britomart:

> her angels face, unseene afore,
> Like to the ruddie morne appeard in sight,
> Deawed with silver drops, through sweating sore,
> But somewhat redder, then beseem'd aright,
> Through toylesome heate and labour of her weary fight.
>
> And round about the same, her yellow heare
> Having through stirring loosd their wonted band,
> Like to a golden border did appeare,
> Framed in goldsmithes forge with cunning hand;
> Yet goldsmithes cunning could not understand
> To frame such subtile wire, so shinie cleare.
>   [IV. vi. 19, 20]

Radigund, although smeared with her own blood, is moon-like:

> A miracle of natures goodly grace,
> In her faire visage voide of ornament,
> But bath'd in bloud and sweat together ment;
> Which in the rudenesse of that evill plight,
> Bewrayd the signes of feature excellent:
> Like as the Moone in foggie winters night,
> Doth seeme to be her selfe, though darkned be her light.
>   [V. v. 12]

The first appearance of Artegall to Britomart belongs to this family of images. When Britomart sees him in 'Venus looking glas', he is solar:

> Through whose bright ventayle lifted up on hye
> His manly face, that did his foes agrize,
> And friends to termes of gentle truce entize,
> Lookt foorth, as Phœbus face out of the east,
> Betwixt two shadie mountaines doth arize.
>   [III. ii. 24]

Lunar white dominates two other images in this family, for two different reasons. The figure Concord wears a crown containing white above a gold-threaded gown (IV. x. 31; see chapter 7), and is thus opposite in appearance to the statue of Isis. As the Virgin Queen, Concord would properly rule as a female principle.[9] For a different reason, Amoret when she first appears to Scudamour in the Temple of Venus wears pure white 'with silver streames amongst the linnen' (IV. x. 52; see chapter 7) suggesting the white, silver-trimmed, lunar garment of Isis in her Temple. Amoret, a woman, not also a principle like Britomart, has still to be won: she presents Scudamour with what is essentially the same problem with which Radigund presents Artegall, and the responses of the two men are opposite and equally wrong. Radigund is so vicious an example of womanhood as to give Artegall little room for manoeuvre. She should in all equity have been dominated, but was surrendered to. Amoret should have been sued for but was mastered, because Scudamour was not a grown gentleman like Artegall but a callow youth. He had heard that all women enjoy being pulled about. Like Britomart, Amoret is first imaged as the dawn, but a white and silvery one.

A proper course for human sexual relationships is framed macrocosmically by this series of images. A relationship of love and mutual freedom is established between Artegall and Britomart when the woman initially quells the male libidinous mastery and competitive violence directed against her. The quelling is accomplished, however, without the establishment of a Radigund-like regiment over the male. The male then adopts the art appropriate to the situation, which is to woo the female with *gentilesse*. The result is a successful marriage from which flow momentous historical consequences. The troubles of Scudamour and Amoret are avoided; those of Marinell and Florimell scarcely enter the question.

9. Perhaps the 'crowned little Ermilin' which is painted upon Artegall's shield (III. ii. 25) is symbolic of the more typical, Isis-like situation: the crown of gold above and the white-furred animal below.

10

Spenser and Chaucer

It is impossible to imagine what kind of narrative poem Spenser might have written if he had not undergone the influence of the Western European literary Renaissance and if he had not shared with its other poets the ambition to emulate the ancients' genre of the epic. For much of his narrative framework as well as for many narrative motifs in *The Faerie Queene* he was as dependent upon contemporary Italian writers of heroic poetry as Chaucer had been dependent on Boccaccio, although in a partly different way. Spenser copies, but transforms and transvalues, the episodes of Italian heroic poems. He often follows Ariosto in narrative tempo and the articulation of plot; he often follows features of Tassonian style, imagery, and sensibility, occasionally to the extent of paraphrase and translation. Chaucer's most important borrowing from Boccaccio is a matter of entire plots, taken over bodily, restructured, and transformed to fit Chaucer's milieu and purpose. In the matter of ancient epic, *The Faerie Queene* makes more extensive use of the ostensible structural features of Classical heroic poems than does Chaucer, who thinks at this level in terms of the romance; and Spenser mobilizes in greater detail the device of episodic allusion to Classical epic, as, for instance, when Paridell's story of Troy, and Hellenore's receptivity to it, recall the similar episode of Aeneas and Dido.

There is no reason to say that Spenser was turning his back on the

Middle Ages in imitating the devices of Classical epic, for medieval Latin writers copied these devices constantly. There is a more positive respect, however, in which Spenser, sharing as he does in the European literary Renaissance, is a continuer of the English Middle Ages and stands close to Chaucer and William Langland. Spenser carries a medieval literary procedure to its logical and historical conclusion up to the time of Blake in his use of a series or 'field' of moralized landscapes. Each of these in *The Faerie Queene* conveys a significance through dense concatenations and multilayered agglomerations of symbols; all of these landscapes are linked together in a more general symbolic statement, and all relate, usually arcanely, to the simultaneous course of a less densely symbolic level of narrative conducted generally in terms of chivalric romance and adventure.

Medieval literature in other vernaculars besides English makes use of this procedure, but Spenser's strongest medieval affiliation is with Chaucer, extensive as Spenser's knowledge and use of other medieval English and French works seems to have been. That his affiliations with Chaucer are on any comparative basis, not only among medieval authors, more extensive than has been thought is what the present book has attempted to show so far.

Spenser is an epigone of medieval poetry, and as such a not untypical manifestation of Tudor culture, in carrying these allegorical devices to their most complicated, subtle, and extensive stage of development. He does this superbly. Another book might be written on the elegance and precision, down to the level of the individual poetic image and the metrical structure of the stanza, with which Spenser weaves his network of interrelated symbolic and nuclear scenes, related in turn to the more diffuse narrative of the adventures of his knights, ladies, and monsters. Much more than is generally realized, the overarching conceptions of his poem are carried through with boldness, harmony, and grandeur; and its language seconds these schemes with suppleness and detailed surprises which seem the only possible expression of the given idea once they are intuited. It is as though the art of the grand formal garden had been raised to the nth degree by translation into another medium. One sees the vistas, the sculptures which work out the various consequences of a theme with an inconspicuous art, the foci in sculptured fountains or temples, the walled private enclosures, and the delicious groves of trees affording privacy to the waters which they surround.

Spenser is, nevertheless, much more schematic in his chivalric adventures than is Chaucer. Also, as one proceeds through the later books of

The Faerie Queene, one meets symptoms of repetition and exhaustion of the finite vocabulary of narrative motifs by which medieval chivalric romance necessarily finds expression. As well, his preoccupation with themes and thematic patterns sometimes makes Spenser extremely absentminded about such elementary matters as motivation and sheer physical likelihood. Yet many readers exaggerate these symptoms out of a bewilderment about what Spenser was getting at in the middle of *The Faerie Queene* as we have it. Probably they often suspect that in that territory he got himself into a series of muddles. The emergence of a clear pattern of endeavour in Books III and IV may help them perceive that the artifact itself is a highly successful and interesting one, even though *The Faerie Queene* will probably always seem to us more grandly simpleminded than *The Canterbury Tales*.

What comes through in *The Faerie Queene* is not the accurate and evocative miming of character and action viewed from without, but the shape of internal experience, the inscape of our feelings: the sensation of loving and hating, the pathos of subjection to an emotion which is not yet shared by its object, the sense of what it is to be either considerate or thoughtless towards the sharer of an intimate relationship, what it is to woo or be wooed, or to be excited about frivolous or superficial sex. All of that is felt in a kind of total lyrical spectrum or universal field-relation of sensibility, and is given a local habitation and a name (or given a kind of Tudor monumentality) so that we may yield it swifter and more fluent affective recognition the next time that we peruse it.

Spenser shares with Milton the distinction of being the only follower of his greatest English predecessor in his chosen field who built upon that predecessor so remarkably as to become a phenomenon of primary interest in his own right. There were many Spenserian poets in Milton's time, and many Chaucerian poets preceded Spenser. Among these latter the author of *The Kingis Quair* and the poets Henryson, Dunbar, and Skelton are marvellously pleasing and offer any reader much that is important and new. But it is only Spenser who erected upon a Chaucerian base something as important and startlingly new as his master's own works. So with Milton in relation to Spenser.

part II
Spenser and Milton

Faerie Queene II, III and *Comus*

Part II of this book concerns itself first with the potent influence of some of Spenser's poetry on Milton's creative imagination in three of his most important works, and then with the equally powerful originality of Milton in reshaping what Spenser gave him. The latter can be seen only in the light of the former.[1] Early in his intellectual life, Milton seems to have grasped in Spenser's work a series of interlocking mythic patterns, or narrative and poetic embodiments of ideas. These patterns the younger poet seems to have wrestled with and variously transformed through a large part of his career. It is as if Milton frequently found it necessary, or easiest, or productive of a usefully reminiscent literary sensibility, to work within the framework of Spenser's myths, transforming many of their terms and almost all their surface but keeping intact much of their skeletal structure. The ideas embodied in these myths are familiar ones, general to Western culture; the embodiments themselves, which give depth and poignancy to the ideas, are not. The mythic structures of *Comus*, *Paradise Lost*, and *Paradise Regained* are

1. It is a commonplace that Spenser influenced Milton. What is already known on the subject is treated only summarily here. See Joan Larsen Klein, 'Some Spenserian Influences on Milton's *Comus*', *Annuale Mediævale*, 5 (1964), 27–48; and 'Spenser' in the index to Grant McColley, *'Paradise Lost': An Account of Its Growth and Major Origins, with a Discussion of Milton's Use of Sources and Literary Patterns* (Chicago, 1940).

much more closely related to such structures in *The Faerie Queene*, particularly in Book II, than has been recognized. Before we can see this in terms of Milton's two great epics, we must consider how Milton probably understood that Book of Temperance and how, it is maintained here, the rest of us ought to understand its 'iconographic program'. It is only after we have clearly recognized the similar mythic foundations in Spenser's and Milton's works that we can speak about the character of the equally interesting difference between the two sets of structures and their 'orchestrations'—about, in other words, the strikingly original contribution which Milton brought to the genre of epic and heroic poetry, and about what was thereby irretrievably lost from a medieval and English narrative kind onto which Spenser had already grafted the heroic poem in its ancient and its Italian forms.

The significance of Spenser's and Milton's now immemorial mythic formulations, and their pertinence for us, are momentous. The works just referred to embody in our own tongue, but with a living link to the known beginnings of Western thought, the defences which are still the only known ones against the assault upon our wills of violent and self-indulgent bloody-mindedness, and against each blurred and frivolous escapade of the senses. Perhaps Spenser and Milton should have done even better, but they are what we have. They claim our initial attention because they have been esteemed by many generations equal in sensitivity to ourselves. They are the eldest magisterial voices that English speakers can still hearken to without teachers or translators, incarnating models for the most crucial decisions that each of us individually can make. They took the risk of addressing us in the most testing and responsible form of discourse known to their time.

In this chapter I consider the persistence in *Comus* of chains of thought patterns that are apparently inherited from Spenser. This inquiry is in the nature of a finger exercise before going on to the more profound transformations of Milton's later works. It remains to be said that a recognition of the structural influence of Spenser's poetry on Milton's is not likely to weaken our testimony to the richness of interplay among the most various strands of knowledge and of literary traditions in Milton's imagination. It is obvious, for instance, that Shakespeare is near the surface of *Comus* at many points, in language and in the concept of an Ariel-like Attendant Spirit, and elsewhere. Milton could not have written *Comus* without a knowledge of the conventions of the masque, no matter how much he departs from them. What Spenser's work seems to provide, unlike any of the other influences, is a model of what is really going on in *Comus*, in terms of structural mythic formulations for moral ideas. It is in this respect that Milton most often intersects with Spenser. Intellectually, and perhaps in most other ways, they differ profoundly.[2]

Spenser was related to three noble sisters of the family of the Spencers of Althorp, to whom he alluded in dedications and otherwise.

> Ne lesse praisworthie are the sisters three,
> The honor of the noble familie,
> Of which I meanest boast my selfe to be,
> And most that unto them I am so nie.
> *Phyllis, Charillis*, and sweet *Amaryllis*,
> *Phyllis* the faire, is eldest of the three:
> The next to her, is bountiful *Charillis*.
> But th'youngest is the highest in degree.
>   [*Colin Clouts Come Home Again*, 536–43]

This youngest one was Alice Spencer to whom Spenser had dedicated *The Teares of the Muses*. In *Colin Clouts Come Home Againe*, published in 1595, she is shown mourning for her Amyntas, Lord Strange, earl of Derby, poet and patron of poets:

> Helpe, O ye shepheards helpe ye all in this.
> Helpe *Amaryllis* this her losse to mourne:
> Her losse is yours, your losse *Amyntas* is,
> *Amyntas* floure of shepheards pride forlorne:
> He whilest he lived was the noblest swaine,
> That ever piped in an oaten quill:
> Both did he other, which could pipe, maintaine,
> And eke could pipe himselfe with passing skill.
>   [436–43]

It is for the same dowager countess of Derby that, fewer than forty years later, Milton describes his *Arcades* as 'Part of an Entertainment presented . . . by some noble persons of her family'.[3] Having in 1600 married Sir Thomas Egerton, she was now the stepmother of Sir John Egerton, earl of Bridgewater. The noble persons referred to, who are

2. The major part of what follows in this chapter first appeared as 'Milton's Comus and Spenser's False Genius', in *University of Toronto Quarterly*, 38 (1969), 313–18. Permission to reprint is acknowledged in the Preface of the present book.
3. *The Poems of John Milton*, ed. John Carey and Alastair Fowler (London, 1968), p. 156.

conducting a search for her as *Arcades* opens, were this earl's children and household, among whom presumably appeared his daughter Alice Egerton. This girl is the one celebrated two years later as the Lady in Milton's loveliest confection, *Comus*. The Alice, then, who is commemorated in Milton's 'masque', is step-granddaughter to that other Alice, surnamed Spencer, related to the older poet, and variously praised by him. On a number of other occasions Milton's actions reinforce our sense of Spenser's presence in his mind (see chapter 13).

Comus was first performed when Milton was nearing his twenty-sixth birthday. We have long recognized that it owed something to Spenser, if only at the rhetorical level of an epilogue (based on a rearrangement and an addition some time after the initial performance) where comforting answers and counterpositions are set up for any lingering questions raised by the preceding action. The Attendant Spirit there describes his own instant departure to a realm where Iris drenches with Elysian dew[4]

> Beds of hyacinth, and roses,
> Where young Adonis oft reposes,
> Waxing well of his deep wound
> In slumber soft, and on the ground
> Sadly sits the Assyrian queen;
> But far above in spangled sheen
> Celestial Cupid her famed son advanced,
> Holds his dear Psyche sweet entranced
> After her wandering labours long,
> Till free consent the gods among
> Make her his eternal bride,
> And from her fair unspotted side
> Two blissful twins are to be born,
> Youth and Joy; so Jove hath sworn.
> [997–1010]

Although, that is to say, the false pleasure of Comus himself is hollow and must be foresworn at all costs, a real Joy can be brought to birth. The principle of chastity which the Lady has supported against the subtly raddled animadversions of Comus is in fact the guarantor of bliss, not its destroyer. It is Comus himself who is ultimately life-

---

4. Unless otherwise noted, all quotations of Milton's verse are from Carey-Fowler, cited in n.3.

denying.[5] Youth and Joy are the offspring of a Cupid and an unspotted Psyche who are of heaven and are knit in matrimony. A grace note of this freely developed myth is that Cupid seems to bear a new evangel of love over against an earlier, earth-bound, faulty generation of deathliness, for his mother sits sadly upon the ground, mourning a flawed love. Yet even that love will be cured and rise again.

It has long been plain that, in spite of a common source in Apuleius,[6] Milton's imagination is at work here in the context of the similarly 'epilogizing' stanzas in Spenser's Garden of Adonis (*Faerie Queen*, III. vi. 49–51). There Pleasure is borne by a reconciled Psyche to a Cupid who has left the world where he discharges his sad darts and has laid them aside in the Garden. Joined to that Pleasure, and raised with her under Psyche's care, is the infant Amoret, ward of Venus, as we have seen. In one way, then (if not the most important way), Milton's Youth and Joy are Spenser's Amoret and Pleasure. The sadly sitting Assyrian queen and her wounded and sleeping paramour constitute a delicate conflation of the faulty and tragic Venus and Adonis in the lubricious tapestry of the Castle of Malecasta (*Faerie Queene*, III. i. 35–38) with the preserved and living Adonis, lapped in flowers and precious spicery, in the company of his Venus in their Garden (III. vi. 46).

In addition to these parallels, however, a new Spenserian element is both more central and more demonstrable in *Comus*. It has been recognized in a general way that the confrontation of virtue and temptation in this work stands in some kind of relation to Guyon's invasion of the Circean Bower of Bliss in *Faerie Queene*, II. xii.[7] Comus, who turns men to beasts, is a son of Circe; Acrasia, who does likewise, is in some fashion Circe herself. Circe was commonly moralized in the Renaissance as the force of sensuality which bereft men of their reason and reduced them to the animal level. Guyon's overcoming of Acrasia and the Lady's withstanding of Comus are thus parallel Renaissance instances of the allegorization of the Circe story, and it has seemed obvious that, being close to Spenser, Milton had in mind Spenser's earlier instance, as well as many other instances. In fact, however, the parallels between *Faerie Queene*, II. xii, and *Comus* are much sharper than this. For the character Comus himself, the chief constitutive figure

---

5. Cf. B. Rajan, 'Comus: The Inglorious Likeness', *University of Toronto Quarterly*, 37 (1968), republished in his *The Lofty Rhyme: A Study of Milton's Major Poetry* (London, 1970), pp. 23–44.

6. *Golden Ass*, IV. 28–V. 24, where Psyche bears Pleasure to Cupid.

7. Cf. *Complete Poetical Works of John Milton*, ed. Douglas Bush (Boston, 1965), p. 110.

in Milton's imagination was Spenser's false Genius who sits within the porch of the gate giving entry to the Bower of Bliss.

This false Genius is

> A comely personage of stature tall,
> And semblaunce pleasing, more than naturall,
> That travellers to him seemed to entize;
> His looser garment to the ground did fall,
> And flew about his heeles in wanton wize,
> Not fit for speedy pace, or manly exercize.
>
> [II. xii. 46]

His departure from the principle of Nature is already suggested in the second line just quoted. In the Bower he is called Genius, but he is not the real Genius, the traditional and literarily popular medieval figure,

> that celestiall powre, to whom the care
> Of life, and generation of all
> That lives, pertaines in charge particulare.
>
> [xii. 47]

The so-called Genius here

> was to that quite contrary,
> The foe of life, that good envyes to all,
> That secretly doth us procure to fall,
> Through guileful semblaunts, which he makes us see.
>
> [xii. 48]

He has the 'governall' of the Bower and 'Pleasures Porter was devised to bee' (48. 7–8). He is like other traditional porters, seen here earlier, who certify the state of mind and body in which a contemplated change can be wrought—Idelnesse in the *Romaunt of the Rose*, Ease in Busirane's Masque of Cupid. The false Genius is the porter of false, or intemperate, pleasure, which is Acrasia: he is, apparently, her chief aide, as the true Genius is of Nature in the medieval tradition (see pages 162–63). He holds a staff in his hand (48. 9) with which he performs enchantments so as to make us see what is not there ('with which he charmed semblants sly', 49. 9; compare 48. 6, just quoted, and 48. 9). At his side 'a mighty Mazer bowl of wine was set' (49. 3). He offers this to all visitors. He does so to Guyon; Guyon 'overthrewe his bowle disdain-fully' (49. 8). A moment later, Guyon also throws to the ground, so that it shatters, a cup in which (with her left, or sinister, hand) the loose damsel Excesse has offered what is represented as wine from the unnatural vine nearby (55).

> In her left hand a Cup of gold she held,
>   And with her right the riper fruit did reach,
>   Whose sappy liquor, that with fulnesse sweld,
>   Into her cup she scruzd, with daintie breach
>   Of her fine fingers, without fowle empeach,
>   That so faire wine-presse made the wine more sweet:
>   Thereof she usd to give to drinke to each,
>   Whom passing by she happened to meet:
> It was her guise, all Straungers goodly so to greet.
>
> So she to *Guyon* offred it to tast;
>   Who taking it out of her tender hond,
>   The cup to ground did violently cast,
>   That all in peeces it was broken fond,
>   And with the liquor stained all the lond:
>   Whereat *Excesse* exceedingly was wroth,
>   Yet no'te the same amend, ne yet withstond,
>   But suffered him to passe, all were she loth;
> Who nought regarding her displeasure forward goth.
>   [56–57]

Correspondingly, Milton's Comus is the son of Circe (as the false Genius is the helper of a Circe figure).

> Bacchus that first from out the purple grape,
> Crushed the sweet poison of misused wine
> After the Tuscan mariners transformed
> Coasting the Tyrrhene shore, as the winds listed,
> On Circe's island fell (who knows not Circe
> The daughter of the Sun? Whose charmed cup
> Whoever tasted, lost his upright shape,
> And downward fell into a grovelling swine)
> This nymph that gazed upon his clustering locks,
> With ivy berries wreathed, and his blithe youth,
> Had by him, ere he parted thence, a son
> Much like his father, but his mother more,
> Whom therefore she brought up and Comus named.
>   [46–58]

And Comus himself, as the next quotation shows, turns men into beasts through their sensuality, as the false Genius helps to do. (Guyon and the Palmer meet such beasts just before encountering him, and at the end of Book II). Comus

Offering to every weary traveller,
His orient liquor in a crystal glass,
To quench the drought of Phoebus, which as they taste
(For most do taste through fond intemperate thirst)
Soon as the potion works, their human countenance,
The express resemblance of the gods, is changed
Into some brutish form of wolf, or bear,
Or ounce, or tiger, hog, or bearded goat,
All other parts remaining as they were,
And they, so perfect is their misery,
Not once perceive their foul disfigurement,
But boast themselves more comely than before
And all their friends, and native home forget
To roll with pleasure in a sensual sty.
[64–77]

Comus first appears 'with a charming-rod in one hand, his glass in the other' (following 92), as the false Genius had borne a staff for enchantment and had had a drinking vessel of wine at his side, and as an associate figure, Excesse, had appeared with a goblet of wine. Comus attempts to persuade the Lady to drink from his glass, as both the false Genius and Excesse had attempted to persuade Guyon to drink.

Comus appears with his rabble, and the Lady set in an enchanted chair, to whom he offers his glass, which she puts by....

see, here be all the pleasures
That fancy can beget on youthful thoughts,
When the fresh blood grows lively, and returns
Brisk as the April buds in primrose season.
And first behold this cordial julep here
That flames, and dances in his crystal bounds
With spirits of balm, and fragrant syrups mixed.
Not that Nepenthes which the wife of Thone,
In Egypt gave to Jove-born Helena
Is of such power to stir up joy as this,

To life so friendly, or so cool to thirst.
Why should you be so cruel to yourself,
And to those dainty limbs which Nature lent
For gentle usage, and soft delicacy?
But you invert the covenants of her trust,
And harshly deal like an ill borrower
With that which you received on other terms,
Scorning the unexempt condition
By which all mortal frailty must subsist,
Refreshment after toil, ease after pain,
That have been tired all day without repast,
And timely rest have wanted, but fair virgin
This will restore all soon.

[preceding 658, 667–88]

We note in passing, the parallel spawning, in the above, of false pleasure from two parents, like true Pleasure, and also some touches from Spenser's Garden of Proserpina in II. vii. 63 (see next chapter), as well as a suggestion of the state of Milton's Eve immediately before eating the apple. Comus is no more successful than the false Genius or Excesse, and the guideline, as in Spenser, is acknowledged to be Temperance.

'Twill not false traitor,
'Twill not restore the truth and honesty
That thou hast banished from thy tongue with lies,

. . . .

Were it a draught for Juno when she banquets,
I would not taste thy treasonous offer; none
But such as are good men can give good things,
And that which is not good, is not delicious
To a well-governed and wise appetite.

[689–91, 700–704]

Further, the Lady's brothers rush in, seize the glass, and cast it to the ground so that it breaks (following 812), which is how Guyon had dealt with the mazer and the goblet.

The iconographic parallel is thus remarkably complete. Milton almost surely kept his interior eye on the false Genius as he moulded his new and in many respects quite different figure. He needed a male counterpart of Circe, rather than a female Circe figure, to attempt the seduction of the Lady. Not, indeed, that he would necessarily have conceived of a Circe figure in terms of those of the Bower of Bliss and therefore chose the only male one he could find there; but among figures whose *esse* is to mislead us into false pleasure, the Spenserian one had no doubt entered his imagination early and was close to its centre.

Spenser plays off the false Genius against the true Genius, who is the porter of the Garden of Adonis (III. vi. 31–32). In the medieval tradition from which the latter figure principally springs, we have seen that Genius is the patron of generation (to which word his name was thought to be related) and the helper or confessor of Nature as mother of generation.[8] He may be considered the helper not only of Nature but also of Venus in the Garden of Adonis; and this Venus of the Garden, like the one in the fifteenth-century *Lover's Mass*, also abetted by Genius, is an appropriate substitute figure for Nature. As we have seen, Art (specious artifice) and Nature compete in the Bower; in the Garden, Dame Nature works alone (III. vi. 29, 30, 44). The antithetical characters of Spenser's two Geniuses are very likely to have helped Milton to formulate his own imaginative pattern for *Comus*, for these personae reinforce the contrast between the Circean domain of the enchanter and the other symbols borrowed from the Garden: Venus and Adonis, Cupid and Psyche, Pleasure and Youth (or Pleasure and Amoret in *Faerie Queene*, III. vi. 51).

Another role assigned to Spenser's true Genius in contrast with the false one at II. xii. 47–48 is that of the Classical genius or guardian spirit, 'Agdistes', or 'our true self',

> Who wondrous things concerning our welfare,
> And straunge phantomes doth let us oft forsee,
> And oft of secret ill bids us beware.
> [47]

8. See pp. 86–88; C. S. Lewis, *The Allegory of Love* (London, 1936), pp. 106, 111, 139, 149, 151, and appendix I; Ernst Robert Curtius, *European Literature and the Latin Middle Ages* (New York, 1953; paperback, 1963), pp. 111, 118 and n., 121, 125. See also *OED*, 'Genius 1.', where Gower's use of the word in *Confessio Amantis*, 148; Chaucer's (?) use in *Romaunt of the Rose*, l. 4768 (Frag. B); and an occurrence of ca. 1536 are listed under the wrong meaning. Cf. also an association of Genius with Venus instead of Nature in the fifteenth-century *Lover's Mass*: 'This is the wyl of Dame Venus / And of hyr Bishop Genivs', in *English Verse between Chaucer and Surrey*, ed. E. P. Hammond (Durham, N. C., 1927), p. 211. The *Middle English Dictionary*, ed. H. Kurath et al. (Ann Arbor, 1963), gives other appropriate citations, such as Lydgate, *Reson and Sensualyte*, l. 863; 'Alle tho ... That falsely wirke ageyns kynde, The which ... Ofte falle in the sentence Of my [Nature's] prest called Genius' (*kynde* is of course 'nature'). Unfortunately, the *MED* also gives a false definition of *genius*. See also Variorum commentary on the false Genius and true one. Milton uses the adjective 'genial' in the generative sense: cf. *Paradise Lost*, IV. 712; VII. 282; VIII. 598.

In contrast, the false Genius, who 'good envyes to all',

> secretly doth us procure to fall,
> Through guilefull semblaunts, which he makes us see.
> [48]

The role of Comus in misleading the unwary, and conjuring up '*a stately palace, set out with all manner of deliciousness*' (after 657), patently resembles that of the false Genius, but in addition the role of an adversary true Genius, or personal guardian, seems to have much to do with the development of Milton's notion of the Attendant Spirit, who, after Comus has appeared as a shepherd to mislead the Lady (270), bodies himself forth as a second shepherd to recount the vital circumstances truthfully to the brothers (491ff.). That Spenser's Genius is 'that celestial powre' (II. xii. 47) is consonant with this interpretation, and, moreover, this latter phrase finds a partial echo in the 'Celestial Cupid' of *Comus*, 1003. The case is fairly clinched by the significances of the two terms by which Milton invariably introduced the Attendant Spirit at an earlier stage in the composition of *Comus*, in the Trinity MS (also the Bridgewater MS):[9] 'daemon' and 'guardian spirit'. As Apuleius points out (*De Deo Socratis*, 15), Greek *daimon* is simply Latin *genius*; and Socrates himself, in the *Symposium*, uses *daimon* as the term for the personal inspiring spirit in each of us. 'Daemon' or 'guardian spirit', then, is what Spenser meant in talking about the Agdistes who is the opposite of the false Genius.

The significance of the staff of enchantment held by the false Genius is intensified by an implied contrast to the staff of Guyon's Palmer. In II. xii. 40 the Palmer easily quells the passions of the beasts (that is, transformed men) of Acrasia's isle by holding over them this staff, which is made from the same wood and possesses the same virtues as the caduceus of Mercury: the latter is said in the same passage to have made possible the invasion of the infernal regions and the quelling of the Furies. On the other hand, in stanza 48, only a little later, we are told that the false Genius secretly 'doth us procure to fall, / Through guileful semblaunts'; and these 'semblaunts sly' are said in stanza 49 to be produced by the false Genius' enchanting staff. The significant force of a

9. See *John Milton's Complete Poetical Works, Reproduced in Photographic Facsimile*, ed. Harris Francis Fletcher (Urbana, 1943–48), I, 398–433 (for the Trinity MS); *Milton's 'Comus', being the Bridgewater Manuscript . . . by the Lady Alix Egerton* (London, 1910). John T. Shawcross shows convincingly that the Trinity MS is the earliest that we have. See his 'Certain Relationships of the Manuscripts of *Comus*', *Papers of the Bibliographical Society of America*, 54 (1960), 38–56.

conjuring rod given to Comus would thus be magnified in Milton's mind, although this rod for good reason is not later broken as is that of the False Genius. Milton seems more impressed by the goblet or cup ('By sly enticement gives his baneful cup', 524); and in fact there is an adversary cup, as well as different twins from the Youth and Joy of *Comus*, 1010, in *Apology for Smectymnuus*:[10]

> . . . divine volumes of Plato and his equal Xenophon: where if I should tell ye what I learnt of chastity and love (I mean that which is truly so, whose charming cup is only virtue, which she bears in her hand to those who are worthy—the rest are cheated with a thick intoxicating potion which a certain sorceress, the abuser of love's name, carried about) and how the first and chiefest office of love begins and ends in the soul, producing those happy twins of her divine generation, knowledge and virtue.

It is partly characteristic of the difference between the arts of Spenser and Milton that the false Genius is silently emblematic, while Comus speaks to us through a varied and subtle (if disordered) register of rhetoric. Yet some of the quality which Milton gives to this rhetoric may be thought of as consonant with the subtle verbal integument of other parts of Spenser's Bower of Bliss. The clearest relation is between Comus' traditional employment of the motif of the rose ('If you let slip time, like a neglected rose . . .' 742) and Spenser's Tassonian rose song (II. xii. 74–75) and treatment of time.

Incidentally it should be obvious that at no point in the final version of *Comus* is Milton defending a merely passive virginity.[11] Imagining as the Lady's antagonist a being who finally advocates not youth and joy but sterile chains, he associates the chastity which the Lady defends with that Spenserian principle whose main embodiment is the Britomart of *Faerie Queene* III, IV, and V: the ward of virginity, but also in her full unfolding the witness to the bliss of true lovers, and the righter of those wrongs which enslave or frustrate them. We have already seen that, by

10. John Milton, *Complete Poems and Major Prose*, ed. Merritt Y. Hughes (New York, 1957), p. 694.

11. For a review of the controversy on the doctrine of chastity or virginity in *Comus*, see Carey-Fowler, pp. 172–73, where it is evident that my position has some affinity with that of J. C. Maxwell, 'The Pseudo-Problem of "Comus"', *Cambridge Journal*, 1 (1948), 376–80. Basic to the discussion is A. S. P. Woodhouse, 'The Argument of Milton's "Comus"', *University of Toronto Quarterly*, 11 (1941), 46–71. See also E. M. W. Tillyard's 'Postscript' in his *Studies in Milton* (London, 1960), pp. 97–99, where he meets Woodhouse's argument and also Maxwell's; Kenneth Muir, *Penguin New Writing*, 24 (1945), 141–43, claims that the Lady's views on chastity are one-sided throughout.

calling his Attendant Spirit 'daemon' as early as the version in the Trinity MS, Milton was apparently thinking of this character as a descendant of Spenser's advocate of innocent and pleasurable procreation.[12]

If we step back for a wider view, the pattern of *Comus* seems to us to be dominated by the mythical formulations of Spenser to a surprising, but not to a disconcerting, degree. The advocates of the false joy and of the true one in this work are now seen to be, in actions and attributes, Spenserian. Comus's immobilization of the Lady in a chair through the magic of his staff relates to Busirane's chaining and conjuring of Amoret (*Faerie Queene*, III. xii. 30–31), as do the 'backward mutters of dissevering power' (*Comus*, 816) to Amoret's release (*Faerie Queene*, III. xii. 34–38). The Lady's bracing advocacy of chastity (*Comus*, 755–98) lets us see through to the world and even to the character of Britomart and her invulnerability, and perhaps also, as we shall see, to the Guyon of Temperance in *Faerie Queene* II. The sadly sitting Assyrian queen, the wounded Adonis on the way to health, and Cupid and Psyche with their offspring Youth and Joy in the last speech of *Comus* all have their counterparts in the Garden of Adonis (*Faerie Queene*, III. vi. 46–51).[13] Even Sabrina and her liberation of the Lady (*Comus*, 819–936) may connect, in a largely episodic way, with the sea nymph Cymoent's rescue of the gravely wounded Marinell (*Faerie Queene*, III. iv. 29–34), as Sabrina herself in *Comus*, 825–57, connects superficially with her namesake in *Faerie Queene*, II. x. 19 (of whom the Attendant Spirit says he has been taught by Spenser—old Meliboeus, at 821). Perhaps the Sabrina of *Comus* relates more profoundly with the Florimell who in saving her honour takes to the sea (*Faerie Queene*, III. vii. 25–27; III. viii. 20–35) and finally gets her beloved Marinell (IV. xii), and with Britomart and with her namesake,

---

12. It must, of course, be taken into account that Milton was acquainted not only with the poetry of Spenser but with that of his followers. Tillyard (*Studies in Milton*, pp. 90, 91, 94) feels that the Lady in *Comus* has affinities with Parthenia, who is virginity, contrasted with Agnia, or wedded chastity, in Phineas Fletcher's *Purple Island* (Agnia, incidentally, resembles Britomart more than she does Belphoebe). This seems to me an unnecessary hypothesis, apart from the point that Milton would have had to read *The Purple Island* in MS to use it in *Comus*, since it was not published until 1633. Britomart is a sufficiently war-like and aggressively chaste damsel to account for everything that the Lady says along that line. Above all, there is a paradigm for the action of *Comus* in *The Faerie Queene*; there is none in *The Purple Island*. Similarly for Agnia. In terms of married bliss, the end of the episode of the Garden of Adonis, with Amoret as the companion of Pleasure under the tutelage of Psyche, is sufficient, and already obviously in Milton's mind.

13. With a touch from the Venus and Adonis of Malecasta's lubricious tapestry (III. i. 35–38).

the Cretan deity Britomartis, who, fleeing Minos, also leaped into the sea.

But whatever the connections of *Comus* with *The Faerie Queene* (and wherever we should draw the limit of likelihood concerning putative connections), every opportunistically borrowed detail used in this work of the twenty-five-year old Milton had been first absorbed by a blissfully self-confident creative mind and finally uttered forth only after having undergone a sea change. The great power of the Miltonic imagination was that it was both vigorously prehensile and boldly independent and original. In terms of Milton's use of Spenser's work, *Comus* is an augury of the future, although the mind in action in that composition startles nearly as much by its economical deployment of Spenserian resources as by its independence and confidence. The structural myth of the whole of Book II of *The Faerie Queene*—the Book of Temperance—seems to have become part of Milton's mental furniture at an early age. Working at a much more profound level and at a greater distance from the fulcrum than the matter of *Comus*, it appears to have exerted great leverage on the choice of incident and the patterns of embodiment for the themes of temptation, ensnarement, and final abstention in Milton's two epics. Milton is at no point Spenser's creature, but the continued presence, in the mind of even the older Milton, of Spenser's fictional projections of ideas is a datum which will give us more help in understanding the genesis of *Paradise Lost* and (perhaps even more) of *Paradise Regained* than has previously been imagined. We had not imagined it, I believe, because we have not understood what Milton saw in the second book of *The Faerie Queene*. We must first turn to an interpretation of that book as Milton would have seen it and as I believe Spenser intended the rest of us to see it, particularly with reference to the Cave of Mammon and the Bower of Earthly Bliss.

My conclusions in this chapter have concerned the final version of *Comus* as Milton left it, but it would be interesting if the various extant earlier verse and song MSS shed any further light. John T. Shawcross's most recent article on the subject of such MSS shows that additional considerations regarding the failure of the various MSS of the songs and their music to correspond with MSS of the masque itself throw into greater doubt the form of the masque as originally presented.[14] It seems most unlikely, however, that any of the differences could have been so great as to modify the conclusions already reached here. The only

14. 'Henry Lawe's Setting for Milton's "Comus"', *Journal of the Rutgers University Library*, 28 (1964), 22–28.

concrete question of interpretation that Shawcross raises in his sum-
marizing paragraph concerns that material in the epilogue of the final
version going beyond those cancelled lines in the Trinity MS which are
located in that MS between what are now lines 4 and 5 of the final
version. This question, he says, concerns 'Adonis and Venus as carnal
lovers who languish far below the celestial heavens and, in
contrast, . . . Cupid and Psyche as the legitimate union of heart and soul,
which union brings forth Youth (eternal life) and Joy (heavenly bliss)'.
We have seen that this proceeds (as far as anything can be said to
proceed from the creation of one author through another's imagination
to that other's creation) from a conflation of the tapestry in Spenser's
House of Malecasta (*Faerie Queene*, III. i) with the Garden of Adonis
(III. vi) (on the supposition, by the way, that Joy is innocent wedded
pleasure, not literally heavenly bliss, as Shawcross says). Had the third
book of *The Faerie Queene* made a tremendous impression on Milton
after he had composed an earlier version of his masque, in which he had
already extensively employed material from the second book? Conceivably. But it seems at least as likely that—at a chronological distance
from that first version—Milton realized he wanted a complementary
element, going beyond mere virginity, and injected this element, *more
Spenseriano*, in the form of wedded love.

A postscript to this chapter is that the dependence of Milton's character Comus on Spenser's false Genius was anticipated by a versifying
divine in 1679. Samuel Woodford, D.D., published in that year *A
Paraphrase upon the Canticles*, to which he annexed certain 'English
Rimes', of which the first is *Epode* (to transliterate his Greek title) in
three cantos. This composition is demonstrably, and even slavishly,
Spenserian. Canto ii is largely devoted to examining the followers of
False Love, or Anteros. This series of personages is primarily, but not
entirely, derived from the Masque of Cupid at the end of *Faerie Queene*
III. Idleness, Fancy, Desire, Folly, Mirth, and Dalliance are followed by
Genius (II. xi. vii), who is associated with the preceding three. Lust, Sin,
and Death follow after. Genius is thus described:

> Next after her in order *Genius* came,
> Of Body somewhat gross, but Humours free;
> Whom part call'd Comus, as by his Sirname,
> Tho both, or either with him well agree,
> Without whom Love, nor merry life can be:
> A right good fellow, as his Belly show'd,
> Which in a swath reacht almost to his Knee,

And made him passage through th' admiring Crowd,
Which shouting to him louted, as to them he bow'd.

No wrinkle in his Counte'nance did appear,
Nor careful thought seem'd to come near his Mind,
Of what should be; but things, which present were,
Variously turn'd him, as did sit the Wind,
And this way now, now that way he inclin'd:
Tho if 'Twere still (and sometime still it lay)
Diversions to himself he'd make, or find;
And sometimes only muse a live-long Day,
Tho askt on what, he or nought knew, or nought could say.
                    [liv–lv]

Writing long after the publication of *Comus*, Woodford, the convinced Spenserian, has almost surely recognized the association between Spenser's and Milton's relevant figures. To his Genius he gives dissoluteness (over against the concern with licit and loving procreation of Spenser's true Genius and Milton's Attendant Spirit, and the latter's concern with chastity per se, subjoined to virginity and flighty imaginativeness (over against the concern with each individual's truth on the part of Spenser's Agdistes-Genius and Milton's Attendant Spirit). He flattens and trivializes the whole issue, but his evidence supports the identification defended here.[15]

15. Perhaps the large belly (but not, certainly, the more important feature of lust) relates to Jonson's character Comus in the masque *Pleasure Reconciled to Virtue*.

12

Milton's and Our

Faerie Queene II

Good and evill we know in the field of this World grow up
together almost inseparably; and the knowledge of good is so
involv'd and interwoven with the knowledge of evill, and in so
many cunning resemblances hardly to be discern'd, that those
confused seeds which were impos'd on *Psyche* as an incessant
labour to cull out, and sort asunder, were not more intermixt. It
was from out the rinde of one apple tasted, that the knowledge of
good and evill as two twins cleaving together leapt forth into the
World. And perhaps this is that doom which *Adam* fell into of
knowing good and evill, that is to say of knowing good by evill. As
therefore the state of man now is; what wisdom can there be to
choose, what continence to forbeare without the knowledge of
evill? He that can apprehend and consider vice with all her baits
and seeming pleasures, and yet abstain, and yet distinguish, and
yet prefer that which is truly better, he is the true wayfaring
Christian. I cannot praise a fugitive and cloister'd vertue,
unexercis'd and unbreath'd, that never sallies out and sees her
adversary, but slinks out of the race, where that immortal garland
is to be run for, not without dust and heat. Assuredly we bring not
innocence into the world, we bring impurity much rather: that
which purifies us is triall, and triall is by what is contrary. That
vertue therefore which is but a youngling in the contemplation of

evill, and knows not the utmost that vice promises to her followers, and rejects it, is but a blank vertue, not a pure; her whiteness is
but an excrementall whitenesse; Which was the reason why our
sage and serious Poet *Spencer*, whom I dare be known to think a
better teacher than *Scotus* or *Aquinas*, describing true temperance
under the person of *Guion*, brings him in with his palmer through
the cave of Mammon, and the bowr of earthly blisse that he might
see and know, and yet abstain. Since therefore the knowledge and
survay of vice is in this world so necessary to the constituting of
human vertue, and the scanning of error to the confirmation of
truth, how can we more safely, and with lesse danger scout into
the regions of sin and falsity then by reading all manner of
tractats, and hearing all manner of reason? And this is the benefit
which may be had of books promiscuously read. [John Milton,
Areopagitica[1]]

Faerie Queene II seems a narrow base from which to derive the
Spenserian presence in Milton's imagination, yet as with *Comus* so with
Milton's two epics the important congruity seems to rest there. This
congruity consists almost entirely in the extension and permutation of a
series of Spenserian mythic formulations. Notionally, the resemblances
between the works of the two poets depend almost entirely upon a
shared intellectual tradition rather than upon Spenser's influence,
which in this respect is trifling. Equally and more obviously, Milton
'orchestrates' these interconnected, mythic image-structures quite differently from Spenser, so that (in the fashionable term) Milton's works
are 'cosmetically' and in their intellectual fibre an enormously original
phenomenon.

Many of the principles of the partly traditional interpretation of Book
II offered here,[2] and of this book's relation to *Paradise Lost* and
Paradise Regained, were succinctly formulated by Edwin Greenlaw
over fifty years ago (see chapter 13).

Like what I have already discussed in *The Faerie Queene*, the Book of
Sir Guyon or Temperance can be usefully thought of as a combination
of chivalric adventure and moralized landscape (see chapter 1). In Book
II what Spenser seems to have considered the most significant structural

1. Ernest Sirluck, ed., *Complete Prose Works of John Milton*, II (New Haven, 1959),
514–17.
2. The interpretation here leans heavily on my 'Three Fearful Symmetries', in *A Theatre
for Spenserians: Papers of the International Spenser Colloquium*, ed. Judith Kennedy
(Toronto, 1973), pp. 19–52. In it I have expressed my indebtedness to works by Professors Kathleen Williams, Frank Kermode, Robert L. Kellogg, and Oliver L. Steele.

positions are given to two such landscapes: the House of Mammon, whose culminating episode lies at the arithmetical centre point of the book; and the Bower of Bliss, which culminates at the end. Spenser's narrative of the House, in canto vii, brings us by way of a subterranean journey, through a tiny, carefully guarded door adjacent to hell's mouth, and through a series of outskirts and precincts, to, finally, an underground garden. The central point of this garden is the silver seat of Proserpina. It lies not only 'in the midst' of her garden, but is introduced and described in the mid-most three stanzas of Book II (vii. 53–55). These correspond to the arithmetical centre points of the other books of the first edition.[3] The last-seen figures in the Garden of Proserpina bid fair to be the most heinously wicked ones of Guyon's underground journey; after seeing them, he leaves the Cave. The Bower, on the other hand, is located in its entirety on an island at the end of a long sea voyage. Spenser's description of the Bower takes us through a broad, flimsy, wide-open portal, through various outlying dependencies and purlieus, to a central area in which Acrasia, mistress of the island, has accomplished the seduction of young Verdant; in dealing with this central area Spenser ends the book. The last figure shown to us here is the most degraded: Grill. The Palmer then indicates to Guyon that it is time to leave.

Three propositions are integral to my subsequent discussion of these two landscapes and of Book II at large. They are necessary preliminaries in presenting what it was here that Milton may have ruminated on for many years while he was evolving the embodiments of temptation and response in *Paradise Lost* and *Paradise Regained*. First, these two systems of symbolic landscape should be considered together as a *divisio*— as an analytical, bifurcating myth—of the two opposed forms of intemperance. Second, these two opposed divisions of intemperance are treated in various ways throughout Book II at large, and form the main propellant of the narrative. These two, along with the third

---

3. See chap. 6, n.6, and pp. 102 and 86–88. The second line of the three central stanzas of Book II, just referred to, begins 'And in the midst thereof a silver seat...'. The two central stanzas (vii. 12, 13) of Book I give us the striking down of Redcross by Orgoglio, the low point of Redcross' quest, corresponding to the failure, seven stanzas before this, 'in middest of the race' of the nymph from whose weakening waters Redcross had drunk. Edwin Greenlaw's analysis of the situation anticipates mine in principle, without reference to precise numerical structure: 'In the first three books, the section of the poem first completed by Spenser, the principal crisis, or fundamental motif of each book comes in the sixth or seventh canto, midway of the story...' ('Spenser's Influence on *Paradise Lost*', *Studies in Philology*, 17, 1920, 331). His footnote to this shows that he means here 'the captivity of Redcross', 'the journey of Guyon through the underworld', 'the Garden of Adonis'.

category, temperance itself, derive ultimately from a Platonic triad of concepts, which, as Spenser knew it, had undergone so many eclectic accretions (including Aristotelian ones),[4] that the word 'Platonic' must be understood very loosely here. The literary and moral interest of Book II lies in its development of a symmetrical, complex, elegant, abstract structure embodying the varieties of the human, living, inward, felt experience of these two realms of sensibility and emotion. Third, one of the ways in which the various embodiments of the two forms of intemperance are related to each other is through a set of images having to do on the one side with fire and with violence—stabbing and rending into pieces—and on the other with water, as a shifting, inconstant, weakish element.

In a way that is customary with Spenser, the two divisions of intemperance with which he is concerned are explicitly presented in the episode with which the treatment of the virtue temperance properly commences in canto i. At the beginning of this episode Guyon and his Palmer have discovered the dead knight Mordant ('death giver'), and his dying wife Amavia ('lover of life'), and their infant (subsequently named Ruddymane). Amavia, disguised as another palmer, we learn, had earlier recovered her husband from the same seductress, Acrasia, who in canto xii will be holding bewitched the similarly named young knight Verdant whom Guyon and the Palmer will rescue. But Mordant had drunk the potion of Acrasia (Milton's preoccupation in *Comus* again), and Acrasia had laid the following spell upon him:

> *give death to him that death does give,*
> *and losse of love, to her that loves to live,*
> *So soone as Bacchus with the Nymphe does lincke.*
> [II. i. 55]

He has in consequence died as soon as he drank from the fountain of the local nymph. Amavia has then stabbed herself and is expiring as Guyon and the Palmer enter. Ruddymane ('Bloody-Hand') is innocently dabbling his hands in her blood, which is becoming mixed with the water of the fountain. Guyon's and the Palmer's definitive comment on this scene, with its apparently somewhat strained application to Amavia, contains the indicated programmatic definition of the two forms of intemperance and the mean between them.

4. On Ernest Sirluck, '*The Faerie Queene* Book II, and the *Nicomachean Ethics*', see chap. 13, n.18. For his 'Milton Revises *The Faerie Queene*', see chap. 13, n.14.

Behold the image of mortalitie,
And feeble nature cloth'd with fleshly tyre,
When raging passion with fierce tyrannie
Robs reason of her due regalitie,
And makes it servant to her basest part:
The strong it weakens with infirmitie,
And with bold furie armes the weakest hart;
The strong through pleasure soonest falles, the weake
through smart.

But temperance (said he) with golden squire
Betwixt them both can measure out a meane,
Neither to melt in pleasures whot desire,
Nor fry in hartlesse griefe and dolefull teene,
Thrise happie man, who fares them both atweene.
[i. 57, 58]

It requires no great effort to see how Spenser generalizes these polar terms into two controlling concepts throughout Book II, but it is well to be clear about the meaning of these terms so as to avoid later the charge of imprecision or of changing ground. What Guyon is saying of the moral world as seen through the examples of Mordant and Amavia is that when passion (of whatever kind, whether pertaining to the appetite or to the will) overcomes reason, certain natures ('the strong', Mordant) are weakened with 'infirmitie', that is, they are subjected through their senses to weakness of purpose and to vacillation, and to being 'unmanned' through self-indulgence: such a one 'soonest falles' through pleasure; but other natures (the 'weake', Amavia) are driven into the opposite form of intemperance, 'bold furie', so that they fall through 'smart'. That this fury results in Book II generally from frantic envy, pride, or contentiousness directed against rivals applies to Amavia only in the ultimately important sense that her despair begins and ends through the machinations of a rival. Spenser touches on this rivalry when he shows Amavia conditionally reproaching heaven for not imposing a just revenge upon Acrasia, and for tolerating Amavia's own unmerited wretchedness (truly unmerited in the sense that unlike Acrasia she herself had not been the agent of a sanguinary reprisal):

But if that carelesse heavens (quoth she) despise
The doome of just revenge, and take delight
To see sad pageants of mens miseries,

> As bound by them to live in lives despight,
> Yet can they not warne death from wretched wight.
> Come then, come soone, come sweetest death to mee,
> And take away this long lent loathed light:
> Sharpe be thy wounds, but sweet the medicines bee,
> That long captived soules from wearie thraldome free.
>   [i. 36]

Because Spenser here needs an innocent victim, not an accomplice to violence against others, Amavia is shown, not acting out contentiousness, but performing violence against self. As the reader sees above, Spenser gives her over to the particular 'bold furie' which in the language of Book I is called Despair, the other half (annexed to Book I's Sloth) of the mortal sin of *Acedia*, from which Una at the end of I. ix had rescued Redcross.

One objection to this line of argument, however, is the name Amavia itself. If she is given over to a fatal despair, why does her name mean, in etymological fact as well as in the etymology of Acrasia's charm, '*her that loves to live*' (i. 55)? The best answer to this question is Milton's own in *Paradise Lost* X, where he shows us Eve suggesting to Adam that their own suicide is a way of protecting their yet unborn descendants from Death. It appears that Milton can be shown here to have been thinking of (and wanting us to reminisce on the subject of) Amavia's case. Eve begins

> Then both our selves and seed at once to free
> From what we fear for both, let us make short,
> Let us seek death, or he not found, supply
> With our own hands his office on our selves;
> Why stand we longer-shivering under fears,
> That show no end but death, and have the power,
> Of many ways to die the shortest choosing,
> Destruction with destruction to destroy.
>   She ended here, or vehement despair
> Broke off the rest; so much of death her thoughts
> Had entertained, as dyed her cheeks with pale.
>   [x. 999–1009]

Like Amavia, Eve is deeply moved, and sees the heavens making no sense of our lives. Adam disapproves of the solution, and analyses her motives thus:

> Eve, thy contempt of life and pleasure seems
> To argue in thee something more sublime
> And excellent than what thy mind contemns;
> But self-destruction therefore sought, refutes
> That excellence thought in thee, and implies,
> Not thy contempt, but anguish and regret
> For loss of life and pleasure overloved.
>
> [1013–19]

To paraphrase: 'Your contempt for life and pleasure might suggest that you are rising above them and spurning them in seeking suicide. In fact, however, your seeking it signifies not your contempt of life and pleasure but rather your regret and anguish over those two things, both of which you have loved more than you ought.' Milton's explanation of Spenser's choice of a name, then, is that 'Amavia' suits someone who commits suicide out of anguished disappointment for the loss of the pleasurable life which she loves all too much—which she loves self-indulgently in fact. Moreover, Milton comes even closer here to Amavia's case than the psychological parallel suggests. It is very difficult to believe that when he created the last line just quoted,

> For loss of life and pleasure overloved,

he did not have in mind a line of the haunting charm of Acrasia, italicized in any edition that he would have read:

> *and losse of love, to her that loves to live.*

Surely, in this conceptually so similar context he intended us to experience literary reminiscence, with a kind of anagram on the etymology of Amavia's name.

The words with which Milton's Adam continues his reproof to Eve for her despair show a connection between this kind of anguish and other forms of 'impatience' which is characteristic of the thinking in *Faerie Queene* II:

> No more be mentioned then of violence
> Against our selves, and wilful barrenness,
> That cuts us off from hope, and savours only
> Rancour and pride, impatience and despite,
> Reluctance against God and his just yoke
> Laid on our necks. . . .
>
> [1041–46]

It is despair like Amavia's which makes another 'impatient' Spen-serian character, Pyrochles, throw himself into the flood, 'readie to drowne himselfe for fell despight', in II. vi, but we shall go astray if we suppose that 'anguish' (i. 58. 7) is the only cause of the fury which is in all cases the sign manual of this second half of intemperance. The clearest example of the dichotomy infirmity-pleasure as opposed to bold fury-smart is in canto xi. There the two helpers of the cause of intemperance, or Maleger, in his battle with Arthur for man's body and soul, are called Impotence and Impatience, two efficient hag-lieutenants. Impotence rushes swiftly on her prey, but is lame in one leg (partly for the same reason, discussed later, that Pyrochles' brother Cymochles receives a wound in the thigh). Because she has at her command the procrastinations and vacillations which are characteristic (for example, for Verdant and Cymochles) of the life of sensual plea-sure, the forgetting of honour, she is equipped with a staff full of little snags (xi. 23). Impatience, on the other hand, is equipped with raging flame. Because in attempting to control one of these forms of intemper-ance we easily fall into the opposite one, Arthur in the act of bending forward over Impotence to bind her is thrown over on his back by Impatience, and the broken chains and bonds with which he had tried to tie her sister became properties and emblems of Impatience herself (xi. 47. 4): impatience brooks no restraint. The situation is close to the unchaining of Furor in canto v.

Spenser carries through the indicated duality into quite detailed effects. Maleger, the leader of the two hags, possesses the qualities of both. Elsewhere in Book II a quality of frantic, resentful, discontented, envious impatience is *disdain* (personified as Disdain in the Cave of Mammon, and present in Pyrochles), and a quality of the impotence which is an effect of inappropriate pleasure is *idleness* (compare Phae-dria's Idle Lake in vi. 10). In the same way, Maleger's breath (his *anima* or *alma*) is characterized by the one and his soul (his *anima* or *alma* or *animus*) by the other. In attempting to kill him Arthur crushes Maleger's body against himself, so (my italics)

> That the *disdainfull* soule he thence dispatcht,
> And th'*idle* breath all utterly exprest.
> [xi. 42]

Two other plain sets of opposed embodiments of the dichotomy first announced in canto i are Pyrochles and Cymochles, who will be discus-sed later in this chapter, and Huddibras and Sans-loy with their lady loves. Huddibras, the lover of Elissa in the House of Medina (canto ii), departs from temperance into impatience in that his reputation is gained by rashness and by foolhardy rather than reasonable exploits (ii. 17); and he suffers from Amavian 'smart' in that his courage is exceeded by his melancholy (ii. 17. 8) in something like the modern sense of this word. In his bottled-up wrath he is an Elizabethan Malcontent (ii. 37. 5–9). His Elissa is full of disdain (ii. 35). Sans-loy and his Perissa are, on the other hand, given over to Mordant-like loose pleasure and lawless lust (ii. 18, 36, 37).

It might be thought in all these cases that Spenser is discussing vice in much the same categories as in Book I, that is, in terms of the Seven Deadly Sins. This idea is in fact partly helpful for anyone who is familiar with the medieval ways of looking at these categories: 'impatience' has to do with the linked, wilful deadly sins of pride, envy, and wrath. Also, the sin of despair, sometimes related to these three, is one into which Amavia, for instance, falls. These four deadly sins, then, are linked generally on the rationale that *Superbia*, or pride, the first of them, is the sin of believing that one's excellences are due to oneself, and that, when these excellences do not lead to personal appreciation and reward, the proud man falls into *Invidia*, or envy, and *Ira*, or wrath, the second and third of the deadly sins. He may also fall into the despairing kind of *Acedia*, often regarded as the fourth. On the other hand, however, there is a difficulty in connecting 'impotence' with all of the other group of the deadly sins. It is certainly true that this kind of intemperance has to do with excessive appetite, both for drink and dainties and for sex, corresponding to the sins of *Gula*, or gluttony, and *Luxuria*, or lust, and to the slothful kind of *Acedia* which follows upon intemperate indulgence. Yet the sin of avarice, which is almost always linked with gluttony and lust, has no precise equivalent of any importance in Book II. What Mammon offers to Guyon in canto vii is yoked to 'impatience', wilfulness, not to 'impotence' and appetite. It is not mere miserly acquisitiveness that is extended as the initial temptation here, but rather the jealous care involved in keeping money away from others and (above all) the power to deploy money so as to gain honour—that is, power and superiority over others—to which temptation Guyon's very proper answer is that honour, that is, glory, is indeed worth having, but only as a reward for honourable, that is, virtuous and praiseworthy, exploits. 'Impotence', or the path of pleasure, has as its corollary the forgetting of honour; 'impatience', or vaunting rivalry, is so hydroptic for honour as to adopt any means, foul or fair, to get it. It has been many times remarked that what Mammon's daughter Philotime offers is exactly what Lady Mede offers us in *Piers Plowman*—graft, the pay-off, to get ourselves a fine place in the world.

It happens, then, that Spenser does not really fall into the language of the deadly sins in Book II. He is concerned instead with a semi-Aristolelian differentiation of what may be called the irascible passion of the will from the concupiscible one of the appetite, between which two lies the 'golden squire', or carpenter's square, of temperance. The classic description of the original doctrine is that of Plato in the *Republic*, IV. 435E–441B, where Socrates discusses the correspondences of the three classes of his perfect society to the individual soul. The doctrine was current, with many changes in detail and combination with other matters, from Plato's time through the Renaissance. A passage in which these divisions of the soul are implicitly defined is useful to us, because, starting with Homer's Circe and her transformation of men into beasts, its author goes on (with some reliance on Plato's *Phaedo*, 81, 82) to indicate that Homer's lines signify allegorically the state of those (after death) who suffer from the two indicated forms of intemperance. Spenser's own mythic formulation ascribes bestial form, under the charm of his Circe-figure Acrasia, to only one of the two forms of intemperance; equally, he is describing the living, not the dead. Nevertheless this passage may have been familiar and useful to him. It survived in the so-called *Eclogae*, a series of selections from Greek authors gathered by the fifth-century Macedonian John Stobaeus and published in a Greek-Latin version in 1575. The passage is ascribed to Porphyry but apparently belongs to Plutarch. Transmigration of souls according to Pythagoras has just been discussed. An English translation of the sixteenth century Latin follows;[5] the italics are mine:

> Homer's account of Circe also contains an admirable interpre-
> tation of the soul's condition. The words are as follows:

5. Translated from the Latin of: Ioannis Stobaei / Eclogarum / Libri Duo: / Quorum prior Physicas, posterior Ethicas complectitur; nunc primum Graece editi; / Interprete Gulielmo Cantero. /.... Antverpiae, / Ex officina Christophori Plantini /.../1575. The passage is on pp. 141–42 of Stobaeus' book, corresponding to I. xliv. 60 in modern editions. The most easily available modern version of the relevant passage is that of the Loeb Classical Library: *Plutarch's 'Moralia'*, XV, ed. F. H. Sandbach (London, 1969), Fragment 200 (pp. 368–75). The translation which appears here is Sandbach's, rather heavily modified so as to correspond to Canter's Latin in the 1575 edition. Canter's Latin version of the quoted passage (printed continuously, without my omissions in English) appears here as appendix C. This edition is the only sixteenth-century one. The Bodleian possesses John Dee's copy, dated by him 1576, and with the Latin heavily annotated. The *Eclogae* should not be confused with the *Sententiae* of the same John Stobaeus, of which there are a number of sixteenth-century editions.

They had the heads of swine, the voice, the hair,
The shape; yet still unchanged their former mind.
Odyssey, X. 239–40.

The story is a riddling version of what Plato and Pythagoras said about the soul, how although imperishable of nature and eternal, it is in no way immutable, but at the time of its so-called death and destruction it experiences an alteration and recasting which bring a change of outward bodily shape; it then follows its own tastes by looking for a shape that suits it and is appropriate by reason of a familiar similarity in its way of life. And there, they say, is the great benefit that each individual derives from education and philosophy, should his soul remember virtue and feel distaste for evil, illicit pleasures; then it will be able to retain control and look to itself and guard against the danger that, before it knows what has happened, it may become a beast, having taken a liking to a body that is naturally gross and irrational, one unclean and without innate disposition to goodness, one that strengthens and feeds in it the source of *appetite* and *anger* rather than that of *reason*.

Now, fixed sequence and nature, the causes of the actual re-fashioning, are designated by Empedocles as the goddess 'that wraps in unfamiliar shirt of flesh', that is, gives the souls their new dress, but Homer has called the cyclical revolution and recurrence of rebirth by the name of Circe, the child of the Sun, since the Sun forever joins every death to birth and birth again to death in unending succession.[6] The island of Aeaea is that appointed region of space which receives every man when he dies, where the souls wander on their first arrival, feeling themselves strangers and lamenting their fate, and not knowing in what direction lies the West.

Nor where the Sun that gives its light to men
Descends beneath the Earth.
Odyssey, X. 190–91.

Longing, according to their tastes, for their accustomed and familiar way of life in the flesh, they fall once again into that potion [Circe's transforming draught is meant] where birth commingles

---

6. This notion is of interest in connection with the discussion in part I of the Bower of Bliss and the Garden of Adonis. Circe in relation to the sun who is the father of recurrence would be very convenient to Spenser in providing an ironical counterpart to Adonis, who has a corresponding relation to the sun in his Garden. Acrasia, then, would be to Adonis as her false Genius is to the true Genius of the Garden of Adonis. Circe as a figure of the sun's recurrence, and consequently of generation and recurrence, is described in Natalis Comes, *Mythologia*. See Variorum note, II, 193–94. See the passage from Macrobius, *Saturnalia*, in appendix B.

and literally stirs together what is eternal and what is mortal, thought and emotion, the heavenly and the earth-born; they are bewitched and enfeebled by the pleasures that draw them back to birth.... Here, it seems, is the right interpretation of that belief in the underworld crossroads of which men tell; the parting of the ways refers to the *parts of the soul,* the *reasoning,* the *irascible,* and the *appetitive,* each of which contains the seeds of the manner of life appropriate to itself. And with this we pass from mythology and poetic invention to truth and the laws of nature. The men whose *appetitive element* erupts to prevail and dominate at this time of change and birth suffer a transmutation by reason of their gluttony and sensuality, so Homer means, into the bodies of donkeys [modern editors add a reading which gives 'and swine' here—an addition for which anyone who had read the initial quotation from the *Odyssey* would see the need] to lead their lives in defilement. Another soul has grown utterly savage through stubborn rivalries and hateful cruelties; when such a one comes to his second birth, full of fresh bitterness and indignation, he unites himself with the shape of a wolf or lion, receiving such a body as an organ that will serve his dominant passion. [The *spirited* or *irascible* part of the soul is obviously meant.] So one should never keep oneself so pure as at the time of one's death, as if taking part in a rite of initiation; one should be free from all evil passions, put all troublesome appetites to sleep, keep feelings of envy and anger remote, and thus withdraw from the body. This is the true Mercury; that is, *Reason,* the mistress of virtue, who keeps the soul from the potion, or, if the soul drains that potion, keeps her in a human life and character for so long as is feasible.

It may be remembered in passing that the rod (of temperance) carried by Guyon's Palmer is likened to the caduceus of Mercury when the Palmer quells the passions of the beasts (that is, men transformed by appetite) before the walls of the Bower of Acrasia (II. xii. 39–41).

It is unnecessary here to go any further than the still useful article of V. B. Hulbert on 'A Possible Christian Source for Spenser's Temperance'[7] to see that a doctrine concerning the reasonable, irascible, and concupiscible parts of the soul was readily adaptable to Christian purposes, for it recurs frequently either by itself or along with

7. *Studies in Philology,* 28 (1931), 184–210. Robert Ellrodt, *Neoplatonism in the Poetry of Spenser* (Geneva, 1960), points out that the distinction among the rational, irascible, and appetitive elements is a commonplace. He gives a number of early and late references (p. 54), of which the most important is probably Macrobius, *In Somnium Scipionis,* I. vi.

other often related sets of categories, particularly the Seven Deadly Sins (a point which she does not take up). With so much eclecticism in discussions of evil-doing in the most varied kinds of writings, and with so grandly eclectic an author as Spenser, it is probably beside the point to talk about definite sources. Yet the popularity of the doctrine is obvious from the sources cited by her. Among early ones, Ambrose gives almost a textbook definition of the dichotomy of intemperance, the spirited passions being *secundum animam*, the appetitive ones being *secundum corpus*.[8] Hulbert's chief point is that Aristotle in the *Nicomachean Ethics* treats temperance as a matter of controlling pleasurable desire, while for both Spenser and the Christian Middle Ages not only the *passiones concupiscibilis* but also the *passiones irascibilis* enter into the calculation, with frequent discussion of the mean without reference to Aristotle. Even the greatest Aristotelian of them all, Saint Thomas, allows for the two in his scheme (page 199).

Hulbert follows the matter of 'Christian temperance' into vernacular treatises and into the Renaissance[9] where the best-known instance is provided by Burton's *Anatomy of Melancholy*.[10] In that work, in I. 2. 3. 3, he speaks of: 'Perturbation and passions which trouble the phantasy, though they dwell between the confines of sense. They are commonly reduced into two inclinations, irascible and concupiscible.' He continues in the following subsection 15: 'These concupiscible and irascible appetites are as the two twists of a rope, mutually mixed one with the other, and both twining about the heart: both good, as Austin holds, *lib.* 14, *cap.* 9, *De Civ. Dei,* "if they be moderate; both perni-

---

8. Ambrosius, *De Iacob et Vite Beata,* I. ii, in *Patrologia Latina,* XIV, col. 630. Translation in Hulbert, p. 193.

9. An instance which she was unable to note turns up, as usual in disguised form, in Lorenzo Valla, *De vero falsoque bono,* III. viii. 2 (ed. Maristella de Panizza Lorch, Bari, 1970):

> Nam omnia vitia in hec duo genera dividuntur: in ea que alteri nocent et in ea que non nocent. Priora sunt huiusmodi: malicia, crudelitas, avaricia, iracundia, perfidia, periurium; posteriora ut pigritia, desidia, somnolentia, hebetudo, sordes, gulositas et similia.

> [All vices, in fact, are of two kinds: those which harm others, and those which do not. To the former kind belong malice, cruelty, avarice, wrath, treachery, lying; to the latter, indolence, idleness, somnolence, dullness, dirtiness, gluttony, and the like.]

Boccaccio, incidentally, connects the irascible element with Mars and the concupiscible with Venus in his gloss on the Temple of Venus, *Teseida,* VII. 1 ff.

10. On the relation of Spenser to Burton, see Merritt Y. Hughes, 'Burton on Spenser', *PMLA,* 41 (1926), 545–67 (excerpted in Variorum, II, 459–62, but the location of article is omitted). Hughes does not take up the difference between the psychology of the *Anatomy* and Spenser's in Book II.

cious if they be exhorbitant".' In the subsections intervening between these two quotations, Burton lists and describes the irascible perturbations as sorrow, fear, shame and disgrace, envy, malice, hatred, emulation, faction, desire of revenge, anger, discontents, cares, and miseries. It is a measure of how swaying and uncertain the lines of demarcation are in this kind of literature that, when he comes to list the concupiscible perturbation, he indeed includes 'love of gaming, etc., and pleasures immoderate' (referring to 'sensual epicures and brutish prodigals, drink, and women'), but he also includes ambition, covetousness, self-love, vainglory, pride, love of learning or overmuch study. These are not included by many other authorities, or by Spenser, who here is closer to Plato and to the other sources just quoted. (Probably Burton was thinking of distinguishing between the two categories in terms of one's being based on love and the other on hate.)

Spenser, then, was drawn in Book II towards what happened to be a stylish Platonic dichotomy in the description of intemperance. This dichotomy suited his structural purposes well, and it is from that point of view that I shall be discussing it. Yet one feels the need on one occasion for a concrete *topos*, or a more specific tradition than seems to be available. For the purposes of so programmatic a description of the moral categories as the verses in which he first set forth this dichotomy, one suspects there may be a specific ancestor, particularly since the weakness attributed to the impatient does not always seem important to Spenser's own working out of the matter in Book II (see Guyon's and the Palmer's definitions at II. i. 57, 58).

In a French emblem-book published in 1555,[11] which Spenser may have seen, is an illustration of Grillus, the pig immortalized by Plutarch.[12] As one of Ulysses' sailors transformed by Circe, he was unwilling to accept his leader's help so as to be turned back into a man (figure 5). He is shown in conversation with Ulysses, and the verses below the picture elaborate on the vicious circle in which all are caught who embark on a career of sensuality. Grillus is the original of Spenser's hoggish Grill, rankest of those transformed by Acrasia, and abandoned to voluntary swinishness at the very end of *Faerie Queene* II. It is tempting to see in Guyon's definition in the first canto of this form of intemperance, 'The strong through pleasure soonest falles', a reflection of the title of this emblem:

11. Petrus Costalius (Pierre Coustau), *Petri Costalii Pegma, cum narrationibus philosophicis* (Lyon, 1555), p. 176.

12. In his *Bruta animalia ratione uti*, 986 f., printed in all editions of his *Moralia*. The Greek form of the name means 'pig'.

Figure 5. Ulysses and Grillus. From Petrus Costalius (Pierre Coustau), *Petri Costalii Pegma, cum narrationibus philosophicis* (Lyon, 1555), p. 176.

Voluptatem immanissimus Quisque Sequitur Lubens:

[He who is fiercest (?) (most violent?) willingly follows pleasure]

Mordant, the immediate object of Guyon's definition, is, after all, not only 'strong' but also 'violent' and 'fierce' in the terms of Acrasia's charm, two stanzas above this, where his name is directly etymologized as he *'that death does give'* (55.5). He is also, more routinely, a knight whose 'high courage' moved him 'his puissant force to prove' (50). Like Grill he has, of course, been caught up in intemperate appetite under the domination of Circe-Acrasia. Yet tempting as this association between the first and last cantos is for a structural interpretation of the book, not much evidential weight can be put on this title because it is unlikely that Spenser would have understood 'immanissimus' to mean 'fierce, violent'. By this word the creator of the emblem, Pierre Coustau, probably meant something like 'most inhuman' or 'most monstrous'. The verses beneath the cut begin 'Qui tibi Grille feri stomachum moveri parentes? [What parents impelled you, Grillus, to the proclivities of a wild beast?] 'Immanissimus', therefore, doubtlessly carries an implication connected with the monstrous interlocutor of Ulysses. Coustau's French adaptor gives the simple title 'Le Vice Plait au Mechant'.[13] It follows, therefore, that we should continue to look for the source, if any, of Spenser's definition, although the emblem itself is of great interest. In connection with all this discussion, Spenser's statement at the beginning of II. vi that pleasure is more difficult to resist than pain ought, no doubt, to be taken into account. As Hulbert points out, there is a general medieval tradition for this opinion, and it is not strictly correct to say (as she does) that Aristotle maintains only the opposite of this. In *Nicomachean Ethics*, II. iii, he expresses the sentiment (which he attributes to Heraclitus) that it is hard to fight against anger, but harder still to fight against pleasure.

Before examining the moralized landscapes of Acrasia and Mammon, we may look at the other important ways in which Spenser deploys the two kinds of intemperance in Book II. In chivalric adventure, Guyon struggles alternately with the two brother-knights, sons of Acrates: fiery, raging Pyrochles, whose heart is consumed with disdain for all rivals, and Cymochles, lascivious, wavering, and unsteady in his knightly commitments as the waves of the sea, to which his name refers.

---

13. *Le Pegme de Pierre Coustau...*, adapted into French by Lantaume de Romieu (Lyon, 1560).

In accordance with this name, Cymochles is most at home floating at hazard in the boat or on the island of the pleasure-loving Phaedria (vi. 5–8) or on the sea-swallowed isle of Acrasia's Bower (v. 28, 35). Trifling with Phaedria, Acrasia's dependent, or glimpsing through apparently sleep-closed eyes the impudicity of loose ladies and lascivious boys (v. 28), he happily abandons himself to titillating lewdness and sloth. As a knight he can be awakened to action only fitfully. Pyrochles, on the contrary, is the seeker of Occasion (iv. 44) and the victim of Furor (v. 23); he has as his touchingly devoted squire one whose name properly means in Old French 'challenge', 'incitement to battle':[14] 'His am I *Atin*, his in wrong and right' (iv. 42). Pyrochles tries to end his suffering in the same lake where his brother and Phaedria are most at home, but his inward fire, corresponding to the meaning of his name, is too strong to allow him to feel the effect of the watery element (vi. 44).

It is a significant feature of the plot of Book II that Guyon struggles with each brother in turn, but that Arthur, who combines all virtues in himself and embodies as well at this point (canto viii) the grace of God, fights and destroys both brothers together in chivalric adventure. In the tradition of symbolic blows, Arthur's most telling one against Cymochles is in the seat of desire.

> His poinant speare he thrust with puissant sway
> At proud *Cymochles*, whiles his shield was wyde,
> And through his thigh the mortall steele did gryde;
> He swarving with the force, within his flesh
> Did breake the launce, and let the head abyde:
> Out of the wound the red bloud flowed fresh,
> That underneath his feet soone made a purple plesh.
> [viii. 36]

And because, in the language of wounds, reason in both brothers is deprived of her due regality, Arthur kills Cymochles with a blow to the brain and cuts off Pyrochles' head. Like Mammon on another occasion, Pyrochles, held helpless on the ground, did not 'upward cast his eye, / For vile disdaine and rancour . . .' (viii. 50).

As in chivalric adventures, Arthur deals simultaneously, not consecutively, with the two forms of intemperance in moralized landscape. In

---

14. See A. Kent Hieatt, 'Spenser's Atin from *Atine?' Modern Language Notes*, 62 (1957), 249–51. Clarence Steinberg, 'Atin, Pyrochles, Cymochles: On Irish Emblems in "The Faerie Queene"', *Neuphilologische Mitteilungen*, 72 (1971), 749–61, offers an Irish derivation of 'Atin', but acknowledges (p. 755) that 'polyglot etymologizing' is likely here.

the battle to save Alma and her house—the soul and the body—from the onslaught of the vices in canto xi, it is Arthur, not the otherwise occupied Guyon, who defeats their leader Intemperance, or Maleger, and his hag-helpers Impotence and Impatience, the most obvious of all the embodiments of the dichotomy which had been presented to us in the first canto: Cymochlean Impotence, tempting by the delaying devices of indulgence; Pyrochlean Impatience, armed with raging flame and holding broken chains and bands. When Arthur succeeds in killing their leader, they destroy themselves.

The pattern of their fates is reversed, however, from that of 'Cymochlean' Mordant and 'Pyrochlean' Amavia, for each overwhelms herself with the opposite element. Impatience, like her opposite Mordant, takes her end by water (as Pyrochles had been unable to do), throwing herself headlong into a lake; Impotence, much like her opposite Amavia, rives herself to the heart with a dart taken from her master. The reversals make sense in one way, because with the soul's conquest of intemperance, its two forms cancel each other out in the achievement of the mean which is between them; but this sudden reversal of roles—sensual relaxation resorting to violence and disdainful 'teene' turning at last to the element which has been emblematic of appetite—will also be paralleled in the two landscapes of Mammon and Acrasia. Likewise the story of Phedon in iv. 17–33, a man so subject to Occasion and Furor as obviously to suffer in the same way as Pyrochles, shows that he was caught up in a rivalry involving sensual desire, much as were Acrasia, Amavia, and Mordant. The sensual bliss which Acrasia offers is faulty not simply in deflecting the sensualist from the paths of honourable achievement, but also in another social consequence. In trying to safeguard that bliss from interlopers he, or she, may suddenly reverse the moral field by resorting to jealous violence. That Amavia did not resort to violent revenge, as did Acrasia and Phedon, is a reason for Spenser's twice stressing Amavia's lack of criminality.

The case may seem forced until we have looked carefully at Acrasia, but we may visualize one more opposed possibility in advance. Just as appetite may fall over into jealous rivalry, so a quality which is primarily prideful—disdainful exclusivity—may be reinforced by appetite. This is a more arbitrary association than the first one, but it is a generally admitted observation that temptations to vice often seem to be reinforced by a totally extraneous attraction at the last moment. The Spenserian mythic embodiment of this experience in the Cave of Mammon seems not to have been lost on Milton.

The episode of Belphoebe and the fabulously spurious *miles gloriosus* Braggadocchio in canto iii is really the pendant satyr-play on the subject of the two forms of intemperance. In *Faerie Queene* III and IV, Belphoebe is by definition temperate, because of her natural virginity. For the purposes of Book II, her natural honourableness is also stressed. Braggadocchio tries to entice her first with the vain and invidious honours of court life, very much as Mammon is later to offer them to Guyon. Her response is the same as Guyon's except that it springs from the pastoral source of the similar response to court life in Book VI and *Colin Clouts Come Home Againe*: for the truly innocent, honour is incomprehensible except as a consequence of honourable deeds:

> Abroad in armes, at home in studious kind
> Who seeks with painfull toile, shall honor soonest find.
>   [II. iii. 40]

From his risibly ineffective proffer of his own kind of hollow honour Braggadocchio now modulates without pause into the opposite intemperance, that of appetite, and burns in filthy lust (iii. 42) when Belphoebe, still discoursing loftily on true honours, happens to mention the always wide open doors of Pleasure's palace. It goes without saying that she repulses this tentative (and slams this door) as briskly as the other. Like Arthur and unlike Guyon she dispatches both forms of intemperance almost simultaneously. Since she is also Elizabeth I, it is just that she should equal Arthur in ability (and expeditious that she should honour the toil 'in studious kind' of a poet, as well as her own noted scholarship), even if this ability is mimed in a farce.

Just as Guyon deals at the level of chivalric adventure quite separately with the two forms of intemperance exemplified by Pyrochles and Cymochles, and as Arthur at the same level defeats them in combination, so at the level of moralized landscape Guyon finds and defeats only one of the forms of intemperance in the House of Mammon, and only the opposite form in the Bower, while Arthur, in the moralized landscape of the House of Alma, dispatches intemperance in both its forms in one battle. This quadripartite pattern is really the main structural feature of the plot of *Faerie Queene* II. The main sticking point for anyone faced with this theory for the first time is the ascription of only one kind of intemperance to the Cave of Mammon, but it is best to turn first to Acrasia and her forces, among whom Phaedria represents most plainly the opposite form of intemperance to that of Mammon.

Phaedria differs significantly at one point from her mistress, giving no suggestion of the violence latent in Acrasia as a rival rather than merely as a seductress. She is a plain case of one alternative in the Renaissance *topos* of Hercules at the crossroads: she is pleasure against Guyon's virtue or honourable exploits,[15] like Samuel Daniel's siren debating on honour:

> Ulysses, O be not deceiv'd
> With that unreal name,
> This honour is a thing conceiv'd,
> And rests on others' fame;
>   Begotten only to molest
> Our peace and to beguile
> (The best thing of our life) our rest,
> And give us up to toil.
>   ['Ulysses and the Siren', 17–24]

When rivalry arises between her apparent admirers, Phaedria's behaviour is at its most attractive, and answers the sentiment of Campion's (and Catullus') lover of Lesbia:

> If all would lead their lives in love like me,
> Then bloody swords and armour should not be;
> No drum nor trumpet peaceful sleeps should move,
> Unless alarm came from the camp of love.
>   ['My sweetest Lesbia', 7–10]

Phaedria says:

> But if for me ye fight, or me will serve,
>   Not this rude kind of battell, nor these armes
>   Are meet, the which doe men in bale to sterve,
>   And dolefull sorrow heape with deadly harmes:
>   Such cruel game my scarmoges disarmes:
>   Another warre, and other weapons I
>   Doe love, where love does give his sweet alarmes,
>   Without bloudshed, and where the enemy
> Does yeeld unto his foe a pleasant victory.

15. Cf. the treatment of the theme in terms of Mars as a knight unmanned by Venus and sleeping while putti play with his arms, in Botticelli's 'Mars and Venus' in the National Gallery, London (reproduced in Edgar Wind, *Pagan Mysteries in the Renaissance*, 2nd ed., London, 1967, plate 74).

Debatefull strife, and cruell enmitie
    The famous name of knighthood fowly shend;
    But lovely peace, and gentle amitie,
    And in Amours the passing houres to spend,
    The mightie martiall hands doe most commend;
    Of love they ever greater glory bore,
    Then of their armes: *Mars* is *Cupidoes* frend,
    And is for *Venus* loves renowmed more,
Then all his wars and spoiles, the which he did of yore.
            [II. vi. 34–35]

This compares favourably with hundreds of other such instances of this commonplace in the verse and plastic arts of the Renaissance. After pacifying Guyon and Cymochles, Phaedria very beautifully, if meretriciously, forces the reader to pause with her in the middle of the first line of stanza 36, when she 'sweetly smyld'. It is not simply a commonplace that, with the most delicate but vital of differences, Spenser makes the whole scene and her speech mirror the episode and speech of Medina, also in Book II, with Guyon, Huddibras, and Sans-loy, the three scufflers in her parlour:

And were there rightfull cause of difference,
    Yet were not better, faire it to accord,
    Then with bloud guiltinesse to heape offence,
    And mortall vengeance joyne to crime abhord?
    O fly from wrath, fly, O my liefest Lord:
    Sad be the sights and bitter fruits of warre,
    And thousand furies wait on wrathfull sword;
    Ne ought the prayse of prowesse more doth marre,
Then fowle revenging rage, and base contentious jarre.

But lovely concord, and most sacred peace
    Doth nourish vertue, and fast friendship breeds;
    Weake she makes strong, and strong thing does increace,
    Till it the pitch of highest prayse exceeds:
    Brave be her warres, and honorable deeds,
    By which she triumphs over ire and pride,
    And winnes an Olive girlond for her meeds:
    Be therefore, O my deare Lords, pacifide,
And this misseeming discord meekely lay aside.
            [ii. 30–31]

The wars of Phaedria are those of Cupid; Medina's wars are those of Concord. There is pleasure in considering the symmetry between the entire speech of Medina along with its effects on her three fighters (ii. 30–32), and that of Phaedria and its corresponding effect on her two.[16] Phaedria has the right answers, as far as they go. In the triadic organization of the soul, she spells out the knowing criticism of the senses and the appetite against the excesses of the spirited and impatiently contentious irascible part. Instead of a song about a rose, such as is sung in the presence of Acrasia, she sings of the lily of the field (vi. 15–17). Christ's message is distorted to the slackness of her Idle Lake, yet there is more here than meets the eye: again she has the right answer, but not the full one. The following are the relevant verses (Matthew 6: 25, 26, 28, 29) taken from the Gospel for the fifteenth Sunday after Trinity in the Second Prayer-Book of Edward VI:

> Therefore I saye unto you; be not carefull for your lyfe, what ye shall eate or what ye shall dryncke: nor yet for your body, what raymente ye shall put on. Is not the life more than meate? and the body more of value than raymente? Beholde the fowles of the ayre, for they sowe not, neither do they reape, nor cary into the barnes; and your heavenly father fedeth them. . . . And why care ye for rayment: Consider the Lylies of the fielde how they growe. They laboure not; neither do they spynne. And yet I saye unto you, that even Solomon in al his royaltie, was not clothed like one of these

In the second place, however, the twenty-fourth verse, immediately preceding this passage and in the same Gospel for the fifteenth Sunday after Trinity, reads as follows:

> No manne can serve two Masters, for either he shal hate the one, and love the other, or els leane to the one, and despise the other: Ye canne not serve God and Mammon.

For the song of the representative of the simply appetitive part of the soul, then, Spenser has chosen a suitable biblical passage, which is immediately annexed to a passage about the chief representative in

16. This is treated at length in A. Kent Hieatt, 'A Spenser to Structure Our Myths: Medina, Phaedria, Proserpina, Acrasia, Venus, Isis', in *Contemporary Thought on Edmund Spenser*, ed. Richard C. Frushell and Bernard J. Vondersmith (Carbondale, Ill., 1975).

Book II of the purely irascible part, Mammon, described also in Luke 16: 9–13 as the Mammon of unrighteousness. Phaedria is for pleasure at any cost; Mammon is for worldly honour at any cost. Little wonder that she retorts ably upon him. Yet her answer is insufficient, for it rises no higher than the vegetable and animal souls; human reason is not in her.

Acrasia and her Bower have already been considered in chapter 7. We need to remember that those in the Bower seem to be awarded the most natural and innocent of affectionate pleasures and to evade the problem of the evanescence of beauty and bliss through having accepted a natural, delicious setting which escapes from time. In effect, however, the artful durability of the Bower is a mineral sterility, the opposite of the eternity in mutability of the Garden of Adonis and its teeming vitality. The suggestion of that latter Garden in the name Verdant of Acrasia's latest youthful victim is a further characteristic touch, as is the vegetative image applied to Mordant, dead through the agency of Acrasia: 'Now in his freshest flowre of lustie hed/... fiers fate did crop the blossome of his age' (i. 41). Ultimately Acrasia is transparently modelled on the enchantress Circe of the *Odyssey*. Like Circe, she rules an island on which the men whom she entices to love her are turned to beasts. The commonly moralized meaning of the Circe story in the Renaissance is that under the influence of sexual appetite man's reason loses its due regality, and he thus descends the chain of Being to the next lower, animal degree. In the Bower, Guyon's object must be to defeat the exclusively Cymochlean variety of intemperance. Such animals reappear as the unruly servants of Milton's son of Circe, Comus,

> And they, so perfect is their misery,
> Not once perceive their foul disfigurement,
> But boast themselves more comely than before
> And all their friends, and native home forget
> To roll with pleasure in a sensual sty.
> [*Comus*, 73–77]

Like these, the hog Grill refuses at the end of the book to leave his sty so as to be restored to manhood. Milton seems to take notice above of Spenser's preparation of this point in canto i, where Amavia says of her husband's situation on Acrasia's island, 'so transformed from his former skill / That me he knew not, neither his own ill' (54).

One curious point concerning the Bower of Bliss could not have been missed by so close a reader of Torquato Tasso's *Gerusalemme liberata* as we know Milton to have been. Much in Spenser's Bower (as Dryden, for instance, knew) is straightforwardly adapted, or even, sometimes, translated, from canto xvi of the Italian heroic poem, reciting the similar situation of the hero Rinaldo and his seductress Armida. The descriptions of the entry of the rescue party of two into Armida's domain and of the entry of Guyon and the Palmer into the Garden are markedly similar. Yet precisely at the point where certain pictorial representations on the face of the gate are described, Spenser departs from his original and substitutes a new feature, leaving something like a neatly cut out hole in the close fabric of his conversion of the Italian narrative to his own purpose. In one representation on his gates, Tasso gives us Hercules in woman's garments, spinning wool among the maids of 'Iole' (presumably meaning Omphale): she carries his club and wears his lion's skin. In another he gives us both Antony following Cleopatra as she fled from the Battle of Actium, and Antony's suicide (xvi. 3–7). The commonplace *significatio* of the first scene is that Hercules has deserted virtue and honour, and for pleasure's sake has accepted a womanish, inactive role, allowing his female partner to pre-empt the man's dominant part; the *significatio* of the second is that Antony has given up the honour of ruling the world for the sake of his desire for a fearful woman. These representations, then, would seem to have been as well tailored to the relationship of Verdant and Acrasia as to that of Rinaldo and Armida, for both men have surrendered will and honour to their beloveds. Yet Spenser avoids both scenes. What he gives us instead are two incidents from the stormy life of Medea with her lover Jason. In one she has dismembered her brother Aegialeus and thrown the gobbets of flesh overboard to deflect their father, who is pursuing in another ship as she escapes with her lover:[17]

> Ye might have seene the frothy billowes fry
>   Under the ship, as thorough them she went,
>   That seemd the waves were into yvory,
>   Or yvory into the waves were sent:
>   And other where the snowy substaunce sprent
>   With vermell, like the boyes bloud therein shed,
>   A piteous spectacle did represent.
>   [II. xii. 45]

Elsewhere on the portal, at the later stage when Jason had transferred

17. For the sources of this and the following, see Variorum note, II, 372–74.

his affections to a rival, Medea has already sent the enchanted robe to this rival, Creusa. When the bride dons the garment, the spell materializes: she is burned to death (xii. 45. 8–9).

To understand why Spenser has chosen to place these scenes at the entrance to the Bower instead of using what Tasso offered him, we need first to compare the passage just quoted from canto xii with another one describing Amavia's condition from canto i:

> Pittifull spectacle of deadly smart,
>> Beside a bubbling fountaine low she lay,
>> Which she increased with her bleeding hart,
>> And the cleane waves with purple gore did ray.
>>> [i. 40]

There is considerable verbal and conceptual similarity between the 'piteous spectacle' of the later lines and the 'Pittifull spectacle' of the earlier ones. Blood which is shed in violence melts in water in both cases, and in both cases the violence is finally a consequence of intemperate sexual passion—Medea's and Acrasia's. Furthermore, when we turn our attention to the destruction of Creusa, we perceive a closer similarity between the cases of the two enchantresses: in opposing her rival Amavia, who seems to have stolen back her husband, Acrasia maliciously works a spell at a distance in order to destroy her lost lover and indirectly to compass the destruction of the rival; when Jason, on the other hand, is to be joined in the bands of true wedlock with Creusa, Medea destroys the rival herself by a spell worked covertly at a distance. Thus, no enormity is too great for sensualists like Acrasia and Medea. If it seems that Acrasia herself is too coldly devoted to vice to be caught up like Medea in her emotion for a lover, the reader might remember that the actual love scene between Acrasia and Verdant is ambiguous on just this point, and that, if Spenser seems to have left us an impression of Acrasia as a cold-blooded adder, he himself had before his mind's eye Circe in love with Odysseus, and the seductress Armida, swept away for the first time in her passion for Rinaldo. The clinching point here in showing that Spenser is mysteriously suggesting to us a lethal resemblance between violent Medea and the apparently lethargic Acrasia of the Bower is that Acrasia's, and Armida's, clearest prototype, Circe, was the aunt of Medea according to a tradition that Spenser would have known.

That Milton would have recognized the whole pattern involved in the departure from Tasso seems next to certain. He would have immediately perceived the appropriateness of, and the reason for, linking the two enchantresses in violence, for he thus linked Medea and Circe in a poem of his own as early as his seventeenth year:[18]

> Si triste fatum verba Hecatëia
> Fugare possint, Telegoni parens
>   Vixisset infamis, potentique
>   Aegiali soror usa virga.
>   ['In Obitum Procancellarii Medici', 17–20]

[If witch-spells could banish sad fate, then the mother of Telegonus would have lived on in her infamy, and the sister of Aegialeus lived on to use her potent wand. 'On the Death of the Vice-Chancellor, A Physician']

That is, life would have continued for the witch Circe, mother by Odysseus of Telegonus, who later unintentionally killed his father, and for the witch Medea, who dismembered her brother Aegialeus and threw the pieces overboard to distract her father from the pursuit of her lover and herself.[19] Conceivably, of course, Milton may have been alerted to one aspect of this association by first seeing it in his actual reading of *Faerie Queene*, II. xii; in any case he would have been ready to recognize what Spenser intended.

In terms of the formal, mythic structure of Book II, what Spenser has done in this initial episode of the Bower of Bliss is to suggest the same inherent instability and tendency to fall into an opposite form of intemperance which he ascribes, for instance, to the end of Impotence in Arthur's struggle before the House of Alma and which we shall see in the final episode of the Cave of Mammon. Water is the general emblem of the intemperance of appetite in Book II at large, as in Cymochles' name, in the Idle Lake and boat of Phaedria, and in the Odyssean sea journey to the floating isle of Acrasia herself. Here, however, Pyrochlean fire and daggered violence like that of impatient Amavia or Phedon in their extremity appear mysteriously on the very portal of what appears to be sensual bliss.

Beyond that portal pleasures as enchanting as professional expertise can concoct await Verdant and his kind. Oblivious of honour, arms laid aside, they bathe in slumbrous bliss in Acrasia's lap. In time, having lost

---

18. Carey-Fowler, p. 28.
19. According to Apollodorus, I. 112–13. The brother's name is Absyrtus in another account.

all discourse of reason, they take on the shape of brutes. Of them all Grill is the worst, because when offered salvation by one who has harrowed this hell, he cannot conceive an advantage in leaving his brutish kind at that crucial point in the affairs of men when the tide is at the full and a brisk wind stands in the right quarter to carry him and his companions away from desolation. The Palmer, using the wand which is the antidote of the one belonging to Acrasia's servant, the false Genius (and of the one belonging to Milton's Comus), has turned them all back to men, but Grill must be left behind.

> Streight way he with his vertuous staffe them strooke,
>   And streight of beasts they comely men became;
>   Yet being man they did unmanly looke,
>   And stared ghastly, some for inward shame,
>   And some for wrath, to see their captive Dame:
>   But one above the rest in speciall,
>   That had an hog beene late, hight *Grille* by name,
>   Repined greatly, and did him miscall,
> That had from hoggish forme him brought to naturall.
>
> Said *Guyon*, see the mind of beastly man,
>   That hath so soone forgot the excellence
>   Of his creation, when he life began,
>   That now he chooseth, with vile difference,
>   To be a beast, and lack intelligence.
>   To whom the Palmer thus, The donghill kind
>   Delights in filth and foule incontinence:
>   Let *Grill* be *Grill*, and have his hoggish mind,
> But let us hence depart, whilest wether serves and wind.
>   [xii. 86–87]

It is perhaps more our own metaphor than Spenser's when we see Adam in Verdant (or in Verdant's predecessor, the more advanced case, Mordant), and think of Guyon as a Christ figure restoring reluctant man to the 'excellence of his creation' and determinedly harrowing a Satanic kingdom:

> But all those pleasant bowres and Pallace brave,
>   *Guyon* broke downe, with rigour pittilesse;
>   Ne ought their goodly workmanship might save
>   Them from the tempest of his wrathfulnesse,
>   But that their blisse he turn'd to balefulnesse:

Their groves he feld, their gardins did deface,
Their arbers spoyle, their Cabinets suppresse,
Their banket houses burne, their buildings race,
And of the fairest late, now made the fowlest place.
[xii. 83]

For Spenser does not really include a cloud of symbols bearing
Christian witness in this adventure. Rinaldo, in the Tassonian ensemble
closest to Spenser's imagination here, had given up for love what was at
least a Christian cause, the recovery of the Holy City from the Infidel.
Verdant, his counterpart, has forsaken only the cause of honour in
general, playing the part of Mars to Acrasia's Venus; and Guyon's main
prototypes here seem similarly distant from the Gospel.

Yet when we turn to the adventure of the House of Mammon and to
the conquest of that part of intemperance that is rooted, not in pleasure,
but in pride and rivalry, we find a hero whom modern criticism fairly
generally recognizes as re-enacting Christ's part in his Temptation by
Satan during the forty days in the Wilderness. Spenser even limits
Guyon's stay in the House of Mammon to the substance of forty stanzas
(from line 3 of stanza 26 to line 4 of stanza 66) in a surely numerological
gesture.[20] At the end of his ordeal in canto vii, Guyon, like Christ,
receives angelic ministration, with the difference that Guyon is not
Christ himself but a soldier enlisted under him and an imitator of him.
Although Guyon's unaided human powers are greatly human ones, they
are insufficient to save him from mortal danger in the exhaustion after
his ordeal, so that the agency of the ministering angel becomes that of
divine grace to a mere man. Arthur, the subsequent instrument of that

---

20. There are thirty-nine complete stanzas between Guyon's entrance and exit (stanzas
27 through 65). Guyon actually effects entrance at line 5 of stanza 26, the stanza
immediately preceding this series (adding this line and the four remaining lines of this
stanza to the series). He exits in line 4 of stanza 66, the stanza immediately following the
series 27 through 65, so as to add four more lines. The odd lines total precisely one stanza,
making a stanza total of forty, or 360 lines. The only objection to this assumption is that
Guyon might be construed to have entered the House of Mammon at line 3 instead of line
5 of stanza 26. I quote five lines and part of a sixth of this stanza:

So soone as *Mammon* there arriv'd, the dore
  To him did open, and affoorded way;
  Him followed eke Sir *Guyon* evermore,
  Ne darkenesse him, ne daunger might dismay,
  Soone as he entred was, the dore streight way
  Did shut....

I suppose, however, that in line 3 we are being told that Guyon continued the course of
action of following Mammon ('followed...evermore', in normal sixteenth-century
idiom), undeterred by the darkness and danger now evident as the door is opened,

grace, saves Guyon in his swoon by defeating the combined forces of Pyrochles and Cymochles, as we have seen.

Although Guyon is obviously occupied with the conquest of Cymochlean, appetitive intemperance in the Bower, it has apparently not been suggested previously that in the House of Mammon he is occupied exclusively with the intemperance belonging to the 'spirited', 'impatient' part of the soul, caught up in the violent search for paramountcy by every means. The evidence for this notion, is, however, extensive. At the beginning of the encounter, Mammon, the tempter, is characteristically Pyrochlean:

> Thereat with staring eyes fixed askaunce,
> In great disdaine, he answerd; Hardy Elfe,
> That darest vew my direfull countenaunce,
> I read thee rash, and heedlesse of thy selfe,
> To trouble my still seate, and heapes of pretious pelfe.
>
> [vii. 7]

In a debate, say, like Samuel Daniel's *Musophilus*, between the idealist and the seeker of honours in this world, Mammon would be on the side of Philocosmus ('World-lover'). Mammon is not a heavenly god: 'God of the world and worldlings I me call, / Great *Mammon*, greatest god below the skye' (vii. 8). But in the ensuing discussion we hear of none of the promised fleshly joys that moved Marlowe's Faustus or any of the libidinous fancies that so exercised Ben Jonson's Sir Epicure Mammon. Rather, what is promised is what Satan offered to Christ, invidious distinction, the intemperate wish of the spirited part of the soul: 'Riches, renowme, and principality, / Honour, estate and all this worldes good' (vii. 8). Guyon's retort is close to the one made by Belphoebe

---

towards the door and perhaps right into the portal, but that the process of entering through it is not complete until line 5.

A similar intrusion of the mensurating device upon gradual process in *Epithalamion* occurs (as I point out in *Short Time's Endless Monument*) in lines 296–300:

> Now cease ye damsels your delights forepast;
> Enough it is, that all the day was yours;
> Now day is doen, and night is nighing fast:
> Now bring the Bryde into the brydall boures.
> Now night is come, now soone her disaray.

The gradual descent of the sun below the horizon, watched in the previous stanza, now brings night at the end of precisely sixteen and one-quarter stanza-hours, in the last line above, conforming to the prescription in *De sphaera* for the longest day of the year in the northernmost clime. See my description of Spenser's symbolic use (parallel to this one) of forty stanzas elsewhere: 'A Numerical Key for Spenser's *Amoretti* and Guyon in the House of Mammon', *Yearbook of English Studies*, 3 (1973), 14–27.

to Braggadocchio: worldly principality is a worthwhile goal for the temperate man called to it, but must be contended for with the true coin of knightly valour:

Regard of worldly mucke doth fowly blend,
And low abase the high heroicke spright,
That joyes for crownes and kingdomes to contend.

[vii. 10]

The frantic thirst for such honours in the House of Mammon (honours which are completely forgotten in the slumbrous Bower) distorts the right relation between virtue and reward. Rewards, says Mammon, can be most easily purchased with money (vii. 11). Guyon moves on to argue that wealth is a source of disquiet, 'got with guile and preserved with dread', a sentiment fully supported by the landscape of the suburbs of hell into which Mammon now introduces him. Spenser's other hell, in Book I of *The Faerie Queene*, shows us a Cymochlean lecher almost as soon as we enter: Sisyphus, punished for his attempt on Juno (I. v. 35). Guyon, however, is met by Pain, Strife, Revenge, Despite, Treason, Hate, Jealousy, Fear, Sorrow, Shame, Horror, and 'sad Celeno'; neither here nor later do we encounter merely sensual intemperate figures.

Unlike the wide open portal of Acrasia's realm, the shut door of the House of Mammon is tiny, hidden, and closely guarded (II. vii. 24–25). It is largely on the basis of narrative expediency that Spenser, or any of his great visionary predecessors, chooses which variety of landscape to moralize at any particular point. It would have been possible to show Acrasia's garden leading as surely to an actual hell as does Mammon's gold; and the fact that Acrasia's gates stand always open may relate not only to the commonplace that, at the crossroads, the way to pleasure is broad and easy, but also to Virgil's

facilis descensus Averno:
noctes atque dies patet atri ianua Ditis;
sed revocare gradum superasque evadere ad auras,
hoc opus, hic labor est.

[*Aeneid*, VI. 126–29]

[Easy is the descent to Avernus: night and day the door of gloomy Dis stands open; where work and trouble lie is in retracing your steps and getting out into the open air.]

Of these two propositions, the second, but not the first, holds for the House of Mammon as well.

The significant figures whom we meet as we pass through the adytum and carefully cumulated sanctuaries of this underground dwelling, in our progress towards its Holy of Holies, are motivated by infernal pride; that is, they are animated by disdainful exclusivity, hateful competitiveness, angry insistence on personal deserving, and the determination to get ahead of others at all costs. At first we see no figures at all. Mammon begins his temptation with coin—chest upon chest, surrounded with skulls, and said to be warily guarded by one 'covetous Spright' against many other 'covetous feends' (vii. 32). When this is seen to have no effect on Guyon, Mammon takes him on to its physical source, the vast chamber of glittering fiery furnaces where the gold is wrung from the earth by busy, gleaming-eyed demons. We remember the name and fiery quality of Pyrochles, and the so different approach to Acrasia's domain, over wastes of heaving water in which Cymochles' name is memorialized. When the gold of worldly advantage is seen not to move Guyon, Mammon uses a still more direct method. He shows Guyon what, in its more intestine reaches, the House of Mammon is really about: worldly advantage itself, to which money is an adjunct. The evidence for this demonstration is the chamber of his daughter Philotime ('love of honour'), of which the porter who guards the entrance is, again, Disdain.

> There, as in glistring glory she did sit,
>> She held a great gold chaine ylincked well,
>> Whose upper end to highest heaven was knit,
>> And lower part did reach to lowest Hell;
>> And all that preace did round about her swell,
>> To catchen hold of that long chaine, thereby
>> To clime aloft, and others to excell:
>> That was *Ambition*, rash desire to sty,
> And every lincke thereof a step of dignity.

> Some thought to raise themselves to high degree,
>> By riches and unrighteous reward,
>> Some by close shouldring, some by flatteree;
>> Others through friends, others for base regard;
>> And all by wrong wayes for themselves prepard.
>> Those that were up themselves, kept others low,
>> Those that were low themselves, held others hard,
>> Ne suffred them to rise or greater grow,
> But every one did strive his fellow downe to throw.
>>> [vii. 46–47]

At this point in the narrative money loses its primacy, and only in order of enumeration is first among those ways of gaining honour which do not relate to merit. In our concern with Milton, we note that until Philotime fell from heaven she had been a spirit heavenly fair, but that now she has had to seek hypocritical counterfeits to cloak her crime (vii. 45). As well, she must be defended by a lie. Mammon calls her

> The fairest wight that wonneth under skye
> But that this darksome neather world her light
> Doth dim with horrour and deformitie,
> Worthy of heaven and hye felicitie,
> From whence the gods have her for envy thrust.
>   [vii. 49]

The horror is her own, and her own Satanic pride has felled her. Mammon offers her to Guyon:

> But sith thou hast found favour in mine eye,
>   Thy spouse I will her make, if that thou lust,
> That she may thee advaunce for workes and merites just.
>   [vii. 49]

The marriage is not to give Guyon sensual delight; the point is that she can get him ahead. The same holds true for her counterfeited beauty's beam which is designed to call more lovers to her, in stanza 45. They are to be lovers of glittering pomp, not of a fleshly woman. Tudor regality is all that Spenser has in mind. Mammon is showing to this *Microchristos* all the kingdoms of the world, and the glory of them.

Something very strange occurs in Guyon's reply to the offer to him of Philotime. Instead of the scornfully low valuation which he has put upon Mammon's other offered boons, he speaks here, with humility, and without irony, as though Philotime were really worth having:

> Gramercy *Mammon* (said the gentle knight)
>   For so great grace and offred high estate;
>   But I, that am fraile flesh and earthly wight,
>   Unworthy match for such immortall mate
>   My selfe well wote, and mine unequall fate.
>   [vii. 50]

It is true that he goes on to avow that his love belongs to another lady; but why the sudden gentleness and the emphasis on the unsuitability of a human's aspiration to divine commerce? Why does he not continue roundly in the immediately preceding vein of 'Suffise it then, thou Money God (quoth hee) / That all thine idle offers I refuse. / ... With such vaine shewes thy worldlings vile abuse' (39)? It seems clear that Spenser's only motive here is to prepare the ground for what Mammon is now to offer Guyon as his greatest dainty in his sanctum, the Garden of Proserpina. The silver seat of this queen of Pluto's, under a central tree that covers her whole island and dips into the filthy river around it, is 'in the midst', at the very centre of the whole of Book II. Even here, money remains in evidence, for in addition to the silver of the seat, the apples of the tree are of gold, and Tantalus, one of the figures here, was, according to Renaissance authority, traditionally rich. But money is subordinated to something else.

The principal new temptation offered to those who enter here, illustrating the more drastic form of prideful intemperance, is that they should be seduced into attempting to rise above their allotted level of existence to the highest—that of the divine; or that they should, each for his own ego's sake, be led to commit enormities to reach that level, should infringe upon divine prerogative, or should even kill God. The final end of Acrasia's Bower was to deanimate men so that they would descend out of their proper being into that of beasts. The final end of Mammon's most abominable temptation, at the lowest point of hell, is that they should be misled by pride into an attempt upon the highest level of all being.

The extraordinary richness and multifariousness of symbolism in Proserpina's Garden is such as to have puzzled commentators repeatedly in the past, to the extent of leading one of them to point out that, whatever this particular ideal landscape may signify, it is an aesthetic failure because the temptations miss the first point of a temptation: they do not tempt.[21] Spenser may indeed have cancelled out some of his effects by showing as unattractive what is supposedly desirable, but in doing so he was working, in the whole of the Cave of Mammon, within a tradition of the tortured saint or Christ figure. Not only temptation is the goal; Guyon must be worn down to the point where his human powers collapse. In criticizing the unpleasantness of Spenser's images one might as well say that fifteenth- and sixteenth-century paintings of the Temptation of St. Anthony are unsuccessful because the various unspeakable beings who bedevil the saint do not tempt us.

In addition, however, Spenser suffers here from a probably drastic limitation of space owing to his numerical projects. He had vowed to himself to get Guyon out of the House of Mammon in exactly forty stanzas—no more. Further, the centre point of the entire book was to fall upon the central spot in the Garden of Proserpina—the silver chair and the golden-fruited tree—fairly late in the narrative of the events in this House (vii. 53–55). It is possible that stanza totals which had already accrued in completed sections of the two halves of Book II led Spenser to accept a location for his centre point that was inconvenient for the amount and intricacy of material which he had in mind to insert in the Garden after the description of its central feature. Or he may have been embarrassed simply by the straitness of a forty-stanza unit—360 lines—for all that he wanted to say.

For purposes of the entire action of the House of Mammon before reaching the Garden—the entry hall, the chamber of stored riches, the chamber where the riches are forged, and the audience chamber of Philotime—Spenser uses only about twenty-five stanzas, leaving fifteen for the Garden: two before the central point, three for that central point, and ten thereafter. These are not nearly enough. One datum seems sufficient to demonstrate this. It is Spenser's clear intention to show that Guyon is faint with hunger and fatigue towards the end of his stay in the House: at the end of that stay we are told so, and Guyon faints. It seems plain, then, that the final temptation which Mammon angrily offers Guyon in the Garden is meant to capitalize on this condition, yet Spenser neglects to develop the premise properly in connection with the temptation itself. Mammon asks Guyon why he does not eat one of the apples and rest his 'wearie person' in the seat; that is, Mammon suddenly reverses the field of temptation and, knowing his intended victim to be exhausted, tries for the first and only time to induce Guyon to accept through the promptings of sheer appetite what is really an emblem of prideful, invidious striving, the opposite kind of intemperance.

Milton was apparently sharp-eyed enough to see Spenser's intention (see next chapter), yet we are not really given what we need to know here about the hero's condition. Mammon's meagre and doubtful two-word attribution is not enough. Faced with such a situation in the case of any of his other heroes, Spenser himself, in his persona as narrator, typically makes very clear in five or six lines, or a stanza, that exhaustion has taken its toll (for example. I. vii. 11. 4–9, and xi. 28). Here we get almost nothing from him. He gives us the evidence of exhaustion only once—immediately after the temptation is over, but too late for most readers to feel it in connection with Mammon's words and Guyon's refusal. It is a most un-Spenserian procedure. As I have contended elsewhere, the particularly puzzling character of the last stanzaic unit of *Epithalamion* results from a numerical need to carry that unit's freight of meaning, with tremendous compression, between the 359th and 365th long line of the poem. Considering the necessary compression in the Garden of Proserpina, then, we are not really surprised that its intricate program can elude us. Spenser may have consoled himself with the reflection that that appropriate adjunct of moralized landscape, an air of the vatically arcane, was being imposed upon him merely by limitation of space. It may finally seem to the reader that what is lost in intensity of sense impressions is recovered in another way in the decorous, elegant marshalling of a multitude of interlocking symbolic systems.

The apples on the tree chiefly point to two most important figures of this symbolic nexus who are not even present in the Garden. Since we as spectators are watching a reenactment by Guyon of Christ's temptation, we reflect that the chief significance of that temptation was that it reversed and neutralized the earlier and successful temptation of Eve by Satan to eat the fruit of the tree. In the fourth chapters of the Gospels of St. Matthew and St. Luke, when the famished Jesus is urged by the tempter to turn stones into bread, he refuses (man does not live by bread alone). Similarly, when Mammon wrathfully (and no doubt with a Pyrochlean sense of reckless hopelessness) plays his last card and tries to cause Guyon to eat the golden apple (and sit in the silver seat), Guyon refuses even though he is near to fainting with hunger and fatigue.

Eve herself, then, who took the apple when Satan promised her and her husband that in eating it and gaining wisdom they should be as gods (Genesis 3:5), is a chief feature of this symbolic structure. As usual, Spenser elaborates the point with a Classical analogue: Proserpina, carried off to hell by Pluto, its god, ate half the fruit (not the apple, *malum*, but the *malum punicum*, according to Natalis Comes) which was offered to her and thus condemned herself perpetually to the Lower Regions for half of every year. It is true that, in providing a parallel to Eve, Spenser does not show us in Proserpina someone motivated by prideful aspiration to divinity, but the parallel in terms of the pathos in the loss of a fragile beauty, accompanied by the disappearance of flowers from the earth, does not seem to have been lost on Milton (see pages 236–37).

Remembering his memorable imagery on the vulnerable flower-like quality of both Eve and Proserpina, we may see another satisfying symbolic symmetry in Spenser's choice of Proserpina as an image. This anti-Garden, or anti-*locus amoenus*, of black and poisonous plants is a counterimage to the fertile and fructifying Garden of Adonis at the centre of Book III. At the arithmetical centre of each book is the seat of a god who is the basis of a seasonal myth: Adonis, who dies at the beginning of winter and is reborn in the spring, and Proserpina, who is condemned to her underground existence for the winter months;[22] both figures live with their divine paramours.

Among others in the group of those concerned with the golden apples of the tree, Atalanta (vii.54) is otherwise prideful: she has overcome many others who have raced with her in order to gain her, but now she is brought to a fall by the three golden apples which her lover throws before her. The most popular version of this tale in the Renaissance is moralized so that the lover signifies the devil and Atalanta herself man's soul.[23] This offers an obvious parallel to the stories of Eve and Proserpina, as does the parallel story of how Acontius trapped his unwilling beloved by the use of a golden fruit (vii. 55). Hercules, we are told, had originally presumed to steal the golden apples from a god (vi. 54), and Paris had been otherwise presumptuous in daring to judge among

22. In this connection cf. Natalis Comes, *Mythologia* (I quote from Lyon, 1605): 'Proserpina. Ceres: Verum cum illa tria grana mali punici, vel novem, ut alii maluerunt, edisset, indice Ascalapho, filiam liberam educere omnino non potuit' (p. 246). 'Qui igitur Lunam & Hecaten, & Proserpinam esse putarunt? unam, illam sex menses, apud inferos esse alterne diserunt; quia antundem sub terra, quantum supra terram Luna in toto anno commoretur. Physici praeterea ac Mythologi antiqui superius hemisphaerum, quod nos incolimus, Veneris appellatione coluerunt, inferius Proserpinam nominarunt. qua ratione Proserpinam a Plutone sub terram deportatam in fabulis tradiderunt' (p. 249).

23. In the much-beloved *Gesta Romanorum*. According to Herrtage in the EETS edition (Extra Series, No. 33, 1879), there was an English edition by Wynkyn de Worde between 1510 and 1515; Herrtage cites testimony for seven more editions before 1602. STC lists one in 1557 and a number from 1595 onward. In the Wynkyn de Worde edition, parts of which are reprinted by Herrtage, the first story is the one of Atalanta. It corresponds in all important respects to the one in the Folger Library copy of an edition of 1610 (1609 O.S.), which is included in the collection University Microfilms 'Early English Books, 1475–1640', Reel 648. The first 'history' in this latter volume concerns 'a mighty Emperour which had a fayre creature to his Daughter, named Athalanta....' The story continues in the usual way. The successful lover is named Pomeis ('Pomeys' in Wynkyn de Worde), presumably because of his connection with apples. He provides himself with 'three bals of Gold against the running' (not described as apples, however, in the story) and proceeds in the usual way. The 'morall' at the end of the history reads in part thus: 'By this Emperour is understood the Father of heaven, and by the Damsell is understood the Soule of man, with whom many Divels desire to run, and to deceive her through their temptaciouns, but she withstandeth them mightily, and overcommeth them. And when they have done their worst, and may not speede, then maketh he three bals of gold, and casteth them before her in the three ages of man, that is to say, in youth, in manhood, and in old age.' Incidentally, 'Pomeis' is also a shortening of 'Hippomenes'.

contentious goddesses and in depriving two of them of the apple which he awarded to one, whence the Trojan War, the great, disastrous contention of mythical antiquity. Tantalus also belongs among the group for whom the golden apples have significance, in the senses that he continually and unsuccessfully reaches for them from his submerged position in the water surrounding the island, and that the Renaissance considered him to be concerned with riches. He is chiefly relevant, though, as part of another group in the Garden, of which the symbolic significance is much less diffuse.

Of the rest of the first group only Eve in addition joins this second group in their presumptuous readiness to usurp the divine prerogative most gravely. Pilate has been continually unsuccessful in his attempt to wash his hands in the water of the stream, because his soul is soiled with having allowed the Jews, through his unjust decision, to kill the Son of God (vii. 61–62). Similarly, the presence of poisonous plants of all kinds in this Garden creates an opportunity for another parallel: as the Jews had killed Christ with the permission of Pilate, so the unjust Athenians had caused the man whom many in the Renaissance considered a precursor and 'type' of Christ, a god-like and divinely inspired man—Socrates—to drink Cicuta, apparently at the instigation (in Spenser's conflation of two stories) of his faithless friend Critias (vii. 52).[24] Finally, and most mysteriously and allusively, Tantalus had desired so strongly to join the gods in their inward secrets, and to know everything about them,[25] that he dismembered his own son to make a meal and tempted them to feast on what he had prepared. Among them only Ceres, mother of Proserpina, who was distracted by the recent loss of her daughter to these infernal regions, had failed to see through the stratagem. She partook of what had been the shoulder of Pelops. Now Tantalus, former guilty banqueter of the gods, is condemned to the realm of Ceres' daughter Proserpina, perpetually denied the water in

24. See appendix D.
25. In Spenser's *Virgil's Gnat*, 348–88, Tantalus is punished because 'he did the bankets of the Gods bewray'; that is, he revealed the secrets of the gods' banquets. The passage in the Garden of Proserpina (stanza 59) seems, then, to include at least the meaning that Tantalus aspired to traffic with the gods—that he wished to commune with them on even terms in a way unsuitable to humankind, and banqueted them ostentatiously in order to do so. The further story—that Tantalus was ambitious to test the gods' omniscience and served his son Pelops to them as a meal in order to see whether they could perceive the composition of the dish—is a very familiar one in the Renaissance. Cf., for instance, 'The white of Pelops' shoulder' (white because the gods had replaced his consumed shoulder with an ivory one) in Marlowe's *Hero and Leander*, I. 65. For a more detailed treatment, in some respects (including sources), of the material of this note and of the preceding one, see my 'Three Fearful Symmetries', cited in n.2.

which he is submerged and the fruit of the branches dangling over his head.

Tantalus is probably the most radical of the Garden's exhibits; in him many lines of symbolism converge. His disdainful wrath, his insolent belief in his own desert, his blank ignoring of his own motives, and his inability to benefit from the water in which he is immersed take us back to Pyrochles and his like, but he is a more extreme case of the intemperance of arrogant pride in his unrepentant assertion that the gods, injured by him, owe him, a man, gratitude:

> Lo *Tantalus*, I here tormented lye:
>   Of whom high *Jove* wont whylome feasted bee,
>
>   .   .   .   .
>
>   Then gan the cursed wretch aloud to cry,
>   Accusing highest *Jove* and gods ingrate,
>   And eke blaspheming heaven bitterly,
> As author of unjustice, there to let him dye.
>   [vii. 59, 60]

This is the frame of mind which Guyon had rejected in saying that he, a mere man, did not deserve Philotime. Grill had fallen into 'Impotence' and sensuality's sty so irrecoverably that he found the centre of his world in his dungheap when salvation was offered him; Tantalus, caught up in the opposite vice, is unconscious of his overweening state, and of how, having murdered and dismembered his son to feed the gods, he is now justly denied sustenance. All that he can remember is that he is important and that he did Jove the favour of feasting him. Pilate's complicity in the murder of the one true God is the graver sin, but at least he is remorseful; Tantalus rages. Tantalus and Grill are, then, Spenser's opposite poles of intemperance.

The variety of symbolic parallels which open out here is so great that one needs to resort to constant syntactic parallelism and verbal repetition to describe them. As the 'impotence' of appetite, which has for its sign manual shifting water in Book II, undergoes, in the episodes depicted in the first scene of Acrasia's sea-surrounded, Cymochles-serving Bower-island,[26] an initial symbolic reversal in the fiery garment

26. The characters connected by their names with the sea in Books II and III are Cymochles (who is unstable as the waves of the sea, is the servant of a witch on a sea-surrounded island, and is the lover of Phaedria on her lake) and Marinell (who is son to Dumarin and Cymoent, and beneficiary of the sea, beside which he lives). Both are negative characters: the first forgetting honour for sensuality, the second deserting due

of Creusa and the violent carving up of Aegialeus, and is elsewhere reversed in the self-inflicted death (like impatient Amavia's) by stabbing of Maleger's lieutenant Impotence, so the 'impatience' of irascibility, whose chief symbols are fire and stabbing or rending, undergoes, in the last scene of the House of Mammon, a final symbolic reversal: a garden is islanded by water in which weltering malefactors are continually drenched. As we are indirectly reminded at the end of the episode of the moralized landscape of Mammon's Cave that vaunting pride had led Tantalus to dismember his son, so at the beginning of the episode of the Bower of Bliss we are fleetingly reminded by a mysterious picture that Medea had dismembered her brother to protect the course of her sensual passion (and we may add that variations on this theme in different keys are Acrasia's destruction of her lover, the rending of Christ's body by 'Jewes despiteous', the poisoning of Socrates, and—for Guyon—'that dreadful fiend, which did behind him wayt' and who 'would have him rent in thousand peeces strayt', vii. 64). As the bloody consequences of Acrasia's crime cannot be washed from the hands of Ruddymane in the pure water of the fountain, so Pilate's incessant efforts to rid his hands of blood in the filthy water around him are in vain (and on the difference in waters Guyon has remarked to Mammon in vii. 15: 'At the well head the purest streames arise: / But mucky filth his braunching armes annoyes, / And with uncomely weedes the gentle wave accloyes.') As we have seen, the concupiscible and sensual modulate into the opposite intemperance of violent and ego-serving rivalry which is figured at the beginning of the episode of the Bower in the emblem upon the portal; so in the Cave the attractions of appetite appear at the very end, where the most extreme forms of contentious pridefulness are reached. We are surrounded by examples of eating and drinking and of physical relaxation, as never earlier in the Cave: Eve and Proserpina have succumbed to the temptation of the fruit; Tantalus wants to eat and drink; his banquet for Jove is referred to; even Socrates, we are told, was made to partake of a plant that grows here. Principally, of course, in the matter of food, Mammon tries upon the

---

love for safety. In contrast with them are Pyrochles (full of fire and all too obsessed with honour), Mammon (with his fiery furnaces and promise of glory), and Busirane (obsessed by sexual conquest, and owning a home that is protected with sulphurous fire). Guyon's ultimate victory in his twelfth canto is over a water-defended isle; Britomart's, in hers, is over a fire-defended dwelling. In the former case, temperate Guyon must arouse sodden Verdant to a sense of right honour; in the latter, loving Britomart must cool the fiery, masculine masterfulness of Scudamour with the arts of friendship, whose true home is the water-surrounded Isle of Venus in IV. x.

exhausted Guyon, for the first and last time, a temptation of the flesh, not of the spirited part—that he should eat the apple and sit upon the seat.[27] Yet all refreshment and sustenance offered in the Garden of Proserpina are spurious. The seat is a trap, the water is filthy, and the apples, like some of the fruit of Acrasia's Garden, are of gold—hard, mineral fruit, with no nourishing inwardness. Neither these nor the counterfeitings of the Bower of Bliss can measure up to the true article, which is neither more nor less than fruit furnished forth by Nature alone in the Garden of Adonis. True Pleasure, who lives in the earlier Garden, not the false one, was the one to be borrowed by Milton in *Comus*.

The thematically organized structure of Book II can be summarily stated by cantos, in the accompanying diagram, with considerable pairing of episodes at equal distance from the common centre of Proserpina's seat. Italics are intended to show matching features.

The new material in this diagram should be self-explanatory except, perhaps, for two cantos. In iv Phedon falls into Pyrochlean fury. Having murdered his beloved and his false friend, he is seeking to murder another betrayer. The case has roots in a rivalry which apparently involves the opposite intemperance of sensual passion (so, at last, the Palmer explains), and thus has affinities with the cases of Acrasia and Amavia.[28] At the practical level of analysis and homily the whole range of the two sides of intemperance, tailored to this example, is again surveyed by the Palmer:

> Then gan the Palmer thus, Most wretched man,
>> That to affections does the bridle lend;
>> In their beginning they are weake and wan,
>> But soone through suff'rance grow to fearefull end;
>> Whiles they are weake betimes with them contend:
>> For when they once to perfect strength do grow,
>> Strong warres they make, and cruel battry bend
>> Gainst fort of Reason, it to overthrow:
> Wrath, gelosie, griefe, love this Squire have layd thus low.

27. Which is ultimately the seat upon which Theseus, once persuaded to sit in hell, was condemned to remain eternally. See Variorum commentary.

28. Now that the whole case concerning spiteful vengeance in Book II has been set forth, it is well to point out that Medina is speaking to it, and not just to the argument before her, when she says in ii. 30: 'And were there rightfull cause of difference, / Yet were not better, faire it to accord, / Then with blood guiltinesse to heape offence, / And mortall vengeaunce joyne to crime abhord?'

Structure of *Faerie Queene* 11

i. Beginning of Book. The object of Guyon's quest is Acrasia's Bower, *false intemperate pleasure,* which has precipitated deaths of Mordant and Amavia, exemplifying reversal into *opposite intemperance* of violent rivalry. The two forms of intemperance are here called 'impotence' (Mordant) and 'impatience' (Amavia).

ii. Medina's House. She *quells two forms of intemperance* in *moralized landscape.*

iii. The Queen as Belphoebe *conquers both forms of intemperance.*

iv. *Guyon saves Phedon from intemperance of fury;* interpolated *story of irascible passion* provoked by rivalry in *love* (cf. Acrasia and Amavia): an instance of *surrender to both forms of intemperance.*

v. Pyrochles. *Guyon overcomes furious rivalry* in sphere of *chivalric adventure,* together with

vi. Phaedria, Cymochles. Guyon *overcomes false pleasure* in sphere of *chivalric adventure.*

vii. *Centre of Book.* Guyon *overcomes fateful rivalry and pride in moralized landscape.* Cave of Mammon. *Human attempt to ascend to,* or infringe upon, *divine.* At end, *appearance of opposite intemperance,* appetite: golden apples and the seat.

viii. In *chivralric adventure,* Arthur *destroys the two forms of intemperance together:* Pyrochles and Cymochles.

ix. House of Alma. *Both natural tendencies,* that of Arthur towards spirited part of soul and that of Guyon towards appetitive, *are temperately controlled.*

x. *Royal lineages,* with earlier *intemperance in both forms.*

xi. In *moralized landscape,* Arthur *conquers both forms of intemperance* and assures temperance of Alma's House.

xii. *End of Book.* Guyon accomplishes his quest by *destroying false pleasure* in sphere of *moralized landscape* of Bower. *Human descent to animal.* At beginning of episodes, *appearance of opposite form of intemperance* in violent rivalry (pictures on gate).

> Wrath, gealosie, griefe, love do thus expell:
>   Wrath is a fire, and gealosie a weede,
>   Griefe is a flood, and love a monster fell;
>   The fire of sparkes, the weede of little seede,
>   The flood of drops, the Monster filth did breede:
>   But sparks, seed, drops, and filth do thus delay;
>   The sparks soone quench, the springing seed outweed,
>   The drops dry up, and filth wipe cleane away:
> So shall wrath, gealosie, griefe, love dye and decay.

[iv. 34–35]

With syntax as difficult as this, a tentative paraphrase is needed:

> The Palmer said to Phedon, 'You are the most wretched of men, having given the bridle to the passions: in their beginnings these passions are weak, but if passive allowance is given to them they reach a fearful maturity (and accomplish fearful ends). Fight with them promptly while they are weak, for having reached their full strength they wage strong battle against the fort of reason, and direct a cruel artillery at it in order to overthrow it. This squire [the Palmer now speaks of him in the third person] has been laid low by wrath, jealousy, grief, and love. [The Palmer now returns to direct address.] Expel wrath, jealousy, grief, and love according to the following method. Wrath (you should know) is a fire, jealousy a weed, grief a flood, and love a fell monster. The fire is bred from sparks; the weed from a small seed; the flood from drops; the monster from filth. Hinder the sparks, seeds, drops, and filth thus: quench the sparks immediately, weed out the germinating seed, dry up the drops, wipe the filth away. Then the products of these small things, namely wrath, jealousy, grief, and love, will be destroyed.'

In this effusion a number of images from the rest of the book are recalled. The values of a few of them are transposed, with what further conscious effort at symmetrical effects it is difficult to say. The filth and the weed recall Guyon's speech to Mammon at the end of vii. 15. The fire has an obvious significance, the monster less so, although one monster follows Guyon through the Cave. The central image which most keeps one puzzling is the one which seems a compressed metaphor for the whole vice-assaulted House of Alma in canto ix: 'Strong warres they make, and cruel battery bend / Gainst fort of Reason, it to overthrow.' As we are told in connection with the story of that House,

What warre so cruel, or what siege so sore,
    As that, which strong affections do apply
    Against the fort of reason evermore
    To bring the soule into captivitie:
    Their force is fiercer through infirmitie
    Of the fraile flesh, relenting to their rage,
    And exercise most bitter tyranny
    Upon the parts, brought into their bondage:
No wretchednesse is like to sinfull vellenage.
                [xi. 1]

It is as though Phedon's case were being described over again. Alma's rigorous resistance is contrasted with this weakness in the next stanza, but the metaphor, again with verbal similarity, is continued in connection with the assault of the vices on her castle:

They all that charge did fervently apply,
    With greedie malice and importune toyle,
    And planted there their huge artillery,
With which they dayly made most dreadfull battery.
                [xi. 7]

Cantos iv and ix are of course matched in the diagram.

Further clarification is needed concerning canto ix in which the House of Alma is described. As J. L. Mills has pointed out,[29] the interior of Alma's parlour is that part of the sensitive soul where the concupiscible and irascible functions operate, with simple, rudimentary images painted upon its walls. In this parlour Arthur and Guyon meet those qualities with which they have a natural affinity. Arthur meets Prays-desire, 'That by well doing sought to honour to aspire' (39). He desires honour and praise, tending magnanimously as he does towards the 'spirited' part of the soul, but controlling the tendency temperately so that his search for undying fame is always conducted honourably: Prays-desire's dissatisfaction is subdued; she does not, for instance, grate her teeth in immoderate and invidious striving. Guyon, on the other hand, meets Shamefastness (Verecundia) because, having a natural tendency in the appetitive direction, he correspondingly tempers it suitably (43). Verecundia is described by many commentators as naturally the controller of the concupiscible element.[30]

29. 'Symbolic Tapestry in The Faerie Queene, II. ix. 33', Philological Quarterly, 49 (1970), 568–69.
30. See V. B. Hulbert, as summarized in Variorum, II, appendix IV, 426.

A serious difficulty for the study of Book II has to do with the persistence of two ideas. One of these is the conviction that Guyon's whole history somehow falls under the dichotomy Nature-Grace. The other, larger, idea, of which most of the expressions of the first are only a species, is that Guyon grows, or progresses meaningfully in experience and wisdom, through Book II, or somehow emerges from the book a better man than when he began.

The transmogrifications of the notion of the thematic function of Nature and Grace in Book II since A. S. P. Woodhouse stated the problem have resulted in too much weight's being put on the idea.[31] The opposition between the two concepts is indeed posed in canto viii, where divine grace, with an angel and Arthur as its instrument, saves another example of our wretched species, none of whom deserves saving: no matter how strong and virtuous he may be, natural man cannot survive without supernatural aid. This intervention is parallel to the similar appearance of Arthur as divine grace in Book I to save Redcross, another wretch of a natural man. Further, this latter intervention is crucial in Redcross's development; in spite of the drastic backsliding in his meeting with Despair, he has begun—or because of what has happened to him will shortly begin—to take off the old man and put on the new. For the first time, he is really dressing himself in the armour of a Christian knight; a great change has been wrought in him. It does not follow, however, that the parallel between Books I and II extends to a necessary reorientation of Guyon's character after the experience of grace. Although there is abundant evidence for the change in Redcross, there is no convincing evidence at all that Guyon is a new man after the supposedly climactic point in Book II. The story of Redcross necessarily follows the terms of the myth of *Heilsgeschichte* or of a typical morality play; man is evil, man is saved from his evil and becomes good. The protagonist of allegory as a form, however, does not necessarily follow this developmental or transformational kind of pattern. Allegory is not *Bildungsroman,* even though allegory can on occasion capitalize on the notion of serial development of a character, or on the notion of a character's transformation. Usually it is to the most flimsy fiction of the protagonist's continuing identity that sixteenth-century and earlier allegory opportunistically attaches its own developing series of ideas; the notion of the scarcely perceptible, steady growth of a consistent novelistic character is alien to it.

31. Woodhouse's article is 'Nature and Grace in *The Faerie Queene*', *ELH*, 16 (1949), 194–228; often reprinted.

Here, perhaps, has been our largest mistake about Guyon. One of the points which Spenser wishes to make about the temperate man is that he cannot stand alone; but this point is not the pivot on which the plot of the whole of Book II turns. Spenser may be momentarily making something of the developmental notion—*Bildung*—when we hear that Guyon

> evermore himselfe with comfort feedes,
> Of his owne vertues, and prayse-worthy deedes.
> [II. vii. 2]

This speech immediately precedes his experience of the House of Mammon; immediately after that experience he falls prey to Pyrochles and Cymochles. But after he is saved from them, there is no suggestion, as with Redcross, that he needs more training. His visit to the House of Alma is instructive, but it is not educational like Redcross's stay in the House of Holiness. An allegorical protagonist exists in a story to display certain truths for which aesthetically satisfactory opportunities, given supreme art, are made to arise; he is not there to grow in his own right, obsessively taking over the course of the story as in much of the best work of Dickens and Dostoyevsky. Typically, also, he is not there to be transformed suddenly and massively, as in a melodrama, from one distinct, heavily characterized persona into another. Both kinds of transformation are available to the allegorist of the Middle Ages or the Renaissance, but neither is obligatory to the form. Those who look for, or are disappointed by the lack of, consistency of character in medieval or Renaissance fiction could with profit read the destructive criticism of the idea, in A. T. Hatto's discussion of *The Nibelungenlied*,[32] as inconsistent, and as great, a work as *The Faerie Queene*. The modern myth of Progress knows no greater excesses than those of the modern myth of universal character-development in fiction.

The convention that a hero must have a development does not hold in the case of Guyon, and it does not hold for Britomart, either, except insofar as she takes one quantum-jump to the knowledge of love when we are first introduced to her. What undergoes development and growth in Book II is a structure of ideas; they are lively and compelling for us because they are embodied from the inside, so to speak, of our experience. We recognize the very feel of bitter, hopeless, jealous anger or of the drawling tides of deep-drowning sensuality. The concept of

---

32. In the Penguin edition of his English translation.

experience mimetically rendered is fundamental to Spenser's kind of allegory; the concept of an individual sundered from other individuals and developing a set of nonreversible characteristics called personality is not. In his Book II Spenser embodies in a satisfying symmetrical formal pattern the two opposed forms of intemperance and their conquest by God-given reason and grace. Equally, the substance of these mythic embodiments is experienced life—pathetic, tragic, comic, or heroic experience seen by the inner eye. In them our feelings can find a home.

All of this latter being so, it is difficult to understand how a reader could find morally irrelevant Spenser's embodiment of the following imperatives: that we should not be deterred by momentary attractions from taking a line of action in accordance with the pattern of living with others which we are conscious of having accepted; and that we should not out of envy and exasperation sacrifice our loose and large-minded detachment from cut-throat competitiveness so as to take shortcuts to the traditional rewards of beneficial action, without having actually done anything worthwhile. Losing one's nerve for the sake of creature comforts, and becoming inauthentic in order to grab public acclaim and credit away from one's competitors, are probably as generally reprobated today as they were in Spenser's Book II. A typical source of confusion in reading Spenser is to suppose that he gives prime importance to the historical, overt content of one pattern of action from the past, namely, the pattern of the knightly ethos which was outmoded before anyone ever thought of acting on it. Yet for Spenser this particular content is almost as purely symbolic and mythic, not concretely chivalric, as it ought to be for us. Otherwise, for instance, he would not have dared to add intellectual activity to the active life when he made Belphoebe his spokesman for temperance. She says that in front of the gate to the mansion of Honour high God stationed the porter Sweat. This latter is a striking personification. Through him we perceive another adversary relationship, like that of the true Genius to the false one. Sweat stands over against Ease, the introducer of the Masque of Cupid. The whole passage would be worthy of Rabelais, one of the great haters of chivalric postures.

13

Spenser and

Paradise Lost

Faerie Queen II is one vast conceit, or series of interlocking myths, of the operation of the two forms of intemperance by which God-given reason falls in us from its due regality, and, of how, contrariwise, the regality of reason can be maintained. Passionate, invidious selfhood and abandoned, besotted pleasure-seeking are shown to be at equal and equally unfortunate removes from the pursuit of honourable action. In canto vii, the House of Mammon is a conceit of intermediate size—a myth embodied in moralized landscape—of both the success and the failure of enticement towards the first of these two forms of excess. We see the success of this temptation and its sequel when First Man (here First Woman), and other men fall prey to the tempter who implants egotism in their hearts by the specious offer of a state higher than their due. Simultaneously, we see the failure of this temptation when an imitator of the Second Adam or Christ rejects the same temptation of prideful selfhood, as Christ himself had rejected it in the Wilderness.

In a purely logical sense these two patterns—that of *Faerie Queene* II as a whole and that of the Cave of Mammon—obviously reappear in Milton's two epics. In *Paradise Lost* the falls of Satan, Eve, and Adam follow a twofold pattern corresponding to that of *Faerie Queene* II as a whole: rancorous or too easily implanted egotism primarily brings about the falls of Satan and Eve—the deep fall of those too high

aspiring; Adam is damned primarily by attachment to a lower, crea-
turely pleasure. We are shown that we must find the divinely enjoined,
reasonable path between these two extremes. In *Paradise Regained* the
pattern is that of the Cave of Mammon; Christ, shown continually in
contrast with First Man, withstands all steps of the temptation to
personal glorification.

> I who erewhile the happy garden sung,
> By one man's disobedience lost, now sing
> Recovered Paradise to all mankind,
> By one man's firm obedience fully tried
> Through all temptation, and the tempter foiled
> In all his wiles, defeated and repulsed,
> And Eden raised in the waste wilderness.
>   [I. 1–7]

But to what extent, in the light of these purely logical parallels, may
Milton be thought of as following Spenser? Each of the items, taken
separately, is a commonplace of Christian tradition. Part of the answer
to the question seems to be that, to an extent surprising for so original a
mind, Milton consciously followed these patterns very far. His imagination seems at some point or points to have reacted intensely to the
stimulus of Spenser's narrative so as to accept consciously and preserve
what amounts to a kind of local Spenserian mythology and Spenserian
picture of the psychology of temptation and evil-doing (although never
the finer points of doctrine such as one finds in *De Doctrina Christiana*.
For that Milton always looked elsewhere). With something of the same
economy with which he mined motifs for *Comus* from the Bower of
Bliss and the Garden of Adonis, Milton found certain larger patterns
ready to his hand in *Faerie Queen* II, and used them. In part, no doubt,
he took satisfaction in the mere fact of continuity with the only great
epic predecessor in his own national language, as the Italian heroic
poets, so well known to him, had already built up a line of continuators.
He seems, indeed, to have wanted his reader to recognize these iconic
reminiscences because the echo of an earlier voice and an elder tradition
strikes our sensibility with increased poignancy and gravity, and because a greatly original metamorphosis of an older motif gives its own
delight.

Beyond this, however, the patterns already present in his mind at a
fairly early date may have helped to lead him to the subjects of his two
epics. Among the religious poets of Western Europe, only he made the

two great Temptations of doctrinal history the main subjects of his whole stock of epic writing. The Fall of the Angels and of Man forms a straightforward enough choice; the Temptation in the Wilderness makes equally superb sense on reflection, but it remains an unusual, hard-to-place choice for an epic subject in Milton's time or any other. The assumption that he was early impressed with Spenser's narrative devices in telling the two stories in parallel is an attractive way out of this difficulty.

Even leaving out of account the known facts of Milton's admiration for Spenser's poetry, we recognize that the younger poet is likely to have taken very seriously an epic work in his own language by a man who could have been his grandfather and who was regarded by many of Milton's contemporaries as the first English poet of his time, and indeed of all time in the then sparse known tradition of poetry in English. Between *Faerie Queen* II and Milton's two epics there are many specific resemblances at the episodic and verbal levels. Certain of these resemblances, particularly verbal ones, carry almost immediate conviction. In the transmutation which Milton's imagination worked on Spenser's narrative, the music of a limited number of highly significant Spenserian lines seems to have lodged in his memory.

This is not, however, to deny the hugeness of that transmutation. At first sight there is a very large leap for our fantasy from the Spenserian world to the Miltonic one we know. Milton must have realized that Spenser dealt in realms of experience more than in experience encapsulated in personae, yet sometimes Spenserian characters at a large remove from the ones we might think of in connection with *Paradise Lost* and *Paradise Regained* seem to have made a strong impression on Milton's mind, just as the False Genius so unexpectedly emerged in his imagination when he needed a male Circe figure for a masque of which the essential feature was a heroine rather than a hero. In terms of characters alone, the most seminal ones of Spenser's for Milton's shaping of Satan seem to have been Pyrochles (in his incandescent defiance and gnawing, self-deceiving conviction that he is unjustly deprived of high-astounding victory) and Mammon (in his disdainful manipulation of the propaganda of individual status and of money as the way to that status); Tantalus must also be remembered, but secondarily, in his symbolically impressive role. Perhaps if one thinks of the mythic formulation of two *areas* of wrongdoing in *Faerie Queen* II as having stuck in Milton's mind, this kind of connection is not really so surprising. Yet there must be something preposterous to some imaginations in seeing those characters in and behind Satan. They seem wraith-like and insubstantial; Satan is firmly outlined.

There is, in fact, a useful principle here to pause over. Part of the quality of medieval visionary landscapes, and of Spenser's extension of those landscapes, is that their denizens are positionally or typographically, rather than individually, defined, and that their significance as characters is necessarily liable to sudden slippage. Not only our understanding of them but their affective force upon us is much more dependent on their place in a group of other characters and objects —processional, successive, hierarchical—and upon the momentary use the author is making of them in a larger scheme, than it is upon a fixed, individual orchestration of affective qualities. To this day, for instance, we are ignorant of how Guillaume de Lorris would have concluded his part of *Le Roman de la rose,* because the properties of his Love God are shifting and ambiguous. In one context—that of his initial subjection of the Lover—the morally bracing character of a whole-souled devotion emerges in the set of rules (including those of personal cleanliness) imposed by this lord upon his subject. In another context—that of the goddess Reason, who, we are told, was made in the image of God himself and whom, presumably, we ought to credit—the Love God is full of disreputable folly; and it is quite possible that Guillaume might have concluded on some such note. These two apparently unqualified characterizations are never really adjusted to each other, but are left in suspense in the unfinished work, awaiting their dispensation.

One may not expect of Spenser's characters in a moralized landscape the kind of affective definition that, for instance, derives from the elaborate 'orchestration' which Milton gives Satan. For example, it will not really work to think of Spenser's Proserpina in her Garden, as Northrop Frye seems to do,[1] as a solely 'demonic' Proserpina. She is simply not characterized that radically, with good reason. It is true that as the wife of the lord of the underworld she is in one sense a mistress of a baleful prison. But she is also in the same class as Eve, Atalanta, and Cydippe ('that lover trew') in the Garden in that she is, like them, a pitiable female who has succumbed to the temptation to eat the fruit. These two, in a sense clashing, affective states, which are available to Spenser in *potentia,* are both drawn on very charily as he drafts yet

---

[1].*Fables of Identity: Studies in Poetic Mythology* (New York, 1963), pp. 78–80. It is perhaps not entirely fair to support on the basis of this passage alone the notion that Frye confines himself to a 'demonic' Proserpina in the House of Mammon, although I believe that he does so. This passage, like work by Williams, Kermode, Kellogg, and Steele (already adverted to), anticipates some of my conclusions in chapter 12.

another part of his polysemous emblematic structure, for neither of them can be heavily orchestrated for fear of annihilating the other, and of impeding the nimbleness of the shifting patterns of significances at the primary level of narrative. The Venus in her Temple in *Faerie Queene,* IV. x, for example, similarly shifts: in one sense she embodies concord but in another must smile encouragingly upon male sexual aggression. Similarly with Mammon. He is introduced as a money god, fingering his gold, but it is important for Spenser's purposes that Mammon's significance should be allowed to shift first to the sphere of worldly ambition and then to that of transcendental presumption. He is a loosely tied bundle of characteristics, not a character.

What happens to such characters in Milton's hands is that they are removed from a visionary world into a concrete one (see chapter 15), and are there given an affective weight congenial to the 'Baroque' imagination—'Baroque' being used here only in the loose sense in which we term 'Baroque' the imaginatively imposing individual figures in any group by Rubens, even one that he borrows from an earlier painter. We may thus put a name to this powerful transformation, although how it was wrought remains a mystery, except that Milton no doubt took the trouble to read Spenser very literally: so perused, even Mammon is not simply a ditty of no tone piping to our spiritual ear. With those of Spenser's characters who are involved in chivalric adventure, as opposed to those in moralized landscapes, the leap of transformation does not need to be so great. Where the symbolic coordinates are not so complex, Spenser may make use of the chance to give some affective loading to, for instance, Pyrochles. There would be nothing preposterous for the Romantic imagination (for Hazlitt, for example) in finding in the *superbia* of Pyrochles' death agony a grandeur like that of Satan's unrepentant spirit. There exist, then, passages of dark 'Byronic' splendour in Spenser. They are scattered, however; with Milton such discourse is the rule.

What we know historically concerning Milton's lifelong plans for a *magnum opus* is so fragmentary that even the skilful efforts of Allan H. Gilbert do not permit us to draw up a likely scenario. We know that in 1638 he promised a British epic in *Mansus,* and that in this he was no doubt thinking of following both Tasso and Spenser. We know as well that he announced his British epic in *Epitaphium Damonis* in about 1639,[2] and that in 1641 in the *Reason of Church Government* he

2. Gilbert, *On the Composition of 'Paradise Lost'* (Chapel Hill, N.C., 1947), pp. 80–84, 162–68.

expressed himself as open to suggestions for a British epic-subject of the period before the Conquest.[3] All plans for a war-like or chivalric epic were, however, rejected in the body of *Paradise Lost* itself (IX. 27–41). We know also of his various plans, recorded in 1640–42 in the Trinity MS,[4] for a tragedy entitled *Paradise Lost,* for a play called *Adam Unparadised,* and for other dramatic compositions. It is plain that they have little to do in matter, and less in spirit, with what finally emerged.[5] Thereafter there are no more plans until the appearance of *Paradise Lost* itself in 1667.

Concerning Milton's knowledge of Spenser, we know that for Alexander Gill Senior, the high master of Milton's grammar school, Spenser was the favourite English poet, 'the English Homer': the bright and biddable schoolboy is likely to have taken this estimate seriously.[6] The strong formal influence of Spenser's poetry on Milton's early works is obvious: in publishing Milton's *Poems* in 1645, Humphrey Mosley had said without fear of contradiction that in this book the poems of Spenser 'are as rarely imitated, as sweetly excelled'.[7] Our knowledge of the Spenserian influence on *Comus* has probably been strengthened by what has been said here in chapter 11. Among Milton's very infrequent references in his own poetry to other English poets are the almost certain one to Spenser in *Il Penseroso* (115 ff.) and a possible one in *Mansus,* 30–33, where the English swans singing on the Thames may point to *Prothalamion.* I have quoted as the epigraph to the preceding chapter the favourable mention of Spenser in *Areopagitica.*

Further, Milton was in some fashion behind the restoration to Spenser's grandson of the estate of Kilcoman, when the young man had lost it through temporary recusancy;[8] Milton was surely motivated here by his regard for the grandfather. The testimony at the end of Milton's career is perhaps the strongest. When his widow, with whom he had spent the last eleven years of his life, was asked whom he most approved

---

3. John Milton, *Complete Poems and Major Prose,* ed. Merritt Y. Hughes (New York, 1957), pp. 668–69.

4. *The Uncollected Writings of John Milton,* ed. T. O. Mabbott and J. Milton French (New York, 1938), vol. XVIII of *The Works of John Milton* (New York, 1931–38), pp. 228–45.

5. On this the comments of Edwin Greenlaw are still valid. See his 'Spenser's Influence on *Paradise Lost*', *Studies in Philology,* 17 (1920), 342–44.

6. See comments on Gill's *Logonomia Anglica* in Arthur Barker, 'Milton's Schoolmaster', *Modern Language Review,* 32 (1937), 527n.; and Donald Leman Clark, *John Milton at St. Paul's School* (New York, 1948), p. 74.

7. William Riley Parker, *Milton: A Biography* (Oxford, 1968), I, 635.

8. Ibid., p. 501.

of among English poets, we are told that her answer was Spenser, Shakespeare, and Cowley.[9] Dryden says in the Preface to *The Fables Ancient and Modern* that Milton was the 'Poetical Son of Spencer' and acknowledged Spenser to be his 'Originall' (see the epigraph to the present book). Dryden's choice of this word is in itself suggestive; the acknowledgement was most probably made during Milton's last year when Dryden was consulting him about the possibility of using *Paradise Lost* for the stage.[10] It is true that Spenser is never mentioned in Milton's *Commonplace Book*, but neither are Plato, Homer, Virgil, or any Greek tragedians.[11] As in the case of these authors, Milton probably knew Spenser's works so well that he did not need to take notes on them.

Two points might be added to these generally acknowledged matters. When, in 1629, in *Elegia Sexta*, the approximately twenty-one year old poet comes to speak (whether ironically or not) of the serious matter of epic composition, he singles out incidents from the *Odyssey*, not from the more expectable *Iliad*. The incidents, too, are somewhat curiously chosen: they are those of Circe's Island (along with the sirens) and Ulysses' visit to hell, the latter being very minor indeed in the narrative of the *Odyssey*:

> *Sic dapis exiguus, sic rivi potor Homerus*
> *Dulichium vexit per freta longa virum,*
> *Et per monstrificam Perseiae Phoebados aulam,*
> *Et vada femineis insidiosa sonis,*
> *Perque tuas rex ime domos, ubi sanguine nigro*
> *Dicitur umbrarum detinuisse greges.*
>
> $\qquad\qquad$ [*Elegia Sexta*, 71–76]

[Thus Homer, eating sparely and drinking naught but water, transported Ulysses through vast stretches of ocean and through the hall of Circe, daughter of Phoebus and Perseis, where men are turned to monsters; over shallows made treacherous by women's song; and through your home, king of the underworld, where the story tells us that he detained the troops of ghosts by means of a libation of dark blood.]

9. *The Life Records of John Milton*, ed. J. Milton French (New Brunswick, N.J., 1958), V, 322–23.

10. Parker, I, 635.

11. Ibid, II, 802. Ruth Mohl has edited the *Commonplace Book* in *Complete Prose Works*, I (New Haven, 1953), 344–513.

It is true that, generally, the *Odyssey* was important to the Renaissance for its picture of the virtuous man,[12] but, more specifically, in selecting these two incidents Milton may already have had in the back of his mind, even perhaps as a possible pattern for an epic, the pattern of Guyon's visit to the underground courts and his obviously Odyssean trip (complete with sirens) to Acrasia's isle.

Concerning the selection of the *Odyssey* itself, there is the additional point of Spenser's having implied that *The Faerie Queene* which we have is closer to the *Odyssey* than to the *Iliad*. He says in the Introductory Letter to Ralegh that Homer had shown the good governor in the *Iliad*, but the virtuous individual in the *Odyssey;* similarly, Spenser continues, he will show the private virtues of Arthur in his first twelve books, and if these are well received he will proceed to twelve more books on the political virtues (probably some great Arthurian struggle against pagan armies on the analogy of the Italian use in heroic poetry of Charlemagne's battles and of the Crusades).

In any case, Milton may have been thinking of these two incidents as emblematic of the two sides of the heroic life,[13] and they in fact parallel the mention some fifteen years later of the Cave of Mammon and the Bower of Earthly Bliss in the quoted passages from *Areopagitica*. The date of that quotation is later than that of any of his recorded plans for a drama, and later than any other piece of evidence here until the actual

12. See Douglas Bush, *A Variorum Commentary on the Poems of John Milton*, I (London, 1970), 214.

13. In a somewhat shorter passage earlier in *Elegia Sexta* (55–58), Milton had spoken of likely incidents in heroic poetry without mentioning an author. The subjects—wars, a mature and sober supreme god (not a younger, errant one), heroes who abide by duty and are semi-divine, the counsels of the gods above, hell below—point first at the *Aeneid* and perhaps Tasso's *Gerusalemme liberata*, but they are suggestive also with regard to *The Faerie Queene*. They may as easily apply to Guyon (*Pius*, 'dutiful'), Arthur (sometimes a type of the Godhead), and Mammon in *Faerie Queene* II, and also to *Faerie Queene* I and VII. The choice of detail from the previous epic in *Comus*, 518–19, when the Attendant Spirit is expressing fear to the brothers about the Lady's fate and is about to broach the subject of the sorcerer, is similar, although the choice in this case is easier to motivate solely in terms of the circumstances of the action. The details accord with *Faerie Queene* II as well as with the *Aeneid*. The details are italicized:

I'll tell ye, 'tis not vain or fabulous,
(Though so esteemed by shallow ignorance)
What the sage poets taught by the heavenly Muse,
Stored of old in high immortal verse
Of *dire chimeras and enchanted isles,*
And rifted rocks whose entrance leads to hell,
For such there be, but unbelief is blind.
   Within the navel of this hideous wood,
Immured in cypress shades a sorcerer dwells
Of Bacchus, and of Circe born, great Comus.

publication of *Paradise Lost* in 1667. It is this latter quotation, of course, which contains the strongest external evidence for Milton's having thought along the lines which I have described. He singles out in it each of the two moralized landscapes which have been interpreted here as the summary emblems of the two kinds of intemperance in *Faerie Queene* II: the Cave of Mammon as the chief emblem of Pride, current in the Lower Regions and communicated through temptation to Eve and others, but refused by an imitator of Christ; and the Bower of Bliss as the emblem of surrender (but not Guyon's surrender) to sensuality. The sensuality is disguised with all the courtly, sentimental trappings of love poetry, but ultimately signifies the surrender of rationality, the substituted love of a creature in place of the Creator, and the abandonment of the Christian call to honourable action in this world. Much of this is, as I have said, very close to the pattern of large parts of *Paradise Lost* and *Paradise Regained*.

Not only does Milton pick out the two points in *Faerie Queen* II which most summarily define these mythic categories, but the context in which he does this also seems significant. In it we find man's Fall—out of the rind of one apple tasted. Perhaps, Milton says, it was through eating that apple that we were condemned to knowing good, only by also knowing evil, so as to differentiate the one from the other. That being the case, in our lapsed condition ('as...the state of man now is') it is well, says Milton, that Spenser, a better teacher than any Scholastic, showed us a man discovering evil in the Cave of Mammon and the Bower of Bliss, so that this man might abstain from it and choose the good. *Areopagitica* goes on to say more generally that by the same token it is good that we should be allowed to read promiscuously whatever book we wish, but Milton's choice of these particular examples from *The Faerie Queene* takes on greater appropriateness if we see that he recognized the fallen Eve, whose case he had just been discussing, as 'mystically' communicated through the golden apples of the Cave; he may even have seen the Old Man of sin and death—the old Adam—in the Mordant who fell prey to the cup (perhaps 'scruzed' from the fruit—some of it golden—of the Bower), which Acrasia-Circe, or a Circe-Eve, gave him.[14] In the cave of Mammon and the Bower of Bliss,

14. If Milton saw in Mordant an Adam figure, he would have been likely to go further in the direction of recognizing a kind of Hermetic system in Book II than I have found it tactful to extend my own interpretation. The figures of Proserpina and Amavia, and of Acrasia when violent not sensual, may have seemed to him, not simply illustrations of one form of intemperance in action, but as types of Eve in a mystical communication of a truth of Holy Writ. Also, Mordant, Cymochles, and Grill would then become for Milton

as Milton requires, good is known by evil in a very direct way: Guyon withstood the temptation to pride and glory; Eve and all her sect did not. In the Bower of Bliss it is easy for us as readers to feel how and why Mordant and the transformed beasts surrendered reason and will to appetite; Guyon is all the more remarkable for not having done so.

It smacks of special pleading to claim here that Milton could not have missed the main lines of the interpretation of *Faerie Queene* II sketched in the preceding chapter. Nevertheless, anyone who becomes convinced that this in fact partly traditional interpretation is correct is likely to agree that Milton would have quickly seen *Faerie Queene* II in the same light: possibly more than any other Englishman of his time, Milton would have had at his fingertips the Renaissance developments of pagan mythology, and the correlations of this with sacred history, which we must dredge up doubtfully, with much sweat, from compendia, dictionaries, glossators, commentators, theological treatises, contemporary poets and emblem-books, and from the Classics and Holy Writ themselves. The kind of firsthand knowledge that would almost surely have made plain to him the significance of Spenser's substitution of Medea for Tasso's 'Iole' on the portal of Acrasia's Bower must have been his from a fairly early age. The intimate understanding of certain areas in *Faerie Queene* II and III, suggested by what we have seen in

'mystic' Adam figures, with Verdant hovering between the Old and the New Man. Such a typological interpretation of what has seemed to me in the main a Platonic, 'neo-Aristotelian' allegory is a conceivable next step, once a typological drift sets in with the plain suggestions of the figure of Eve in the Garden of Proserpina, the figure of Christ behind Guyon, and the figure of the Godhead in Arthur as rescuer in canto vii. But I do not see plainly that this step needs to be taken. One other piece of evidence is the anagrammatic resemblances in the names 'Adam' and 'Mordant', 'Eve' and 'Amavia'.

In 'Milton Revises *The Faerie Queene*', *Modern Philology*, 48 (1950–51), 90–96, the distinction which Ernest Sirluck introduces may indeed be useful and correct. He perceives a Guyon temperate in the Aristotelian sense (that is, led by ingrained habit and not needing the help of the rational faculty—of, that is, his Palmer) in the House of Mammon, and, on the other hand, a Guyon merely continent in the Aristotelian sense (that is, needing the help of reason, the Palmer, in order to avoid the various temptations to which he nearly succumbs in the Bower of Bliss). Certainly there is nothing in the theory supported in the present book which excludes the possibility of the eclectic use by Spenser of such Aristotelian distinctions. As has already been shown, Guyon has, in the House of Alma, a natural affinity for 'Shamefastness', *Verecundia*, the temperate (in the general sense) form of a tendency which, when allowed to dominate reason, constitutes surrender to appetite; Arthur, on the other hand, has an affinity for 'Prays-desire', or the temperate desire for honour, which in its intemperate form is surrender to the irascible element of the soul. Whether upon these opposite, natural tendencies of the two heroes Spenser thought to erect the Aristotelian category of the 'continent', as opposed to the Aristotelian category of the 'temperate', is not my immediate concern here. The same holds for Sirluck's associated suggestion that Milton trusted only reason, not habit, in matters of moral choice, and for this reason unconsciously added the Palmer in his reference to Guyon in the House of Mammon.

Comus, also demonstrates his skill in following Spenser's kind of narrative.

It is true that the work of Milton's transforming imagination on thousands of books enters into the composition of *Paradise Lost* and *Paradise Regained*. To consider only the English drama of his time, it seems likely that his thoughts about tragedy may have led him to something like a five-act structure in *Paradise Lost*, for instance, as Arthur Barker suggests,[15] and to an intensification of the rancour of his Satan through reminiscences of the protagonists of revenge tragedy, as is claimed by Dame Helen Gardner.[16] The wealth of other resources on which he drew is staggering. Nevertheless his imagination maintains a basic continuity with, and in a sense a basic structural dependence upon, that of his great English predecessor in epic. 'Long choosing and beginning late', he still preserves in recognizable form, and sometimes even with close verbal echo, many of Spenser's patterns and many details related to those patterns. This Spenserian material had no doubt undergone lengthy, devious underground development after the period leading up to *Comus* when Milton had first encountered and absorbed it.

The notion of Milton's dependence on Spenser, and the interpretation of *Faerie Queene* II upon which the theory of this dependence is based, were formulated *in nuce* in 1917 in a few paragraphs by Edwin Almiron Greenlaw, the inceptor of the Variorum Spenser. Those paragraphs from the original article appear in volume II, appendix V, of that work.

> The apparently episodic structure of one of the books of the *Faerie Queene* is organic, not a matter of chance. The seemingly unrelated episodes in the first six cantos of Book II are *exempla*, illustrating the evil effects of anger or spirit in the unfavourable sense....In the last six cantos the stories of Maleger, Acrasia, etc., illustrate the evils of sensuality. This symmetry of structure is further marked by the fact that the two great 'adventures' in this book as well as in Book I, represent climaxes in the development of the hero.... In both form and content on the one hand and philosophic conception of the relations between virtue and sin on the other, Spenser seemed to Milton a better teacher than Aquinas (I do not for a moment wish to be interpreted as holding that this second book of Spenser's poem is a source in the sense usually

15. 'Structural Pattern in *Paradise Lost*', *Philological Quarterly*, 28 (1949), 16–30, rpt. in *Milton: Modern Essays in Criticism*, ed. Arthur Barker (New York, 1955), pp. 142–55.

16. 'Milton's "Satan" and the Theme of Damnation in Elizabethan Tragedy', *Essays and Studies by Members of the English Association*, NS 1 (1948), 46–66.

understood ... but this similarity in conception yields some surprising parallels in incident).... In the main, the Legend of
Guyon, like *Paradise Lost*, is concerned with two great themes:
the machinations of Satan, and the Bower of Bliss.... Mammon
takes the place of Archimago, representing Satan in another form.
This temptation, the first great crisis in Guyon's development, is of
extraordinary interest. It takes three forms, lasting three days. On
the first day Guyon is tempted by wealth and power; on the
second day by ambition (Philotime); on the third the climax is
presented in the mysterious temptation of the tree laden with
golden apples. Spenser gives many classical references in order to
show the beauty of this fruit; he does not mention Eden; he does
not even make clear why the apples should be a severer test of
Guyon's temperance than Mammon's chest of gold and promise
of power or Philotime's promise of worldly fame. That it is so
regarded by Spenser is clear.... The three days' temptation of
Guyon concludes a series of incidents that pretty certainly
influenced *Paradise Regained*, in which Christ proved his temperance in the sense understood by Spenser and Milton.... One type
of intemperance, the subject of the first great crisis in Guyon's
development, is unworthy ambition and lust for power; the corresponding theme in *Paradise Lost* is the fall of Satan, the first
great 'adventure' in Milton's epic, through yielding to the same
form of intemperance. Guyon's final 'adventure', the overthrow of
the Bower of Bliss, unquestionably influenced Milton's story of
Adam's temptation and fall, not of course as the source of the
story, but in a way fully as significant.

Among a number of other departures, the present book does not follow
Greenlaw's simple division of *Faerie Queene* II into a prideful first and a
sensual second half, or his assumption that Guyon undergoes a development of character, like Redcross. Also, there may be something a
little overdone about the rejection of *Faerie Queene* II as properly a
source for Milton ('not for a moment ... a source in the sense usually
understood'). It is refreshing to hear from the year 1917 an overtone of
deprecation of the aridities and lunacies of some source study, but in
point of fact some things in that book can probably be called sources of
some things in Milton's two epics without profaning of the oft-profaned
operative word. Milton probably desired us to recognize such concrete
and detailed connections as part of his literary effect. In principle,
however, Greenlaw set forth over half a century ago the chief concepts
defended here. The precedent of this great scholar gives much support

to the development of these ideas, perhaps the more so because the path by which he reached them was so different from mine.[17]

On the premise, then, that the patterns of *Faerie Queene* II had a deep and enduring place in Milton's imagination, the manifestations through which we can chieflly trace their agency in his epics are the inward, psychologically detailed depiction of invidious, impatient pride and disdainful anger developed in the character of Satan and of the angels infected by him, and of this pride implanted by him, with a final fillip of voluptuousness, in Eve; the action of sensual desire in Adam; the pattern of human history before the Flood as revealed by Michael; the course of the most significant portion of the temptations in *Paradise Regained*; and a number of verbal reminiscences, motifs, and important isolated episodes in the two poems at large. Of all these substantive matters, to be taken up in turn, those relating to *Paradise Regained* form, perhaps, the strongest evidence. The conclusions with respect to the temptation of Milton's Christ to worldly honour seem very firm. Some of the evidence concerning the imaginative connection between *Faerie Queene* II and *Paradise Lost* seems, not, perhaps, less convincing, but more deeply submerged, as though this material had descended deeper into Milton's imagination and then had had to travel further to re-emerge. Our sure prior knowledge of Milton's strongest interest in and admiration for Spenser is likely to combine with the new evidence of Spenserian influence in many specific areas so as to exert a perfectly proper incremental effect. The larger pattern of Milton's two epics seems plain: first, the preoccupation in the first work with the progress of a temptation to rise higher than other beings—and higher than man ought—to an honour individiously understood as glory, balanced against an opposed temptation to overvalue the most bewitching object of appetite to the abandonment of true honour; second, the preoccupation in the second work with the temptation to false honour, this time successfully withstood.

17. Which was via a theory of numerical structure in Spenser, first set forth in Baybak, Delany, Hieatt, cited in chap. 6, n.6. Reflection on the significance of the numerical centre point in *Faerie Queene* II led to a new interpretation of the Cave of Mammon, in 'Three Fearful Symmetries' in *A Theatre for Spenserians: Papers of the International Spenser Colloquium*, ed. Judith Kennedy (Toronto, 1973), pp. 19–52. Greenlaw's original article is 'A Better Teacher than Aquinas', *Studies in Philology*, 14 (1917), 196–217. J. H. Hanford, in fourteen lines of his *Milton Handbook* (4th ed., New York, 1964, pp. 260–61), touches only very generally, and without much apparent justification to the reader of Milton, on these connections as elaborated by Greenlaw. The reason that Greenlaw's theory has not been followed up is probably that his presentation of it was brief, general, and theoretical.

This concentration on certain motifs is so extensive, and psychologically so elaborated, partly because Spenser was in Milton's mind to help him. Spenser's part in the process may be roughly gauged by the fact that nowhere else among English or Continental writers of epic or drama does one find the elaboration of these features in so pure and extended a form as in Spenser and Milton. At the same time, however, as we note correspondences in general patterns and in detail, we must hold in mind that Milton's transformation of Spenser's patterns along fairly consistent aesthetic, formal, and psychological lines is probably an even more important and interesting matter.

Eve suggests to Adam in Book X of *Paradise Lost* that by taking their own lives they may thwart Death's domination over their yet unborn progeny (1003–6; see page 174). Her rashness here is on a level with her earlier 'How are we happy, still in fear of harm?' (IX. 326). But in this projected resolve for suicide she stands with Amavia, who in her quite different situation says, in impatience with the apparently indifferent or malicious heavens, 'As bound by them to live in lives despight, / Yet can they not warne death from wretched wight' (*Faerie Queene*, II. i. 36). Like Amavia, Eve seems deeply moved, beyond the measured quality of her speech (1007–9). The point of connection between the situations of Eve and Amavia lies in Adam's answer (X. 1013–19). Both Eve and Amavia are like Aristotle's incontinent man in the discussion of intemperance in the *Nicomachean Ethics*, VII. vi. 1, who feels more strongly than he should the lash of deprivation of pleasure.[18] Eve's response, like Amavia's, is the bold fury that arms the weakest heart, and their pain is 'impatient smart' (*Faerie Queene*, II. i. 44). We have seen that, given the context, Milton is unlikely not to have had in his head these words, directed against Amavia, of Acrasia's enigmatic three-line charm, italicized in early editions: '*And losse of love, to her that loves to live*' (II. i. 55) when he shaped Adam's line, 'For loss of life and pleasure overloved'. When Milton composed the reproach of Adam and Eve's proposal of suicide, he was, then, thinking of the complex of ideas surrounding Amavia's own suicide, and his explanation of the name Amavia ('lover of life') is that the resort to despair with his proffered

18. One of the many places where Book II makes contact with the *Ethics*. Aristotle often, as in this chapter, makes use of the bifurcation between irascibility and concupiscence, or the like. Many other points of contact are catalogued in Ernest Sirluck, 'The *Faerie Queene* Book II, and the *Nicomachean Ethics*', Modern Philology, 49 (1951–52), 73–100. I disagree with the tenor of this careful and well-known article, in concluding that Book II makes contact at many places with the *Ethics*, but is not structured by that work. Sirluck allows for the presence of the Platonic triad of categories in *Faerie Queene* II.

knife (or rope) is likely to be the device of the weakly impatient, who, deprived of a parcel of the overloved *voluptas* of life, turn to violent action against self. A confused version of this difficulty is probably at the bottom of the fallen angel Nisroch's comment, just before his party strikes back in heaven by inventing gunpowder:

> Sense of pleasure we may well
> Spare out of life perhaps, and not repine,
> But live content, which is the calmest life:
> But pain is perfect misery, the worst
> Of evils, and, excessive, overturns
> All patience....
> [*Paradise Lost*, VI. 459–64]

The point is several times made in Amavia's case that her violence is not in revenge against others; she is no Acrasia, or Phedon: 'Live thou', she says to her son,

> and to thy mother dead attest,
> That cleare she dide from blemish criminall.
> [*Faerie Queene*, II. i. 37]

And Guyon says:

> sith this wretched woman overcome
> Of anguish, rather then of crime hath beene,
> Reserve her cause to her eternall doome.
> [*Faerie Queene*, II. i. 58]

What Amavia and Eve have both fallen prey to is immoderate anguish. Probably the most important point here, however, is that a continuation of Adam's previously quoted speech connects this kind of impatience with a more general wrathful violence, the attitude typical of both Spenser's Pyrochles and Milton's Satan. The two attitudes seem always to be related in both authors' minds (the continuation of this speech also gives the lie to Amavia's outcry against the 'careless heavens'):

> No more be mentioned then of violence
> Against our selves, and wilful barrenness,
> That cuts us off from hope, and savours only
> Rancour and pride, impatience and despite,
> Reluctance against God and his just yoke
> Laid on our necks....
> [*Paradise Lost*, X. 1041–46]

Among examples of rancour and pride, impatience and despite, in turning one's back on forgiveness and grace and embracing one's own destruction, Spenser's most poignant is indeed Pyrochles, on his back and at Arthur's mercy:

> So he now subject to the victours law,
> Did not once move nor upward cast his eye,
> For vile disdaine and rancour, which did gnaw
> His hart in twaine with sad melancholy,
> As one that loathed life, and yet despised to dye.
> [*Fairie Queene*, II. viii. 50]

It seems clear that this and similar reactions of Pyrochles are an imaginative constituent in Milton's fashioning of the despairing but defiant aspect of Satan. It is not that Satan, after the initial fall, was given the chance of grace as man was, but that the theological aura in which Spenser wraps this episode shows us how Milton would imagine such a being, devilish or human, confronting the fact of divine generosity. Arthur here plainly takes on the role of the Godhead in relation to man, in a context concerned with grace. He offers Pyrochles full remission of his sins, and it is as a stubborn 'Pagan' that Pyrochles refuses this freely yielded gift. He has 'wilfully refused grace'.

> But full of Princely bounty and great mind,
>   The conqueror nought cared him to slay,
>   But casting wrongs and all revenge behind,
>   More glory thought to give life, then decay,
>   And said, Paynim, this is thy dismall day;
>   Yet if thou wilt renounce thy miscreance,
>   And my trew liegeman yield thy selfe for ay,
>   Life will I graunt thee for thy valiaunce,
> And all thy wrongs will wipe out of my sovenaunce.
>
> Foole (said the Pagan) I thy gift defye,
>   But use thy fortune, as it doth befall,
>   And say, that I not overcome do dye,
>   But in despight of life, for death do call.
>   Wroth was the Prince, and sory yet withall,
>   That he so wilfully refused grace;
>   Yet sith his fate so cruelly did fall,
>   His shining Helmet he gan soone unlace,
> And left his headlesse body bleeding all the place.
> [*Faerie Queene*, II. viii. 51–52]

We may notice in passing that the replacement here of divine mercy with divine vengeance in the face of obduracy (removing physically the rational organ which spiritually had already been lost) reminds us a little of the Miltonic God's promises of future punishment. Principally, however, the wilfully embittered, final self-destructiveness of such a one as Pyrochles is seen by Spenser as a passionate search for relief in the same self-indulgent but benighted direction as Amavia's suicide; and similarly with Milton: Adam's condemnation of an initiative of Eve's in which Milton remembers Amavia's character and fate leads us to the wilful rancour and disdain characteristic of Satan and his followers to whom the very thought of repentance is distasteful. As Pyrochles 'for vile disdaine and rancour' 'did not once move nor upward cast his eye', so Satan, preparing to answer Abdiel on the field of battle, refuses to look at him.

> Whom the grand foe with scornful eye askance
> Thus answered....
> [*Paradise Lost*, VI. 149–50]

In the same way Mammon prepares his first speech to Guyon: 'Thereat with staring eyes fixed askaunce, / In great disdaine, he answerd...' (*Faerie Queene*, II. vii. 7).

For it is not only Pyrochles but also Mammon and others filled with rage and envy in *Faerie Queene* II whom Milton makes use of in developing his picture of Satan and his followers. Mammon and others in his realm are like Satan in having been banned from heaven. Although Spenser is obviously inclined to the construction of ad hoc mythological genealogies, varying according to need, the fact that Lucifera, embodiment of disdainful and invidious pride in *Faerie Queen* I, is the daughter of Pluto and Proserpina (I. iv. 11) relates to the character of Proserpina's and Mammon's realm in *Faerie Queene* II. Philotime, the embodiment of worldly, passionate competition for false honours, is the daughter of Mammon. Mammon claims to be the greatest god but adds that he is so 'beneath the sky'. He has no standing in celestial divinity. It was unjustly, he tells us, that Philotime was cast out from heaven (a transparent fiction). Similarly, Tantalus was sure of his right to feast in heaven, although we see him starving in hell. All of these bear on the signal *acharnement* of Milton's Satan. Hardened hearts and closed minds come in many varieties, but, whether smooth and glozing or maddened by wrath, they are likely to originate in a concentration of one's whole being on *revanche*, on turning the tables on a hated, victorious enemy. In that dialogue held with himself at the

beginning of Book IV, paced so much like one in Marlowe's *Faustus*,
Satan's unrelenting quality owes much to these Spenserian characters.
The remnant of a better self asks, 'Is there no place left for repentance,
none for pardon left?' and the hardened answer comes pat:

> None left but by submission; and that word
> Disdain forbids me,...
>
> .   .   .   .
>
> So farewell hope, and with hope farewell fear,
> Farewell remorse: all good to me is lost;
> Evil be thou my good.....
> [*Paradise Lost*, IV. 81–82, 108–110]

The discomposure of the prideful man who thinks himself wronged sits
upon his countenance whenever he forgets himself:

> Thus while he spake, each passion dimmed his face
> Thrice changed with pale, ire, envy and despair,
> Which marred his borrowed visage, and betrayed
> Him counterfeit, if any eye beheld.
> For heavenly minds from such distempers foul
> Are ever clear.....
> [114–19]

Such discomposure is again and again characteristic of Pyrochles:

> So up he let him rise, who with grim looke
> And count'naunce sterne upstanding, gan to grind
> His grated teeth for great disdeigne, and shooke
> His sandy lockes, long hanging downe behind,
> Knotted in bloud and dust, for griefe of mind,
> That he in ods of armes was conquered.
> [*Faerie Queene*, II. v. 14]

Satan's rage is fiery, like that of Pyrochles; one difference between the
two figures is that Satan is at first open to conscientious scruple and
rational doubt, which, of course, he will soon overcome.

> Satan, now first inflamed with rage, came down,
> The tempter ere the accuser of mankind,
> To wreak on innocent frail man his loss
> Of that first battle, and his flight to hell;
> Yet not rejoicing in his speed, though bold,

Far off and fearless, nor with cause to boast,
Begins his dire attempt, which nigh the birth
Now rolling, boils in his tumultuous breast,
And like a devilish engine back recoils
Upon himself; horror and doubt distract
His troubled thoughts, and from the bottom stir
The hell within him, for within him hell
He brings, and round about him, nor from hell
One step no more than from himself can fly.
[*Paradise Lost*, IV. 9–22]

When he has for a moment become 'stupidly good' as he spies on Eve whom he is about to corrupt, what works within him is enough to return him to his accustomed state:

But the hot hell that always in him burns,
Though in mid heaven, soon ended his delight,
And tortures him now more, the more he sees
Of pleasure not for him ordained.....
[IX. 467–70]

In Pyrochles this constant burning is (as his name suggests) the most evident quality. Even when he submerges himself in Phaedria's muddy but cooling Lake of carnal Idleness and forgetfulness of honour, he burns on inextinguishably, self-consumed on the bonfire of his own rancour,

I burne, I burne, I burne, then loud he cryde,
  O how I burne with implacable fire,
Yet nought can quench mine inly flaming syde,
Nor sea of licour cold, nor lake of mire,
Nothing but death can doe me to respire.
[*Faerie Queene*, II. vi. 44]

(The suicide motif is continued poignantly in the following stanza.) As Pyrochles burns, so does Tantalus, consumed physically with thirst in the midst of feculent water, and consumed mentally by what he considers the imposition wrought on him by the highest god. Surely both these characters were in Milton's mind as he shaped his Satan,[19] although it is true that the inexpiable wrath of Milton's devil has much in common

19. A number of 'Pyrochlean' passages appear in connection with Satan and his followers in the battle in heaven in Book VI, of which the most strikingly applicable to the inveterate combatant against Guyon and Arthur is in lines 785–97.

with that of the protagonists in Elizabethan revenge tragedies. Revenge tragedies, however, glory in the spirit of feud and vendetta or at the best are ambiguous on this subject. Milton, like Spenser in the case of his just mentioned characters, firmly identifies Satan's vengeful rancour for what it is on any Christian scale: loss of reasonable control.[20]

The reverse side of Satan's envy and wrath towards those above him is that he and his followers can truly comprehend no good save glory and worldly honour. In this way they follow Mammon, to whom it did not occur to offer anything but this to Guyon. Superficially the devils seem much concerned with liberty and the justice deemed by them to be their due. At this level, the rooted, intoxicated self-deception, supported by a variety of question-begging rhetorical means, which is at the base of the sophistry passing for thought among Satan and his fallen companions, is in a way an elaboration of Tantalus' rhetorical insistence and of his lack of self-knowledge. But when the chips are down and Satan is communing with his immediate confederates in an emergency, it is plain that all that was cant:

> Found worthy not of liberty alone,
> Too mean pretence, but what we more affect,
> Honour, dominion, glory, and renown.
> [*Paradise Lost*, VI. 420–22]

The degree to which the devils take themselves seriously is in fact a measure of the absurd disproportion that Spenser and Milton are both at pains to create through the aspirations of Mammon, Philotime, Tantalus, and Satan, all of whom believe that they belong either with, or in the room of, God or Jove and yet have their seats beneath the earth or at the bottom of the universe: high pride in lowest place.

> For strength from truth divided and from just,
>
> . . . .
>
>   to glory aspires
> Vain glorious, and through infamy seeks fame:
> Therefore eternal silence be their doom.
> [*Paradise Lost*, VI. 381, 383–85]

In relating how Eve is infected with a similar blindness, Milton continues to hold his predecessor in his imagination at various points. As Eve seeks occasion, so had Pyrochles also sought it. Questioned by Guyon, Atin says that his master has sent him to search out the

---

20. I cannot take seriously the opinion, still held by some, that Milton finally means the opposite of this.

personification Occasion, 'where so she bee'. This is the immediate reaction:

> Madman (said then the Palmer) that does seeke
> *Occasion* to wrath, and cause of strife;
> She comes unsought....
>
> [*Faerie Queene*, II. iv. 44]

Eve, wishing to work alone in the garden and affirming our human ability singly to resist the tempter, and to gain honour thereby, gets a similar reply from Adam:

> Seek not temptation then, which to avoid
> Were better, and most likely if from me
> Thou sever not: trial will come unsought.
>
> [*Paradise Lost*, IX. 364–66]

The occasion, of which it is said in both cases (surely with verbal reminiscence in the second) that one should not seek it because it comes unsought, prompts to wrath in the one case and will prompt to pride in the other. Wrath and pride are two intimately associated mortal sins; as well, however, we have already seen them as parts of a single complex in both Spenser and Milton.

Further, when Satan in the shape of the serpent has successfully inveigled Eve to follow him to the Tree of Knowledge, her first, guileless utterance as she identifies the tree is 'Fruitless to me, though fruit be here to excess' (IX. 648). These words are the more heavily fraught with ambiguity because they are not accurately descriptive of the physical scene before her. In what precise sense could the abundant fruit of the tree be called excessive? On the other hand, fruit is ready here to Excess's hand (compare *Faerie Queene*, II. xii. 56, 57, where Excesse plucks and offers to Guyon) and here excess finds its fruition. Upton long ago suggested a reminiscence here of Spenser's lines in the Garden of Proserpina concerning the gaining of the girl Cydippe by Acontius.[21]

> Here also sprong that goodly golden fruit,
> With which *Acontius* got his lover trew,
> Whom he had long time sought with fruitlesse suit.
>
> [*Faerie Queene*, II. vii. 55]

It is easier to believe Upton's suggestion if we accept as Milton's own the interpretation already offered of this episode: that the story runs in

---

21. See Variorum Spenser, II, 265.

parallel with the immediately preceding one of Atlanta and of Hippomenes who gained her with golden apples, and that Spenser intends us to recall the moralization of this latter tale in the immensely popular English sixteenth-century versions of the *Gesta Romanorum*, according to which the lover of Atalanta is the devil and she the soul of man. It is likely that the given interpretation was Milton's stimulus to put his punning lines in Eve's mouth under typologically identical circumstances. He may also have imagined that Spenser (no tyro in Greek if Lodowick Bryskett can be trusted)[22] may have intended the name Acontius to carry an overtone of Greek *akontistikos* ('skilled in throwing the dart') and related words (for example, *akontion*, 'dart', 'javelin') and thus of a Satanic dart thrower as well as an aggressive Cupid figure, or an implication of *akoniton*, 'aconite', a poison-giving plant, like the Tree of Knowledge, and also an association with the list of other poisonous plants two stanzas before this in Spenser's narrative.

Yet another possible object of Milton's imagination in connection with Eve may have been Spenser's association of her with Proserpina. It is true that there is an earlier tradition of Proserpina as a type of Eve,[23] but there is something very pointed and central about Milton's preoccupation with the resemblance between the two who became subject to hell, and who are practically coterminous in Spenser's Garden of Proserpina. We have first the passage in *Paradise Lost* IV (one of Arnold's touchstones) where Proserpina is obviously a type of Eve:

> Not that fair field
> Of Enna, where Proserpine gathering flowers
> Her self a fairer flower by gloomy Dis
> Was gathered, which cost Ceres all that pain
> To seek her through the world....
> [268–72]

Then, Eve is identified with Ceres in what might be called a pre-Proserpina stage before her Fall:

> Ceres in her prime,
> Yet virgin of Proserpina from Jove.
> [IX. 395–96]

22. See Alexander C. Judson, *The Life of Edmund Spenser* (Baltimore, 1945), p. 106.
23. See Don Cameron Allen, *Mysteriously Meant: The Rediscovery of Pagan Symbolism and Allegorical Interpretation in the Renaissance* (Baltimore, 1970), pp. 129, 187, 237, for occurrences in Athanasius Kircher, *Oedipus Aegyptiacus*; Abraham Fraunce, *The Third Part of the Countess of Pembrokes Yuychurch*; Francois Pomey, *Pantheum Mysticum*.

Thereafter we have the series of evocations of flowers, taking us back to her whose removal robbed the earth of all vegetation. As the serpent watches her, Eve stoops to support various unpropped stems,

> mindless the while,
> Her self, though fairest unsupported flower,
> From her best prop so far, and storm so nigh.
> [IX. 431–33]

and the garland of roses which Adam is meanwhile weaving for her head drops its petals as soon as she, fallen, approaches him. Adam calls Eve 'deflowered' at line 901. This linking through flower imagery of the two women who had eaten the fruit may thus suggest a connection with the Garden of Proserpina. If so, the connection must be one of the happiest influences exerted by that unhappy garden. Perhaps nothing is more touching in the whole of *Paradise Lost* than the connection suggested between the fates of this classical figure and the biblical one.

Three cancelled lines in the Trinity MS of *Comus*, at the point where one brother is fearsomely speculating on the fate of the Lady, show Milton using this pathetic instance at an earlier stage of his career, when he was under what has been generally regarded as a more obviously Spenserian influence:[24]

> So fares as did forsaken Proserpina
> When the big rolling wallowing flakes of pitchy clouds
> And darkness wound her in....

For our purposes the point here is that Milton's Lady stands with Spenser's Guyon in succeeding where Spenser's Proserpina-Eve failed.

The temptation of Milton's Eve, like that of Guyon and, by implication, of Eve herself in the Garden of Proserpina, is mainly in the direction of overweening pride and status, with much greater elaboration than in other accounts and with an added fillip at the climax. Satan tries to arouse discontent, vain hopes, inordinate desires, and pride in Eve's mind as she sleeps at IV. 807–9. Her later description of the resultant dream makes plain that her mind has dwelt (whether with repulsion or liking) on being as the gods in heaven. His main attempt upon her in Book IX is spanned by a series of encomiastic epithets, beginning at line 540: 'celestial beauty' (with an appeal like Braggadocchio's to leave desert places and go where she may be 'universally admired'), 'Empress of this fair world', 'Sovereign...universal

---

24. Quoted from Carey-Fowler, p. 194n.

dame', 'Queen of this universe', 'Goddess humane'. At the moment of eating, 'Godhead' was not absent 'from her thought'. Satan had just put to her the soft, terrible question, with its travesty of the Eucharist:

And what are gods that man may not become
As they, participating godlike food?
[IX. 716–17]

In the Spenserian context that we have been suggesting here the travesty is indeed a double one. Tantalus had been self-tempted by what he had anticipated from a meal with Jove, in which we know that the food was his own son. That son should have been, but was not, well beloved of his father: he was sacrificed by that father, not for the sake of man, but in the hope that the father could attain to god-like knowledge or commerce.

Something in the last step of Eve's infatuation as she reaches for the apple is probably familiar to anyone who has been strongly tempted, but is also strikingly reminiscent of the last step in Mammon's unsuccessful temptation of Guyon. There seems to be a certain fatality about strong attractions. At the last moment the ground bass of a long-standing temptation is likely to be supplemented by a descant of an entirely different variety of enticingness so as to make surrender seem a foregone conclusion—seem a revelation of truth that we should have perceived long before. In this case infernal pride is seconded by the disarming voice of appetite:

Fixed on the fruit she gazed, which to behold
Might tempt alone, and in her ears the sound
Yet rung of his persuasive words, impregned
With reason, to her seeming, and with truth;
Mean while the hour of noon drew on, and waked
An eager appetite, raised by the smell
So savoury of that fruit, which with desire,
Inclinable now grown to touch or taste,
Solicited her longing eye....
[*Paradise Lost*, IX. 735–43]

It is difficult to see why Spenser does not make more of the similar expansion, at the last moment, of the field of Guyon's temptation. As suggested in chapter 12, the numerical exigency may have had something to do with this failure. In any case, we know from the form of

Mammon's words and from Guyon's subsequent state that the hero has grown weak with hunger and exhaustion after his three days' test. Mammon speaks with an anger characteristic of the unsuccessful tempter of *Paradise Regained* rather than of the smooth devil who overcomes Eve (although with the epithet 'fearful' he may be trying to elicit the kind of rashness that separated Eve from Adam on the fatal day):

> Thou fearefull foole,
> Why takest not of that same fruit of gold,
> Ne sittest downe on that same silver stoole,
> To rest thy wearie person, in the shadow coole.
>
> [*Faerie Queene*, II. vii. 63]

Guyon himself, then, is being tempted to accept a quintessential embodiment of pride by the appeal of this very embodiment to his appetite: so seamless is the web of moral life.

Milton's Sin, who for the sake of her father and former lover, Satan, is shown acting out in advance Eve's capitulation to him, expresses her own abominable, self-deceived surrender to his will in what is, in principle, the same pattern: first prideful expectation of rising to the highest rule, and then *voluptas*:

> Thou art my father, thou my author, thou
> My being gavest me; whom should I obey
> But thee, whom follow? Thou wilt bring me soon
> To that new world of light and bliss, among
> The gods who live at ease, where I shall reign
> At thy right hand voluptuous as beseems
> Thy daughter and thy darling, without end.
>
> [*Paradise Lost*, II. 864–70]

Imagining herself Satan's darling, she may embody an ironic reminiscence of the darling of the true God, in *An Hyme of Heavenly Beautie*:

> There in his bosome *Sapience* doth sit,
> The soveraine dearling of the *Deity*,
> Clad like a Queene in royall robes, most fit
> For so great powre and peereless majesty
> And all with gemmes and jewels gorgeously
> Adornd, that brighter than the starres appear
> And make her native brightnes seem more cleare.
>
> [183–89]

A little later Sapience is called 'that faire love of mightie heavens king' (235).[27]

The most appalling feature of Eve's sudden, new exclusivity immediately after eating the apple is her thought that she might remain superior to Adam by not offering it to him, as her mind lights on the proposition that no one can be happy except at the top of the heap ('Inferior who is free?'). She is restrained from this step at first only by the further consideration that she might lose him to another woman: 'A death to think'. From this point onward the middle of the stage is occupied by the fall of Adam himself, in which Eve plays the role of another Acrasia, as though she had moved from Eden to a Bower of Bliss, opposite her Adam who plays the part of another Verdant or Mordant gradually moving towards the state of Grill. Milton gives his picture the specious glories of courtly love, as in the Bower. Adam holds the world well lost for her:

> if death
> Consort with thee, death is to me as life.
> [IX. 953–54]

And she blissfully approves the spurious heroism:

> O glorious trial of exceeding love, . . .
>
> .   .   .   .
>
>   So saying, she embraced him, and for joy
> Tenderly wept, much won that he his love
> Had so ennobled, as of choice to incur
> Divine displeasure for her sake, or death.
> [961, 990–93]

Both fallen, they share indifferently in both forms of intemperance. First, 'in lust they burn'; then, recovered from that, they fall to 'anger, hate, / Mistrust, suspicion, discord' (IX. 1123–24). When they encounter God, they show to him and to each other what Satan had felt and what had been displayed in *Faerie Queene* II by Pilate and Tantalus in the Garden of Proserpina, and by the recovered beasts of the Bower:

>   apparent guilt,
> And shame, and perturbation, and despair,

25. Apart from these correspondences it is obvious that Satan, Sin, and Death form a parody of the Trinity in *Paradise Lost* itself. See also, in connection with Sapience, the muse Urania playing with her sister Wisdom in presence of the Almighty Father, in *Paradise Lost*, VII. 9–11.

Anger, and obstinacy, and hate, and guile.
>   [X. 112–14]

Much of the story here of Adam's fall into appetite and of the pair's mutual guilt seems to bear less of the imprint of Spenserian narrative details than does some of the other material at which we have looked. Nor, of course, may we say that a pattern of twofold in-temperance—one produced by wilful striving and recrimination, the other by appetite—defines Milton's vastly more complex theological formulation of the case. Nevertheless the overarching narrative and mythic pattern, supported by much detail elsewhere, persists here as well. Thereafter in Books XI and XII there is something suggestively Spenserian about the descent of an angel not simply to punish, as in other accounts, but also, under grace, to minister to, a repentant Adam and Eve before they leave Eden. In one sense, Michael here parallels the angels who ministered to Christ in the Gospel accounts, and in *Paradise Regained*, after His successfully undergone temptation. It was Spenser, however, who had had the idea of a ministering angel, analogous to the one in the Gospel, descending after the temptation for the sake of a mere mortal, Guyon, in *Faerie Queene*, II. viii; and it is perhaps from this source, and from Spenser's expatiation there on the availability of such grace in spite of our wretched sinfulness, that Milton got the primary notion which he then developed into Michael's descent to Adam and Eve so as to give an exposition, not without hope, of the history of the race through the coming of Christ and beyond.

A large part of even this account follows a structure that is now familiar to us from Spenser. There is a two-stage historical process for the descendants of that 'bevy of fair women' (XI. 582) who come on in dance, and in gems and wanton dress, singing 'Soft amorous ditties', and who consort in the tents of wickedness with the men who, 'though grave, eyed them, and let their eyes / Rove without rein'. In the days of the first generation of descendants,

>   might only shall be admired,
> And valour and heroic virtue called;
> To overcome in battle, and subdue
> Nations, and bring home spoils with infinite
> Manslaughter, shall be held the highest pitch
> Of human glory, and for glory done
> Of triumph, to be styled great conquerors,
> Patrons of mankind, gods, and sons of gods,

Destroyers rightlier called and plagues of men.
[XI. 689–97]

These lovers of false honour aspiring finally to divinity and having
violence as their sign (as in *Faerie Queene* II) are followed by a second
generation whose end is in water, mythically like the sodden followers
of appetite in *Faerie Queene* II, associated with the inconstant lake or
sea on which their islands float errantly. The second group are 'Flood
overwhelmed' (XI. 748) because they are given over to sensuality:

All now was turned to jollity and game,
To luxury and riot, feast and dance,
Marrying or prostituting, as befell,
Rape or adultery, where passing fair
Allured them....
[XI. 714–18]

These who 'now swim in joy' (as Adam and Eve 'swim in mirth') are
'Erelong to swim at large' (625–26); only those in the ark are saved. As
for the others, 'in their palaces / Where luxury late reigned, sea monsters
whelped / And stabled' (750–52). The Flood, a datum of doctrinal
history, is fitted into a pattern that structurally mirrors the conception
of the two forms of intemperance. Milton is likely to have been
reflecting here Spenser's symbolic pattern of intemperance, as well as his
own and Spenser's structuring of the climactic temptations to self-
assertion on the one side and sensual abasement on the other.

We know, however, that Michael's story has a happy ending. The
tradition of such prophecies is a popular one, going back at least as far
as the 'magnus ab integro saeclorum nascitur ordo' and the 'iam redit et
Virgo' of Virgil's Fourth Eclogue, but it would be surprising if Milton
had not thought, while composing that story, of a more secular version:
the brutal history of British kings (read by Arthur in *Faerie Queene*, II.
x), to be followed by the reign of Belphoebe-Elizabeth, who scorns both
false honour and sensuality. Equally, when Milton lets us hear Adam
speak of the end of that prophecy,

How soon hath thy prediction, seer blest,
Measured this transient world, the race of time,
Till time stand fixed: beyond is all abyss,
Eternity, whose end no eye can reach,
[XII. 553–56]

he may have remembered not only the end of the Mutability Cantos but also Spenser's workman-like manipulation of the hallowed machinery for ending such prophecies, after Merlin has finished an equally brutal account of early history for Britomart and her squire (*Faerie Queene*, III. iii. 49–50). Milton would have congratulated himself, however, as a seer blest who had chosen eternal truth over the lying fancy of a merely secular apotheosis.

Before leaving *Paradise Lost*, I wish to discuss two further points concerning Satan's followers. It is no doubt already obvious that in Milton's imagination Spenser's Mammon most often became Satan at large. Nevertheless, Milton's own Mammon is also coterminous with his predecessor's at that point in the Infernal Council of *Paradise Lost* where he speaks out as an artificer (and as an advocate of empty honour as well):

> This desert soil
> Wants not her hidden lustre, gems and gold;
> Nor want we skill or art, from whence to raise
> Magnificence; and what can heaven show more?
> [II. 270–73]

The Ovidian *topos* of man's wounding the earth for gain which leads to crime (*Metamorphoses*, I. 137–40) had already been used by Spenser in one of Guyon's replies to Mammon:

> The antique world, in his first flowring youth,
> Found no defect in his Creatours grace,
> But with glad thankes, and unreproved truth,
> The gifts of soveraigne bountie did embrace:
> Like Angels life was then mens happy cace;
> But later ages pride, like corn-fed steed
> Abusd her plenty, and fat swolne encreace
> To all licentious lust, and gan exceed
> The measure of her meane, and naturall first need.
>
> Then gan a cursed hand the quiet wombe
> Of his great Grandmother with steele to wound,
> And the hid treasures in her sacred tombe,
> With Sacriledge to dig. Therein he found
> Fountaines of gold and silver to abound,
> Of which the matter of his huge desire
> And pompous pride eftsoones he did compound;
> Then avarice gan through his veines inspire

His greedy flames, and kindled life-devouring fire.
                    [*Faerie Queene*, II. vii. 16–17]

And, correspondingly, Milton uses this *topos* in the case of his Mammon and Mammon's helpers:

> Mammon led them on,
> Mammon, the least erected spirit that fell
> From heaven, for even in heaven his looks and thoughts
> Were always downward bent, admiring more
> The riches of heaven's pavement, trodden gold,
> Than aught divine or holy else enjoyed
> In vision beautific: by him first
> Men also, and by his suggestion taught,
> Ransacked the centre, and with impious hands
> Rifled the bowels of their mother earth
> For treasures better hid. Soon had his crew
> Opened into the hill a spacious wound
> And digged out ribs of gold. Let none admire
> That riches grow in hell; that soil may best
> Deserve the precious bane....
>   [I. 678–92]

The special case of this motif in connection with the followers of Satan digging for the materials with which they were the first to fabricate gunpowder probably has one of its sources here. In their spiteful pride, they associate themselves with fire, like Spenser's disdainful ones (no matter what further connections there may be with Milton's early poems on the Gunpowder Plot):

> innumerable hands
> Were ready, in a moment up they turned
> Wide the celestial soil, and saw beneath
> The originals of nature in their crude
> Conception; sulphurous and nitrous foam
> They found, they mingled, and with subtle art,
> Concocted and adusted they reduced
> To blackest grain, and into store conveyed:
> Part hidden veins digged up (nor hath this earth
> Entrails unlike) of mineral and stone,
> Whereof to found their engines and their balls
> Of missive ruin; part incentive reed

Provide, pernicious with one touch of fire.

[*Paradise Lost*, VI. 508–20]

In the second place, the grove of trees (X. 547 ff.) filled with spurious fruit from which Satan's followers eat in enforced imitation of man, after Satan's return from hell to announce the Fall, is (with apologies to Irene Samuel's *Dante and Milton: The 'Commedia' and 'Paradise Lost'*)[26] much closer to the tree overshadowing Proserpina's seat than to the trees towards which those on the Sixth Terrace extend hands in Dante's *Purgatorio*. All of these trees correspond symbolically to the Tree of Knowledge, but Milton's grove is like Spenser's tree in being infernal, not purgatorial. The apples of the grove are filled with dust and ashes; Proserpina's apples are hard, mineral gold, correspondingly lacking in true nourishment. Had Tantalus attained one, or had Guyon wanted one, the practical effect would have been quite similar: sharp disappointment with Dead Sea fruit. A detail which further vaguely suggests that in creating his grove Milton was remembering the Garden of Proserpina, and was suggesting a continuity of tradition with it, is his recall of the name of Proserpina's infernal consort in the epithet at X. 444 for the audience chamber where the devils are first turned to serpents and then rush forth to devour the fruit: *'Plutonian hall'*.[27]

---

26. (Ithaca, N.Y., 1966), p. 246. She cites *Purgatorio*, XXII. 130 ff., XXIV. 103 ff., XXXIII. 52–57.

27. For the idea of the fallen angels turning (at least metaphorically) to serpents, see E. C. Baldwin, 'Milton and Phineas Fletcher', *Journal of English and Germanic Philology*, 33 (1934), 544–46. The passage referred to is *The Purple Island*, VII. 10, 11. The resemblance is very general, but it is adjacent to 'In heav'n they scorned to serve, so now in hell they reigne', a line which looks like being the source of *Paradise Lost*, I. 262–63 and IV. 183–84.

14

Spenser and
Paradise Regained

More than does the Satan of *Paradise Lost*, the one of *Paradise Regained* matches Spenser's Mammon. Partly this follows of necessity. This Satan is unsuccessful in tempting Christ; Mammon is unsuccessful in tempting a man taking Christ's place. There is a natural similarity, for instance, in the formulae with which each of the foiled deceivers shows his growing discontent at each of his successive failures. In *Paradise Regained* the series runs: 'To whom thus answered Satan malcontent' (II. 392); 'Satan stood / A while as mute confounded what to say' (III. 1–2); 'Satan had not to answer, but stood struck / With guilt of his own sin, for he himself / Insatiable of glory had lost all' (III. 146–48); 'To whom the tempter inly racked replied' (III. 203); 'Perplexed and troubled at his bad success / The tempter stood, nor had what to reply' (IV. 1–2); 'To whom the Fiend with fear abashed replied' (IV. 195); 'Satan now / Quite at a loss' (IV. 365–66); 'To whom the Fiend now swoll'n with rage replied' (IV. 499). The corresponding series in the House of Mammon runs: 'The Feend [Mammon's servant, sooner enraged than his master] his gnashing teeth did grate, / And griev'd, so long to lacke his greedy prey' (II. vii. 34); 'Mammon was much displeased yet no'te he chuse, / But beare the rigour of his bold mesprise' (vii. 39); 'Mammon emmoved was with inward wrath; / yet forcing it to faine…' (vii. 51); 'Mammon…roughly him bespake' (vii. 63). Both series have a rising action, but the resemblance between them is not conclusive. Nevertheless, other strong and interesting evidence exists for the persistence of *Faerie Queene* II. vii in Milton's imagination at the time of composition of *Paradise Regained*, whenever that may have been.

There is, for example, the matter of the polar contrast between the garden of *Paradise Lost* and the grove of temptation summoned up by Satan in *Paradise Regained*. I have discussed in chapter 7 how Spenser made a programmatic distinction between the roles of Nature and Art in a series of moralized landscapes, but particularly in the Garden of Adonis and the Bower of Bliss. Milton makes the same distinction in contrasting Eden, created by God, and the grove materialized by Satan's shams. It seems probable that he inherited the idea in this context, and a way of verbalizing it, from Spenser. The widespread dichotomy Nature-Art is not employed elsewhere in this way. Eden:

> Flowers worthy of Paradise which not nice art
> In beds and curious knots, but nature boon
> Poured forth profuse on hill and dale and plain.
> [*Paradise Lost*, IV. 241–43]

The grove in *Paradise Regained*:

> Nature's own work it seemed (Nature taught Art).
> [II. 295]

It follows from the premises with which I began the discussion of *Paradise Lost* that the temptations to which Christ is to be exposed in this moralized garden landscape do not resemble those in the garden landscape of the Bower of Bliss but are like those of the House of Mammon. I have noted, however, that Spenser's or any medieval visionary poet's choice of scene—a garden for one kind of temptation, the Lower Regions for another—is mainly a matter of narrative expediency and of what works best in terms of his total pattern and drift of meaning. Anyone who doubts that the wide open gate of Acrasia's Bower could as easily in another context be Virgil's continually open door to gloomy Dis, or a medieval wide-open hell's mouth, might consider both the contiguity and the ambiguities of scenes of garden and hell in Hieronymus Bosch's triptych 'The Garden of Earthly Delights' in the Prado. Milton was naturally constrained to opt for a garden scene here, and he uses the dichotomy Nature-Art in Spenser's manner in reference to a situation whose terms undergo only a permutation, not an essential change.

Among the temptations which Milton imagines as being inflicted on Christ, the one to accept money in order to gain honours, and then the temptation to accept honours directly, are, conceptually and verbally, startlingly close to the corresponding temptations of Guyon. There is also food for thought, however, in the character and sequence of the Miltonic Christ's temptations as a whole.

Of the two extended Gospel accounts, Luke 4 speaks of Christ's being tempted to change stones into bread, to accept the kingdoms of the world, and to cast Himself from the pinnacle of the temple, in that order. Matthew 4 lists the same three items but reverses the last two. Milton's sequence is like Luke's, except that Milton interpolates the temptation of an offered banquet between the first and the second. Given Luke's sequence, we may ask what use Milton would have been likely to make of Guyon's human version of the forty-'day' (that is, stanza) sojourn in the Wilderness and the Temptation,[1] if this version was vivid in Milton's imagination.

He would have realized that since Guyon was human, not divine, Spenser could have done nothing with the temptations to change stones into bread, or to cast oneself from the pinnacle of the temple: these are for the Son of God alone. For a similar but opposite reason there was no place in *Paradise Regained* for the temptation put to Guyon to be as the gods. Milton would have had to develop these two without help from Spenser's corresponding scene. However, with the Spenserian formulation of the temptation to accept the kingdoms of the world something might be done. As well, beyond the scriptural account, there remains the temptation which Spenser invented for Guyon, the one touch of *volup-*

---

1. As with *Comus*, one must attend to the point that Milton read followers of Spenser as well as Spenser himself. Professor Barbara K. Lewalski, in *Milton's Brief Epic: The Genre, Meaning, and Art of 'Paradise Regained'* (Providence, R.I., 1966), draws attention in this connection to Giles Fletcher's *Christs Victorie and Triumph* (1610), which is also an English biblical poem. As she says, the sequence of temptations in Fletcher's House of Pangloretta (Bacchus, Luxurie, Avarice, Ambitious Honor, and Pangloretta herself—glory) bears some resemblance to the one in *Paradise Regained*, where, however, there is no temptation to *Luxuria* (pp. 119–20). Fletcher's sequence is partly derived from Spenser's House of Mammon, and the temptations of *Paradise Regained* seem to me to be closer to the latter, in detail and in expression. Professor Lewalski points out also that Milton's Satan as 'an aged, pious, but deprived desert dweller' is like Fletcher's (p. 118). This seems valid, although as she says in her note, both Fletcher's and Milton's Satans here resemble Spenser's Archimago. See also pp. 91, 105, 128, 129.

Miss Joan Grundy's *The Spenserian Poets* (London, 1969) is the most recent book in this field. Her penultimate words on the resemblance in texture and detail between the work of the Spenserians (particularly of Drayton) and much that Milton wrote ought to be read by everyone interested in Milton's inheritance (pp. 204–15). See, in her paragraph on Milton's relation to Spenser, her position that Milton 'learned' and assimilated Spenser, rather than imitating him (p. 204).

tas in the House of Mammon: something to eat, on the analogy of Eve's temptation, the point being that Eve accepted but Guyon refused. Milton might also capitalize on this, if, as we premise, he was really interested in Spenser's rendition of the myth. Since Milton is dealing here with Christ only, and not with Eve (Spenser, we remember, had covered both series of temptations, and more, in one large conceit), perhaps a contrast might be worked up between the two instances of offered food. Eve was not able to resist a mere apple; Christ could now be shown successfully rejecting an elaborate banquet. But then the place of this temptation in the sequence of temptations would prove an embarrassment. Spenser had put it last, with good effect, but how could Milton put it *after* the temptation offered to Christ to throw Himself from the pinnacle, with the perhaps already imagined superlative climax of Satan's own, second fall, from that place? It would be much better to move it back in the sequence, but how far? Certainly it should not come after the kingdoms of the world, where it would still be anticlimactic. On the other hand, it would fit in neatly just after the temptation to change stones to bread, for, after that, Satan might be imagined as tempting Christ with actual bread, of the very highest quality, before going on to stronger medicines.[2]

On this line of argument, Milton would have found himself with the following sequence of temptations: to change stones into bread; to partake of a banquet; to accept the kingdoms of the world (with influence of Spenser's extensive modification and development of this item); to cast oneself from the pinnacle of the temple. This is the sequence of events in *Paradise Regained* as we have it, but nothing can be made of this without substantiating detail.

With regard to the temptation directed at Christ in *Paradise Regained* actually to partake of food,[3] it has been generally recognized that there is no tradition at all,[4] except, as I may now point out, the single case of Guyon's being invited to relieve his great hunger by eating a golden apple. It is also true that he is asked to take a seat:

Why takest not of that same fruit of gold,

2. Note that it is at the end of Guyon's temptation in the House of Mammon that he is offered nourishment, but that it is at the beginning of his adventure in the Bower that he is enticed to take the cup.

3. On the banqueting scene in *Paradise Regained*, see Elizabeth Marie Pope, '*Paradise Regained': The Tradition and the Poem* (New York, 1962), pp. 70–79, where there is also a conspectus of other views. Also, on this subject in particular, see B. Rajan, ed., *The Prison and the Pinnacle*, Toronto, 1973 (a collection of papers on *Paradise Regained* and *Samson Agonistes*, presented at The University of Western Ontario in 1971).

4. See Carey-Fowler, p. 110 n. to *Paradise Regained*, II, 337–65.

Ne sittest downe on that same silver stoole.

> [II. vii. 63]

The formula in *Paradise Regained*, is, however, very similar. Milton's paragraph begins:

What doubts the Son of God to sit and eat?

> [II. 368]

and ends:

What doubt'st thou Son of God? Sit down and eat.[5]

In the matter of the temptation involving the kingdoms of the world, the Gospels tell us only that the devil offered to give Christ all this power and glory if Christ would worship him. Spenser departs from this scenario radically and goes into much greater detail. Mammon, god of this world and worldliness, offers Guyon money wherewith to buy all glory and honours—to gain crowns and kingdoms—if Guyon will worship him:

> God of the world and worldlings I me call,
>   Great *Mammon*, greatest god below the skye
>   That of my plenty poure out unto all,
>   And unto none my graces do envye:
>   Riches, renowme, and principality,
>   Honour, estate, and all this worldes good,
>   For which men swinck and sweat incessantly,
>   Fro me do flow into an ample flood,
> And in the hollow earth have their eternall brood.

> Wherefore if me thou deigne to serve and sew,
>   At thy command lo all these mountains bee;
>
>   . . . .

> Vaine glorious Elfe (said he) doest not thou weet
>   That money can thy wantes at will supply?

5. Note George Herbert's beautiful use of this formula in the contrary condition of Communion or the Marriage Feast of the Lamb, at the end of 'Love' (III): '"You must sit down", says Love, "and taste my meat": / So I did sit and eat.'

Christ's demurrer completes the series of refusals to ingest: Guyon has refused the apple in the House of Mammon and the cup in the Bower—two things which may have been allegorized in Milton's mind as the flesh and the blood, both wrongly offered, particularly considering the abominable food of Tantalus; the Lady in *Comus* has refused the enchanter's cup; and now Christ has refused a banquet.

Shields, steeds, and armes, and all things for thee meet
It can purvay in twinckling of an eye;
And crownes and kingdomes to thee multiply.
Do not I kings create, and throw the crowne
Sometimes to him, that low in dust doth ly?
And him that raignd, into his rowme thrust downe,
And whom I lust, do heape with glory and renowme?
[II. vii. 8, 9, 11]

After Guyon has finally refused all the gold spread before him because
he believes that honour is earned not bought, Mammon gives the screw
another turn. He offers Guyon directly, without interposing money, all
rank and honours themselves in the competitive scramble of this world,
that is to say, in the court of Philotime ('love of honour'), whose hand
Guyon is offered.

Milton follows Spenser very closely here in principle. When Christ
has refused the banquet, Satan turns to the general rubric 'high designs,
/ High actions' (II. 410–11) and, under it, immediately offers Him
enabling money.

Money brings honour, friends, conquest, and realms;
. . . .
Therefore, if at great things thou wouldst arrive,
Get riches first, get wealth, and treasure heap,
Not difficult, if thou hearken to me,
Riches are mine, fortune is in my hand.
[II. 422, 426–29]

Christ's answer is in large part Guyon's, with some verbal intermixture
from Mammon's speech. Guyon:

All otherwise (said he) I riches read,
    And deeme them roote of all disquietnesse;
    First got with guile, and then preserv'd with dread,
    And after spent with pride and lavishness,
    Leaving behind them griefe and heaviness.
    Infinite mischiefes of them do arize,
    Strife, and debate, bloudshed, and bitternesse,
    Outrageous wrong, and hellish covetize,
That noble heart as great dishonour doth despize.

Ne thine be kingdomes, ne the scepters thine;

> But realms and rulers thou doest both confound,
> And loyall truth to reason doest incline;
> Witnesse the guiltlesse bloud pourd oft on ground,
> The crowned often slaine, the slayer cround,
> The sacred Diademe in peeces rent,
> And purple robe gored with many a wound;
> Castles surprizd, great cities sackt and brent:
> So mak'st thou kings, and gaynest wrongfull governement.
>
> Long were to tell the troublous stormes, that tosse
> The private state, and make the life unsweet:
>   . . . .
>
> Indeede (quoth he) through fowle intemperance,
> Frayle men are oft captiv'd to covetise:
> But would they thinke, with how small allowaunce
> Untroubled Nature doth her selfe suffiise,
> Such superfluities they would despise,
> Which with sad cares empeach our native joyes.
>   [II. vii. 12, 13, 14, 15]

Christ, following the concluding line of Satan's speech, which is given as the first line here:

> While virtue, valour, wisdom sit in want.
>   To whom thus Jesus patiently replied;
> Yet wealth without these three is impotent,
> To gain dominion or to keep it gained.
> Witness those ancient empires of the earth,
> In highth of all their flowing wealth dissolved:
> But men endued with these have oft attained
> In lowest poverty to highest deeds;
>
>   . . . .
>
> For I esteem those names of men so poor
> Who could do mighty things, and could contemn
> Riches though offered from the hand of kings.
> And what in me seems wanting, but that I
> May also in this poverty as soon
> Accomplish what they did, perhaps and more?
> Extol not riches then, the toil of fools,
> The wise man's cumbrance if not snare, more apt

To slacken virtue, and abate her edge,
Than prompt her to do aught may merit praise.
What if with like aversion I reject
Riches and realms; yet not for that a crown,
Golden in show, is but a wreath of thorns,
Brings dangers, troubles, cares, and sleepless nights
To him who wears the regal diadem,
When on his shoulders each man's burden lies;
For therein stands the office of a king,
His honour, virtue, merit, and chief praise,
That for the public all this weight he bears.
                    [*Paradise Regained*, II. 431–38, 447–65]

The reader will perceive many more similarities if he peruses the context succeeding each of these quotations. (Note as well an interesting admixture above of Shakespeare on Henry IV and Henry V.)

What now follows in *Paradise Regained* has caused one investigator to describe the whole poem as 'built around the contrast between Christian "heroic virtues" and the selfishly ambitious kind of heroism which Satan has to offer'.[6] It is difficult to see in what sense this is not a precise definition of the ensuing stages in *Faerie Queene*, II. vii.[7] Certainly Milton subtilizes the discussion far beyond Spenser's mythic formulation; but in an important sense all that Satan offers Christ upon earth is a travesty of Belphoebe's definition of true honour:

Abroad in armes, at home in studious kind
Who seekes with painfull toile, shall honor soonest find,
                    [*Faerie Queene*, II. iii. 40]

always allowing for the fact that Milton's feelings about chivalry had migrated from that early point where he was ready to write an Arthuriad to a later point (made explicit in *Paradise Lost*, IX. 27–41) where, unlike Spenser or Tasso, he would never accept knightly exploits as an emblem of virtuous activity at large.

6. Merritt Y. Hughes, in John Milton, *Complete Poems and Major Prose*, ed. Hughes (New York, 1957), p. 477, discussing Z. S. Fink, 'The Political Implications of *Paradise Regained*', *Journal of English and Germanic Philology*, 40 (1941), 482–88.

7. M. M. Mahood on the same subject: 'Milton's theory of fame is expounded in the third book of *Paradise Regain'd* which deals at length with Satan's offer...of "the authority and the glory".—Milton...is not greatly concerned with the first and third assays....He concentrates all the dramatic interest of the work on the one temptation...which was within the experience of the human mind at its heroic best' (*Poetry and Humanism*, London, 1950, pp. 233–34).

Paradise Regained, nearly to the same degree as *Comus*, and perhaps more so than *Paradise Lost*, betrays the presence of Spenser's shaping hand in Milton's creative imagination. It is not clear how this bears on the supposition that *Paradise Regained* was drafted before *Paradise Lost*,[8] or whether the degree of Spenserian influence in one or another section of *Paradise Lost* relates to the stages of the latter poem's composition.

8. See John T. Shawcross, 'The Chronology of Milton's Major Poems', *PMLA*, 76 (1961), 345–58.

15

Symbolic Network and Rectilinear Narrative

It may be agreed that in one sense the subjects and many of the details of Milton's two epics are 'given' in *Faerie Queene* II, so that (to state the matter in the most oversimplified way) *Paradise Lost* is Milton's version of the Gardens of Proserpina and Acrasia, and *Paradise Regained* is his version of what Guyon avoided doing in the House of Mammon. Yet it may still be objected that the completely transformed integument of the Miltonic version of the mythic patterns is fully as important a matter. This is surely true, although we have to recognize the patterns themselves before we can talk sensibly about how they are metamorphosed.

Milton is one of the Spenserian poets, but it must be immediately added that he is the only one to transform the Spenserian heritage so completely as to become the more admired son of his esteemed poetic father. Spenser's treatment of the Edenic temptation and of a type of Christ's temptation in the Wilderness is a single, visionary, multilayered allegorical conceit. Milton's is a marmoreal, literal narrative. Compared with Spenser's, it seems to have sorted out the earlier poet's confluent motifs. Yet Milton's narrative is also interspersed with many a metaphorical cross reference, and delicately modulates from one traditional *mise en scène* or traditional role or traditional reference to another so as to suggest yet further juxtapositions or metaphorical convergences. Spenser's metaphors are foreground allegory or vision or ideal landscape; in Milton's hands these things are transformed into concrete fiction in the foreground (for example, the Garden of Eden) or poetic metaphor properly speaking. The metaphorical juxtaposing in Milton's narrative is really marginal. Essentially we have a story, told as Tasso or Virgil might have told it.

Probably we may speak here of an historical, not simply a personal and temperamental, change between Spenser and Milton. Among Renaissance vernacular literary cultures, the English one of the late sixteenth and early seventeenth centuries not only originated lyric poetry in which the new tradition, for England, of formal and complex poetic metaphor had a startling efflorescence, significantly different from the continuation of this tradition in Italy and elsewhere. It was also in English, alone among vernacular cultures, that one work of genius by Spenser chanced to continue an older tradition shared mainly with France and the Low Countries of the large-scale, sacred or profane, visionary narrative metaphor called allegory.[1] In a sense Milton changed all that. He was the first in English to reject habitual allegory at the level of the most exalted and solemn poetic narrative, that is, of the heroic mode. Although he was in many ways a man of the earlier Renaissance, he was not one to perpetuate the medieval narrative allegory that Spenser had carried into that Renaissance.

Milton's is an essentially modern imagination, which is perhaps why he, like Tasso, makes so much more use than Spenser of that Christianized epic device, the angelic messenger between heaven and earth. What Spenser conveys 'mystically', as Milton would say, through a feigned confounding together of realms of being, Milton wishes to convey, at his main level of narrative, in terms of literal truth, or in terms of as possible an account as epic poetry will permit, although he knew as well as we do that the transcendental side of his narrative entailed the use of a fictional clothing for the ineffable.

In the case of Spenser there is some general historical interest in perceiving that his poetry participates in the great outburst of late medieval art and architecture which constituted an initial, conservative adaptation (finally to be replaced by fundamentally new canons) to the growing accuracy of Humanist understanding of the formal aspects of Classical art and literature, to the new nation-state, to the changing

---

1. Extended allegorical narrative of the Middle Ages in Italian and German is a meagre phenomenon compared with that of France, of the Low Countries in the fifteenth and early sixteenth centuries, and of England, in spite of the single great exception of the *Commedia*.

social and economic arrangements, and to the new relation of Western Europe to the rest of the world. The sometimes pleasant kind of *haute vulgarisation* which glories in juxtaposing Portugese Manueline Gothic, the Classicizing medievalism of Flemish town halls, the beauties of French Flamboyant, the early Albrecht Dürer, fifteenth- and sixteenth-century late Gothic German sculpture in wood, the Classicizing style of the Netherlandish primitive Mabuse, the jewelled irrealism and preoccupation with detail of Tudor portraiture, etc., might as well include *The Faerie Queene* in the concoction, for the visionary and allegorical side of that work belongs here. The *Faerie Queene* is a logical extension of certain medieval literary phenomena in that it is an allegorical poem of even greater and more bewildering schematic complexity than earlier medieval ones, with the possible exception of Dante's, and in that it makes even greater use than any such earlier narratives of a long-metamorphosed, medievalized Pagan mythology; at the same time, however, it is partly under the control of the scheme of the Classical epic, and of the narrative habits of Italian writers of heroic poetry who were firmly fixed in a Renaissance mould.[2]

Of these two aspects it has been useful here to emphasize the medieval one. The onward movement of Spenser's poem is characterized by that easy and opportunistic slipping from one level of signification to another, until a whole emblematic structure is achieved, which is equally characteristic of *Le Roman de la rose*, *Piers Plowman*, *Peàrl*, or *The Parlement of Foules*. To some readers, Book II of *The Faerie Queene* has seemed in the first place the story of the adventures of a chivalric hero, recounted in a way made fashionable by Italian writers of heroic poetry in Spenser's century. In fact, however, particularly in the episodes which unroll in moralized landscapes, symbolic elaboration upon a theme takes over to so great a degree from this ostensible narrative line that the subject no longer remains Guyon's adventures and quest but becomes Temptation to Wrongdoing: resisting or succumbing to it.[3] Spenser's aim, for instance, in the Garden of Proserpina (and conceivably in the Bower of Bliss) is an elegantly symbolic amal-

2. Two necessary but not damaging qualifications to this from the point of view of a medievalist are that *The Faerie Queene* also partakes of the English and French kind of medieval chivalric romance, as in Malory; and that, long before *The Faerie Queene*, medieval Latin verse narrative often imitated Classical epic slavishly.

3. That the procedure of *The Faerie Queene* is thematic or emblematic, not primarily narrative, has been pointed out frequently in recent years. See, for instance, William Nelson, *The Poetry of Edmund Spenser: A Study* (New York, 1963); and Jane Aptekar, *Icons of Justice: Iconography and Thematic Imagery in Book V of 'The Faerie Queene'* (New York, 1969).

gam of instances in which the Fall of Man and Christ's temptation in the Wilderness as a reversal of First Man's (as First Woman's) Fall displace knightly adventure, but are in turn embroidered with instances of Man's other infringements upon the divine. Spenser's method in the Garden of Proserpina is to establish a charged field in which one symbolic set seems to attract, or metaphorically to evoke, another having an affinity with it.

This can be shown by going over familiar ground in a somewhat new way. One starts the tally of such symbolic sets with Guyon's temptation, the ostensible narrative occasion for all the rest. As a temperate knight he resists it. In doing so, he imitates Christ as we all should do. But as a *Microchristos* he is also in a position to re-enact Christ's specific acts. Guyon's refusal of food and rest when he needs it is associated with Christ's earlier refusal of *Superbia* at a time when its exercise would have served his needy appetite: instigated by Satan to turn stones to bread he refused. But Eve when tempted took the apple presumptuously. Other parallels of temptation and presumption present themselves. Proserpina was condemned to hell for accepting the fruit; Atalanta and Cydippe each lost her freedom through a tempter's golden fruit; the contention of the Trojan War was caused by a human's presumptuous award of the golden fruit in a contention among goddesses; Tantalus, full of riches, desires fruit but is denied it because, in a presumptuous gesture towards divine arcana, he prepared food for the gods from the body of his own son; Socrates, a Christ figure, was betrayed by a friend and destroyed by the Athenians; Christ was destroyed by the Jews without Pilate's having intervened. Socrates was forced to eat, or drink, the fruit, or vegetable matter, of the poisonous plant Cicuta. Thus not only the temptation of Christ but also His death at the hands of presumptuous man is added to the metaphorical construct. Those hands cannot be cleansed. Perhaps the guiltless death of the Son of Man, whose flesh and blood we consume in a sacramental feast, is related to the feast for the gods prepared from the innocent son of Tantalus. Elsewhere, in another garden, is the cup of secret poison which had killed Mordant, and which is rejected by Guyon when it is offered by the False Genius and by Excesse; in that same place is a picture of dismemberment of an innocent brother in the service of passion. One could extend this symbolic tapestry, but the point is obvious that Spenser's metaphors are often foreground allegory or vision or moralized landscape of a medieval kind.

For Milton, metaphor is marginal, in the modern narrative way, and the foreground is occupied by a nonmetaphorical, suitably paced account of concrete happenings. To decide that the new development in exalted poetic narrative represented by *Paradise Lost* is to be called exclusively 'Renaissance' or 'Mannerist' or 'Baroque' does not as yet seem to be a very useful exercise (in the way it is useful, for instance, for German literary historians to speak of the work of the youthful Goethe as 'Rococo', not yet 'Romantic'). The main point about Milton in this connection is that he achieves in his human and Satanic figures and landscapes a kind of Michaelangelesque solidity.[4]

The Faerie Queene is the last great visionary poem of Western culture before the precursors of Romanticism returned to this form under essentially new auspices. It may be that the particular conditions of literary development in late medieval and Renaissance England had something to do with this survival, and with another already mentioned, quite distinct peculiarity of English Renaissance poetry when it is seen in its Western European setting: the development of certain kinds of imagery in late sixteenth- and seventeenth-century lyric poetry which differ significantly from analogous developments in other Western European vernaculars and in Renaissance Latin. It was not, of course, Milton's hand that wiped out this whole constellation, but his role in part of the process has not yet been justly appraised.

A further point emerges in this connection from our examination of *Faerie Queene* II, *Paradise Lost*, and *Paradise Regained*. It was not necessarily *ex nihilo* that Milton carried on his famous speculations concerning the finally self-defeating character of all epics except the one that most directly presented an embodiment of the central Christian credo, and concerning the frivolity, finally, of allowing Classical mythology or a national myth like an Arthuriad to inhabit the foreground of a completely serious fiction. He had something concrete in the way of an already existing heroic poem to wrestle with, his predecessor's own formulation of the same task which Milton was to set himself; hence, perhaps, his greater interest in the second than in any other book of the *Faerie Queene*. His solution is seen to have been to move Classical and historical material from foreground allegorical vision into reinforcing, occasional imagery. The result is foreground figures of a robust plasticity on which the imagery forms a series of grace notes, pathetic, picturesque, or haunting. Spenser was capable of creat-

---

4. 'Michaelangelesque' is to be taken, not as an effort at art-historical periodization, but as descriptive of firmly delimited, completely filled-in concretions. 'Giottoesque monumentality' would have done as well.

ing such imagery but seems to have had no inkling of such figures, unless, perhaps, in *Epithalamion*. The sustained concentration of the seriously directed gaze upon heroically acting, speaking, and thinking characters in a long narrative is, after all, almost without precedent in exalted English narrative poetry. With the exception of *Troilus and Criseyde*, the best medieval verse romance does not allow its figures to expatiate in character more than fitfully; when they are allowed monologues, these are the working out of *topoi*. One must look to Shakespearean drama for a large precedent in English.

16

Afterthoughts on Chaucer, Spenser, and Milton

Paradise Lost shows some continuity with Spenser's and indeed with Chaucer's notions concerning the relation between man and woman and the status of human life and procreation in universal, mythic terms. This deserves our attention, yet wedded love in Milton has already been written about well and at some length.[1] In addition, discussion from my point of view is partly inhibited by the consideration that Chaucer may never have become a living part of Milton's imagination. Perhaps the English Tityrus took a largely formal and second-rate place as against the singing swans of the Thames in *Mansus*, 30–34. On the other hand, although the choice of the Squire's Tale as the unique work of Chaucer's for mention in *Il Penseroso* (109–15) sounds strange to modern Chaucerians, both the importance and the Platonizing quality (via Boethius) which I have shown Spenser giving to this tale by his continuation of it may have been recognized by Milton; so conceived, the Squire's Tale performs a sound thematic function in Milton's poem. Chaucer is occasionally cited in Milton's *Commonplace Book*, but the suspicion has already been expressed that the authors whom Milton

1. See the review in Carey-Fowler, pp. 172–73, of the controversy on the themes of virginity and chastity in *Comus*; William Haller, 'Hail Wedded Love', *ELH*, 13 (1946), 79–97; and E. M. W. Tillyard, 'Appendix C, The Doctrine of Chastity in Milton', in his *Milton*, rev. ed. (London, 1966), pp. 318–26.

knew really well, like Virgil and Spenser, find no place there.

There is certainly a reflection in Milton of the complex of notions, already considered here in Chaucer and Spenser, concerning the participation of man's successively begotten lives in that conditional eternity of ever-repeated cycles of change, which is a pale reflection of the true eternity of God's realm. Before the Fall, Adam suggests to God that, as a finite being, man would have to be perfected through multiplicity rather than infinitude. This is a conversion of the traditional idea into nontemporal, spatial terms, before the entrance of Death into the world made Time the paramount consideration. Adam speaks first of God's condition:

> No need that thou
> Shouldst propagate, already infinite;
> And through all numbers absolute, though one;
> But man by number is to manifest
> His single imperfection, and beget
> Like of his like, his image multiplied,
> In unity defective, which requires
> Collateral love, and dearest amity.
> [*Paradise Lost*, VIII.419–26]

But the very absence of Time from this expression of the idea suggests that Milton is thinking not so much of Spenser here as of the traditional beginning of this notion in Plato's *Timaeus*,[2] where the best reflection of Infinity and Eternity that the Demiurge can find to implant in a newly created universe is Number, that is, the notion of multiplicity of spatially and temporally measured units. Milton was no doubt well acquainted with Spenser's embodiment of this idea in the Garden of Adonis and the Mutability Cantos, and conceivably he was acquainted with it in *Epithalamion*, yet Adam's speech here seems to go back to Milton's and Spenser's ultimate common source.

On the subject of the sun, the chief measurer of time and bringer of cyclical change and growth in our visible universe, and on the stars, we have in *Paradise Lost* something which might be taken vaguely to illustrate what I have previously attributed to the pattern of *Epithalamion*, and to illustrate as well something which appears also in the Garden of Adonis and *Mutabilitie*.

> above them all
> The golden sun in splendour likest heaven

2. 37D.

Allured his eye: thither his course he bends
Through the calm firmament; but up or down
By centre, or eccentric, hard to tell,
Or longitude, where the great luminary
Aloof the vulgar constellations thick,
That from his lordly eye keep distance due,
Dispenses light from far; they as they move
Their starry dance in numbers that compute
Days, months, and years, towards his all-cheering lamp
Turn swift their various motions, or are turned
By his magnetic beam, that gently warms
The universe, and to each inward part
With gentle penetration, though unseen,
Shoots invisible virtue even to the deep.
                    [*Paradise Lost*, III. 571–86]

Yet Milton could have drawn on any number of sources for this sentiment, except that the last four lines may possibly contain a reminiscence
of the impregnation of Chrysogone while sleeping, by which Amoret
and Belphoebe were begotten (*Faerie Queene*, III. vi. 5 ff.). Spenser
suggests, as we have seen earlier, that the sun and the ever-returning
Adonis ('Father of all formes . . . that living gives to all'; vi. 47) are
mysteriously the same (*Faerie Queene*, III. vi. 7. 5–9, 8. 1–6, 9, 1–5).

The justly praised celebration of marriage in *Paradise Lost* IX stands
in the line of Chaucer and Spenser. Adam first asks God not for a
woman but more generally for a friend, for 'fellowship' (*Paradise Lost*,
VIII. 389) (Chaucer's own term). The notion of an eternity through the
procreation of innocent lovers is movingly invoked in Eden as it was in
the Garden of Adonis. In the same passage all that 'courtly love' which
Spenser described in the life of the Castle of Malecasta is condemned
(IV. 765–70). The inimical role of Time in the Garden of Adonis is very
precisely taken over by Time and Death in *Paradise Lost*. Spenser:

Great enimy to it, and to all the rest,
    That in the *Gardin* of *Adonis* springs,
    Is wicked *Time*, who with his scyth addrest,
    Does mow the flowring herbes and goodly things,
    And all their glory to the ground downe flings,
    Where they doe wither, and are fowly mard.
                    [III. vi. 39]

Milton, letting us hear Sin address her son Death after the Fall:

Thou therefore on these herbs, and fruits, and flowers
Feed first, on each beast next, and fish, and fowl,
No homely morsels, and whatever thing
The scythe of time mows down, devour unspared.

> [X. 603–6]

For the true admirer of *The Faerie Queene*, as C. S. Lewis once said,[3] motifs are continually relating themselves to myriads of other motifs, and are continually falling into new combinations, like the view through a kaleidescope. Milton seems occasionally to be experiencing this process. At the point in *Comus* where the Second Brother speaks of the danger to chaste beauty in desert wastes, Milton is consciously dealing with traditional motifs touched by many other poets (particularly, perhaps, Dante) but, on the grounds of cross reference between the parts, he seems primarily to be combining motifs freely from different sections of *Faerie Queene* II and III:

For who would rob a hermit of his weeds?

. . . .

But Beauty like the fair Hesperian tree
Laden with blooming gold, had need the guard
Of dragon-watch with unenchanted eye,
To save her blossoms, and defend her fruit
From the rash hand of bold Incontinence.
You may as well spread out the unsunned heaps
Of miser's treasure by an outlaw's den,
And tell me it is safe, as bid me hope
Danger will wink on opportunity.

> [*Comus*, 389, 392–400]

If one adds to this certain cancelled lines of the Trinity MS,[4] in a passage which touches on much of this material, the width of reference is very great:

Amidst the Hesperian gardens, on whose banks
Bedewed with nectar and celestial songs
Eternal roses grow and hyacinth
And fruits of golden rind, on whose fair tree
The scaly-harnessed watchful dragon ever keeps

---

3. *The Allegory of Love* (London, 1936), p. 358.
4. Quoted from Carey-Fowler, pp. 175–76n.

His unenchanted eye, and round the verge
And sacred limits of this blissful isle
The jealous Ocean that old river winds
His far-extended arms, till with steep fall
Half his waste flood the wide Atlantic fills
And half the slow unfathomed Stygian pool.

The dragon watch relates to the dragon of chastity with dart-pierced, blind eyes, beneath the feet of the statue of Cupid in the House of Busirane (III. xi. 48), as well as to the corresponding, unsuccessful effort of Gardante, archer of love mastery and embodiment of darted glances in the House of Malecasta, to do more than superficially wound the chaste Britomart. The 'fruits of golden rind' are appropriate to the Garden of the Hesperides, guarded by the dragon Ladon, but also, like the 'eternal roses', are a kind of transfiguration of the flora of the Bower of Bliss (eternal because artificial or, in the rose song, all too subject to change) into their opposite—a truly celestial, blessed garden, the curse removed. The 'unsunned heaps / Of miser's treasure' form a precise description of Mammon first met, turning over his gold in a glen covered from heaven's light (II. vii. 3–5). 'Ocean that old river' and the lines that follow are not, it must be admitted, particularly Spenserian; nevertheless they are included here because they are very lovely and are seldom seen by anyone: they have the expertise so much admired in Milton by the nineteenth century.

When we come to a more precise statement of the marriage relationship, in terms of Adam's and Eve's actions, then for some readers a rift appears in the lute. Milton's notion of the balance of responsibility and of praise and blame in male-female relationships has been discussed from almost every point of view. I might try an historical one. Just as modern readers are often made uncomfortable by the appearance in Chaucer of the fastidious thirteenth- and fourteenth-century convention that a lady first finds love for her hopelessly besotted lover in the *pite* ('pity', 'compassion') which she feels for his case, so in a contrary way in Milton we miss a measured appreciation of the male potentiality for deceit, tyranny, and sadism in the sexual relationship. The condemnation of self-satisfied, unsympathetic *machismo*, a condemnation which we find in Chaucer on *maistrye* and in Spenser on the brash overboldness of Scudamour, will be sought in vain in Milton. The only reference, for instance, to the possibility of physical compulsion on

Adam's part (beyond the idealization of what is normally desired by the
female in lovemaking, at IV. 307–11) is his repudiation of it:

> I admonished thee, . . .
>
> . . . .
>
> beyond this had been force,
> And force upon free will hath here no place.
> [IX. 1171, 1173–74]

This speech comes within the bickering after the Fall. Although what is
in the context of these words is being presented as mere self-justification
on Adam's part, the words themselves appear to be advanced as valid.
Adam has in fact refrained from force, and it is impossible to imagine
Milton's having required it of him before the Fall, in order to restrain
Eve from going off to a distance. It is as though Adam had already
learned all the tricks of connubial sophistry in shifting the blame, but
could not have learned anything about a masculine passion for domination. Perhaps it is not unfair to say that in attempting to fashion his
archetypal pattern of behaviour between the sexes Milton somehow
managed to leave out a male tendency to play the despot, by whatever
means, far beyond the needs of 'leadership' in the putative hierarchy of
man and woman which Milton himself is asserting. Chaucer and
Spenser do not leave out this datum. Milton does not, it is true, put all
blame upon Eve in her relationship with Adam. For instance, she starts
the reconciliation between herself and her husband after the Fall (but
she is more to blame). The grotesque character of opinionated male
fault-finding against women is neatly struck by Milton in this exchange
between Adam and the archangel Michael:

> But still I see the tenor of man's woe
> Holds on the same, from woman to begin.
>   From man's effeminate slackness it begins,
> Said the angel, who should better hold his place
> By wisdom, and superior gifts received.
> [XI. 632–36]

And whatever may be thought of that last line, it is true that for both
parties, male and female, Milton has masterfully rendered the archetypal marriage squabble at IX. 1136–89. Yet there is still something
missing.

It might be contended that a manipulation of a guileless woman by
the deceptive masculine will is furnished in Satan's corruption of Eve.

Certainly the pathos expressed for her (IX. 424–33) as he first eyes her is very close to the note of Chaucer's *Legend of Good Women*, with its instances of innocent womanhood betrayed by a male egotist; yet there is reason to suppose that the irate Love God who imposed upon Chaucer the duty of writing tales to justify the female sex would not have been happy with Milton's legend of Eve and Satan. Milton's point is, after all, that Eve has willed her unsupported state and has wilfully exposed herself to a temptation to which she will submit with unbecoming facility. As an arguable case of male mastery in Milton's poetry, this finds its Spenserian parallel, not in Scudamour and Amoret, but in Paridell and his eager and soon shopworn victim Hellenore. We are at liberty to imagine that a Milton kneeling in the field of daisies before the Love God of Chaucer's Prologue would have found himself unsupported by the only available prop there, the gracious flower-lady Alceste.

The case is similarly weak for another parallel between Satan's perversion of Eve and the situation in Chaucer's Clerk's Tale, on terms borrowed from comparative folklore. In those terms, this tale of Griselda, an instance of extreme male mastery in marriage, has affinities with the motif of the Demon Lover or of Cupid and Psyche, where a male otherworldly visitant imposes extreme trials on a woman for his own reasons. Folkloristic parallels of this kind, however, often suggest what literarily are fallacious connections. At one level the Clerk's Tale gives us in the victimized Griselda a moralized instance of how man ought to accept, with undiminished love for God, the stripes with which He allows us to be scourged in our human journey; at another level Chaucer imposes a certain confusion by injecting reproaches directed at the behaviour of the husband as such, as mere man in a marriage partnership. That is not the role of Satan, even though Satan is an instance of the egotistically unscrupulous being. On this basis one could more easily compare him with Napoleon. In Milton's scene there are no more than secondary sexual overtones, if any; and in any case his Eve is closer here to the Wife of Bath (who is said to be her daughter) than to Griselda.

Despite the magnitude of his genius, something in Milton's narrative method works against him in our minds. Chaucer's embodiments of the relationship between man and woman culminate in idealist and visionary narratives; Spenser's are almost entirely of this kind. Such plainly archetypal formulations of a norm are wonderfully adaptable to social change. The character of the relationships among Britomart, Artegall,

Radigund, Scudamour, and Amoret in their various moralized land-scapes and overtly symbolic adventures awakens no modern questions concerning the precise state of the former Elizabeth Boyle after she entered the household of Edmund Spenser, Gent. On the other hand the graphically envisaged middle-class sobriety of Adam and Eve's ex-changes leads easily on to the best-selling exaggerations of Gravesian fictionalized biography.[5] The specificity of Milton's range of narrative reference, and even perhaps the modern temptation to portray him as a fatuous lover and a malevolent spouse, may be no more than by-products of the historical collapse of allegorical narrative in English at the highest poetic level. This collapse is primarily signalized, of course, by the remarkable originality of Milton's own innovation.

5. See Robert Graves, *Wife to Mr. Milton* (London, 1943).

Appendix A

Osiris, Isis, Horus, Typhon, Busiris

Much material from Classical and Renaissance sources was available to Spenser concerning an Egyptian god, king, and culture-hero Osiris, his wife Isis, his murderer and brother Typhon (Set), his son Horus (Harpocrates), a king Busiris, and a city Busiris. I am mainly concerned here with a putative adversary relationship between the character Busirane in *Faerie Queene* III and the figures Osiris and Isis in *Faerie Queene*, V. vii, but there are other important issues. The tradition is complicated and at times self-contradictory. Only a selection of authorities is cited here. The following points are perhaps the most relevant.

1. Busiris is a city on the Nile in Egypt. It contains a great temple of Isis (Herodotus, II. 59; R. Stephanus, *Dictionarium*, s.v. 'Busiris'). It was founded by Busiris (Stephanus).

2. 'Busiris' was the name, not of a king, but of the tomb of Osiris (Diodorus Siculus, I. 88. 5).

3. Osiris was secretly killed by his brother Typhon (Stephanus).

4. Typhon was an inhuman, fierce king of Egypt who through his cruelty laid the country waste (Natalis Comes, *Mythologia*, VI. xxii).

5. Busiris was a tyrant who immolated visitors to his kingdom, but was

destroyed by Hercules when Busiris tried to sacrifice him as well (Stephanus; Boccaccio, *De genealogia deorum*, XIII. i).

6. Busiris, king of Egypt, used to sacrifice strangers on an altar of Zeus in accordance with a seer's statement that by doing so annually Busiris would stave off a dearth that had lasted nine years. Busiris first sacrificed the seer. When he tried to sacrifice Hercules, the latter broke his bonds and killed Busiris and his son Apollodorus (Hyginus, XXXI, LVI; Apollodorus, II. v. 11; Plutarch, *De Iside*, 73).

7. The Egyptians assigned to Osiris the attributes which others give to Bacchus, or Dionysus. Osiris introduced the vine and taught men the use of wine (Natalis Comes; Stephanus; and others). Osiris is in Greek 'Dionysos' (Herodotus, II. 144).

8. The Egyptians identified the sun with Osiris, the moon with Isis. Isis is represented with horns, either because in her early phase the moon seemed horned, or because the cow is dedicated to Isis among the Egyptians (Alciati, *Emblemata*; and others). Isis may also be represented with a sphere or disk of the moon on her forehead (Alciati) (see figure 3).

9. Typhon killed Osiris. Isis, the queen of Osiris, and his sister as well as his wife, destroyed Typhon in battle, with the aid of her son Horus, begotten by Osiris (Stephanus). Horus deposed Typhon (Herodotus, II. 144).

For further material on Isis and Osiris, see the captions to figures 3 and 4.

Appendix B

Sun, Adonis
Venus, Osiris,
Isis, Busiris

The following syncretic treatment of Adonis, Proserpina, Osiris, and Isis is quoted from Macrobius, *Saturnalia*, trans. P. V. Evans (New York, 1969). This corresponds closely to the text appearing in the sixteenth century. As pointed out earlier, Spenser would have had many opportunities to familiarize himself with this passage, for the *Saturnalia* possessed considerable popularity in the Renaissance.

I. xxi.

[1] That Adonis too is the sun will be clear beyond all doubt if we examine the religious practices of the Assyrians.... Physicists have given to the earth's upper hemisphere (part of which we inhabit) the revered name of Venus, and they have called the earth's lower hemisphere Proserpine.

[2] ... Six of the twelve signs of the zodiac are regarded as the upper signs and six as the lower, and so the Assyrians, or Phoenicians, represent the goddess Venus as going into mourning when the sun, in the course of its yearly progress through the series of the twelve signs, proceeds to enter the sector of the lower hemisphere.

[3] For when the sun is among the lower signs, and therefore makes the days shorter, it is as if it had been carried off for a time by death and had

been lost and had passed into the power of Proserpine . . . ; so that Venus is believed to be in mourning then, just as Adonis is believed to have been restored to her when the sun, after passing completely through the six signs of the lower series, begins again to traverse the circle of our hemisphere.

[4] In the story . . . of Adonis killed by a boar the animal is intended to represent winter. . . . And so winter, as it were, inflicts a wound on the sun. . . .

[5] On Mount Lebanon there is a statue of Venus. Her head is veiled, her expression sad. Her cheek beneath her veil is resting on her left hand; and it is believed that . . . the statue sheds tears. . . . A symbol of the earth in winter . . .

[7] In the same way the myths and religious ceremonies of the Phrygians . . . ; Mother of the Gods and Attis . . .

[Most of the foregoing is cited by Boccaccio, *De genealogia deorum*, II. liii ('De Adone Filio et nepote Cynare').]

[11] In Egypt, too, . . . there is a similar religious ceremony, in which Isis mourns for Osiris; for . . . Osiris is . . . the sun and Isis . . . the earth or the world of nature, and the explanation which applies to the rites of Adonis and Attis is applicable also to the Egyptian rites, to account for the alternations of sorrow and joy which accompany in turn the phases of the year. . . .

[16] . . . Among the signs of the zodiac, the Egyptians have dedicated an animal, the lion, in that part of the heavens where in its yearly course the sun's powerful heat is hottest. And the sign of the Lion they call 'The House of the Sun', because a lion seems to derive its essential qualities from the heat of the sun.

VI. vii.

[5] Busiris is 'a villain who used to sacrifice victims from all over the world, and therefore . . . deserves to be hated and cursed by all mankind'.

Appendix C

Plutarch on Transmigration into Beasts

Canter's Latin translation, from the Greek of the apparently Plutarchan passage, in the 1575 *Eclogae* of John Stobaeus. See pages 178–80; also chapter 12, note 5.

...Quae autem ab Homero de Circe dicuntur, mirabilem continent animae explicationem. Sic enim ait,

> Ast illi vocemque suum, crinesque gerebant,
> Et capita, et corpus: sed mens antiqua manebat. (*Odys.*)

quae fabula Pythagorae ac Platonis de anima sententiam tecte indicat, eam videlicet immortali praeditam natura, sed mutationibus obnoxia, per interitus ac mortes in alias corporum formas transferri, vitae similitudinem studio voluptatis sectantem; eaque in re doctrinae ac philosophiae usum cerni, si honesti anima memor, ac turpes illicitasque voluptates exosa, imperare sibi possit, et cavere, ne in pecus mutetur, corpus brutum et impurum amplexa, quod ineptam et rationis expertem naturam, et cupiditates irasque potius, quam rationem, alat ac nutriat. Siquidem huius transmutationis ordo ac natura ab Empedocle dea praedicatur,

> Externam carnis tunicam circumdare docta, et animas induens.

Homerus autem nascendi ambitum Circem nuncupavit, Solis filiam, qui omnem interitum cum ortu, et ortum rursus cum interitu semper connectit. Aeaea vero insula, quae cadaver suscipit, pars est continentis in quam primum animae delapsae vagantur, et lamentantur, nec sciunt

> qua sint occasus et ortus,
> Nec qua Sol terram lucis dux parte subintrat. (*Odys.*)

Cum porro solitam in carne vitam voluptatis studio desiderent, rursum in ortus misturam incidunt, plane permiscentis aeterna et mortalia, affectibus vacantia et obnoxia, caelestia ac terrena, voluptatibus ad ortum redeuntibus illecta, cum quidem maximam requirunt animae felicitatem et prudentiam, ne pessima quaeque secutae, infelicem ac ferinam vitam adipiscantur. Etenim quod inferorum dicitur trivium, in his fere animae partibus cernitur, rationis et ira et cupiditatis compotibus, quarum unaquaeque vitae sibi convenientis principium continet. Neque haec iam pro fabulis poeticis, sed naturae veritate sunt habenda. Quorum enim in transmutatione cupiditas principatum obtinuerit, hos in asinina corpora, vitamque impuram prae gula et libidine transferri censet. Cum autem gravibus contentionibus et odiosis crudelitatibus prorsus efferata secundum ortum petierit anima, in lupi vel leonis naturam se recentis acerbitatis plena, confert, corpus tale velut instrumentum affectui dominanti asciscens. Quapropter unumquemque decet in morte potissimum, velut in initiis, omni pravo effectu vacare, omnique cupiditate sedata et invidia iraque remota, de corpore decedere. Atque hic verus est Mercurius, ratio videlicet honesti magistra, quae a mistura longissime arcet animam, vel, si eam hauserit, in humana vita diutissime, quatenus licet, conservat.

Appendix *D*

Socrates, Critias, Theramenes (*Faerie Queene* II. vii 52)

Spenser speaks here of poisons 'With which th'unjust *Atheniens* made to dy / Wise *Socrates,* who therof quaffing glad / Pour out his life, and last Philosophy / To the faire *Critias* his dearest Belamy'. The generally accepted explanation of what has happened (offered by Upton; see Variorum commentary) is that Spenser has fused Socrates and Theramenes (since they are lengthily compared in terms of their common fates in Cicero's *Tusculan Disputations*). Theramenes was betrayed by Critias, who had been his friend (see Xenophon, *Hellenica*, II. iii. 15). As one of the Thirty Tyrants, Critias had had Theramenes unjustly condemned to death by poison. Theramenes then drank the poison and, pouring out the last drops as a pledge or toast, said with mordant irony, 'I pledge fair Critias' (or 'beautiful' or 'handsome' Critias, II. iii. 56 in the *Hellenica*; in Cicero's Latin, 'Propino hoc pulchro Critiae'.). As Cicero tells the story, an explicit parallel is drawn with the case of Socrates: 'After a few years Socrates went into the same prison and partook of the same goblet, by the same kind of miscarriage of justice' (*Disputationes tusculanae*, I. xl. 96). Cicero then equates Thermanes and Socrates as men famous for virtue and wisdom. The first syllable of *belamy* gives a literal translation of the adjectives used by Xenophon and Cicero in reference to the friend Critias. I suggest, then, that Spenser—consciously or unconsciously—has substituted

Theramenes for Socrates, and Critias for Phaedo, in the famous death scene in the *Phaedo*, so as to take advantage of yet another case of infringement, not by the 'Jewes despiteous' and Pilate, but by the 'unjust *Atheniens*' and Critias, upon a man-god or god-man who, be it noted, is shown in the *Republic* as the ultimate author of the triadic division of the soul which has here been described as basic in *Faerie Queene* II. Socrates is paralleled with Christ by Ficino, among others, as a man who intellected the one, the true, and the good directly; who offered, by his teaching and his life, an ideal to his people; and who by them was unjustly, but juridically, condemned to death. By using the word *belamy,* Spenser gives Critias—quite unhistorically—the somewhat epicene character of some of the Platonic Socrates' interlocutors. This word is applied in *The Canterbury Tales* by the Host to the Pardoner where some aspersion on full masculinity is intended (Introduction to Pardoner's Tale, 30; 318). Socrates would further mean that, in having willingly drunk of the cup and now pouring out the remainder of its contents and uttering a pledge, he was pouring 'out his life, and last Philosophy'.

T.M. Gang, in a letter in the *Times Literary Supplement*, 3 August 1956, p. 463, drew attention to an emblem showing Theramenes as he empties the last drops of poison from his cup in pledging Critias (see figure 6), in Achille Bocchi (Bochius, Bocchius, called Phileros), *Symbolicarum quaestionum...libri quinque*, Bologna, 1555 (in which this emblem is No. 137), 1574 (in which the emblem—the one reproduced in the present book—is No. 139). The title is 'Contemptio mortis metu cor liberat'. Theramenes' words, 'Propino hoc pulchro Critiae', appear beside the figure representing him, and his name appears beneath. A youth, or boy, stands watching him with folded arms, waiting for Theramenes to finish the cup which the youth has presented. To the right, in a smaller picture, the same youth stands with the cup on a salver before a seated rank of old men, of whom Gang supposes the first one to be Theramenes, to whom the cup would then be in the process of being presented. In fact this latter picture can be made to correspond to nothing in Xenophon's or Cicero's accounts. Possibly the old men are the Council whom Critias forcibly persuaded to condemn Theramenes, and the boy is a messenger to convey the poison. As Gang points out, certain verses on the right allude to Socrates; they are part of a dialogue. The relevant lines are:

Figure 6. Theramenes as a Parallel Figure to Socrates. From Achille Bocchi, *Symbolicarum quaestionum . . . libri quinque* (Bologna, 1555), No. 137.

Mortale quicquam si saperet genus,
  Mortem vel optare inciperet, vel hanc
  Desisteret saltem timere
  Dogmate Socratico ut monemur,
Nam quid potest optabilius dari
  Nostris supremus si ille animis dies
  Mutationem affert loci, non
  Interitum, omniaue auferentem
Extinctionem?

Theramenes' left hand does not point at these verses, as Gang suggests; rather, the hand is open in a gesture of excitement, the open palm facing us, and the wrist on the arm of the chair. I do not understand, either, how Spenser, seeing this emblem, could have supposed that the youth was at the time the friend of the condemned man and thus could have confused him with Socrates' Phaedo, for the expression on the youth's face seems definitely inimical. If Spenser indeed happened to see this emblem, it seems most likely to me that, as Upton suggested, he still conflated Socrates and Theramenes and supposed Socrates to have had a betraying friend, named Critias, as did Theramenes. Possibly Spenser would have supposed (or would have been struck by the possibilities of the idea) that the youth in the picture was a younger Critias (on the analogy of the young Phaedo) who had become an enemy (like the real Critias) and to whom the main figure pours out his life figuratively with the goblet and recites his last philosophic reflection, showing his contempt for death. But this becomes very speculative. In sum, I suppose Spenser to have intended his Critias to be a friend turned enemy of Socrates (and we remember that Spenser has left little space in his forty stanzas to explain himself). If I am wrong, then the parallel still stands between Socrates, a 'type' of Christ, unjustly condemned to death for the sake of the Athenians, and Christ, treated the same way for the sake of the Jews. Critias appears again as a true friend of Socrates In *Faerie Queene*, IV. Proem. 3. If, as P. C. Bayley tentatively suggests in his note to the passage under discussion (in his edition of *Faerie Queene* II, London, 1965), Spenser has confusedly substituted 'Critias' for 'Crito', then 'Critias' does indeed remain Socrates' friend.

Sections of
The Faerie Queene
Discussed in This Book

Index